THE AMELIORATION AND ABOLITION OF SLAVERY IN TRINIDAD, 1812 - 1834

Experiments and Protests in a new Slave Colony

Noel Titus

authorHOUSE®

AuthorHouse™
1663 Liberty Drive
Bloomington, IN 47403
www.authorhouse.com
Phone: 1-800-839-8640

First published by AuthorHouse 11/11/2009

ISBN: 978-1-4389-8557-2 (e)
ISBN: 978-1-4389-8556-5 (sc)
ISBN: 978-1-4389-8555-8 (hc)

Library of Congress Control Number: 2009909306

Printed in the United States of America
Bloomington, Indiana

This book is printed on acid-free paper.

DEDICATION

To my grandmother, Margaret Franklin, from whom I heard my first stories about slavery; and to my immediate family: Glencora, David, Pamela, Nicole, Neil, Andrea, Tiffany and Danielle.

TABLE OF CONTENTS

Contents

PREFACE

It was my privilege to have researched a critical period of Trinidad's history, when British policy-makers were struggling with changes in thought and attitude about slavery. As a new British slave colony, Trinidad became enmeshed in these changes. The island's history as a slave colony lasted only thirty-seven years at most, from its capture from the Spanish in 1797 until slavery was legally abolished in 1834. In that space of time, it was encouraged to import slaves, then forced into a slave policy which other colonies were reluctant to accept. Indeed, it was made the setting of experiments in dealing with the slaves, success in which should have made those experiments exemplary for other colonies.

The experiments were the subject of a number of Orders-in-Council, formulated in London and sent out for implementation in Trinidad since the colony did not have its own legislature. These Orders, with the exception of that for 1812, have not been looked at in any detail. They are related extensively in this work for the purpose of facilitating discussion of the reactions which followed their publication. These experiments did not work well for various reasons. Slave owners in Trinidad were no more accommodating than their counterparts in other colonies, and strenuously resisted the experiments; while public officials were themselves only too willing to circumvent the system. In many ways the machinery for carrying out this programme was defective. Very few of the officials could have been considered impartial; and the planters' hostility, at first partially concealed, became more overt towards the end of the period.

At the back of the minds of most officials and white slave owners was the view that slaves, as well as free coloured and black persons, were violent and untrustworthy. This showed itself in the widespread resistance to changes in government policy towards the slaves, as well as in generally negative attitudes towards the free coloureds. White slave owners in Trinidad considered themselves superior to their coloured counterparts, and naturally superior also to the slaves. They resented the programme of amelioration, which they considered an unwarrantable interference with their property. Coloured proprietors   were simultaneously resentful of the inferiority with which they were regarded by the whites in general, and inclined to haughtiness towards the less educated or affluent of their own class, as well as towards the slaves. In their struggles for improvement in their social status, they wavered in their attitude towards the amelioration programme. Eventually they joined the white proprietors in protesting the final Order in Council for the amelioration of the condition of slaves.

When in 1834 the Act for the abolition of slavery came into force, it came to a slave owning class who accepted it because they felt powerless to prevent it. They continued to look for labour as a means of enrichment. The laws which they passed to implement emancipation showed the continued desire to keep the labourers under strict control. The authority which the individual planter lost was transferred to a judiciary still dominated by the planter class, except for two stipendiary magistrates, while the fear of a servile insurrection lingered on to provide a motive for future policy.

This story formed the basis of a Master's thesis, which was submitted to the University of the West Indies (St. Augustine) many years ago. I owe a debt of gratitude to many persons, who assisted me in the preparation of the work initially: to Prof. James Millette, who has consistently encouraged me to publish it; to Sir Keith Hunte, former Principal of the Cave Hill Campus of the U.W.I., from whom I received very valuable advice; to Prof. Alvin Thompson and Dr. Anthony Phillips, also of the Cave Hill Campus of the University of the West Indies, in the later stages of revision. To students and others, from whom I received comments from time to time, I continue to say thanks.

Noel F. Titus

INTRODUCTION

When, under Sir Ralph Abercromby in 1797 the British successfully invaded Trinidad, they acquired a colony which had suffered nearly three hundred years of Spanish indolence. Following Columbus' chance landing on this island in 1498, it remained unattended for most of the next three centuries. It was not until 1592 that a settlement was established at St. Joseph, and a further period of nearly two hundred years before a substantial population of mainly French citizens was introduced in 1783. Neglected and poorly administered, it has truly been described as "a byword in the history of colonialism for its inefficiency and incompetence".[1] Spain proved unable to defend the island properly, to provide for its economic development, or to promote its development generally. The result was that in 1797 Trinidad reflected, in the size of its population and the extent of its cultivation, the comparative neglect of what was considered a very fertile island.

The change in policy towards Trinidad began with the appointment of Governor Manuel Falquez, who assumed his duties in December 1776. Falquez was instructed to encourage the immigration of foreign Catholics from the French Antilles, especially those islands which were under British rule following their capture from the French. As a result, there was large-scale immigration to Trinidad of planters from the French islands of Martinique, Dominica, and Grenada. The effort of the Spanish crown to promote the development of Trinidad attracted the attention of one who became an enthusiastic promoter of the cause. Though he was not responsible for the expansion of settlement at this time, the Grenadian planter Roume de St. Laurent took an active part in encouraging that immigration. St. Laurent was of the opinion that a large population of whites, along with their slaves was available to settle the island and to expand its cultivation; but he believed that greater advantages needed to be offered them. He travelled first to Caracas and then to Spain to promote the island's cause.[2]

Partly as a result of his advocacy, a Spanish *cedula* or proclamation was issued in 1783 to promote the population of the island. This proclamation provided that the settlers were to be Roman Catholics, and nationals of friendly countries; and that they were admissible after they had taken oaths of loyalty and submission. Each white settler was to receive from the Spanish government a large land grant of 32 acres, as well as an additional grant of half that amount for each slave brought into the island. Each free coloured or black person was to receive 16 acres of land, and an additional eight acres for each slave brought in. Thus anyone entering the island with fifty or more slaves immediately became a considerable land-owner, whether he were white or coloured. Tax exemptions for slave importation during their first ten years, reduction in and exemption from the tithes, the privilege of naturalization after five years, all added to the privileges granted to the new settlers. [3]

To implement this policy, a new Governor was appointed in the person of Jose Maria Chacon, who was fluent in both English and French. He was also well informed, an able administrator, prudent, conciliatory, and affable. The new approach on the part of Spain led to a rapid increase in the population of the island; but even so it was quite small for the size of the colony when the British captured it in 1797. Population growth was rapid in the early years of this policy, reaching 11,533 by 1787. It continued to grow at a slower pace in the following years, but had reached 15,519 in 1794; and in the last three months of Spanish rule it grew rapidly again. At the time of the conquest, the total population was 17,718 persons, and these occupied what is now the county of St. George, the coastal area from Couva to Naparima, the Cedros peninsula, and the north- and south-eastern tips of the island. As a result of the new immigration policy, the bulk of the immigrants consisted of mainly French whites and coloureds with their slaves, to the extent that Spain could be said to rule while France governed. [4] Fraser shows that there were two groups of Frenchmen: those who constituted the more refined class in the society and those who, being of republican views, were thought to be of a more turbulent nature. The French occupied the west coast towards the south; the Spaniards occupied Port of Spain, St. Joseph, and La Brea. [5]

The area settled and under cultivation when the British arrived in 1797 was minuscule compared to the area available for cultivation. A total of 134,688 acres had been granted by the Spanish government, of which over 52,000 acres were in the southern part of the island, and a large proportion of this was in the hands of French planters – white and coloured. Because of the superiority in numbers of the French, and especially of the large number of free coloured proprietors, officials harboured a serious concern for the security of the colony. Many of the whites assumed that the coloured planters would have sympathised with the slave population, apart from being overly influenced by the notions of equality, which the French revolution had made current. Some also regarded the French as republican in their politics, and therefore dangerous. There appeared, therefore, to be a fertile soil for conflict between the various classes of the society.

At the time of its capture the colony was not as thickly populated, nor as well cultivated, as the older colonies of the British West Indies. The population of 17,718 comprised 10,009 slaves, 4.476 people of colour, 1,012 Indians, and 2,151 white persons.[6] As indicated earlier, the chief centres of population were the West coast from Diego Martin to Port of Spain and Maraval, Savaneta to Naparima and Savana Grande, La Brea to Cedros in the south, and eastwards from Port of Spain to Arouca. There were also intermittent settlements between Cumana and Toco in the north east. With respect to its cultivation, there were 468 plantations, which consisted of 159 sugar, 130 coffee, 103 cotton, 6 cocoa, and 70 tobacco plantations, covering an area of approximately 85,268 acres.[7] The amount of cultivable land at the time was calculated to be 2,720 lots – each lot comprising about 320 acres – giving an aggregate of 870,400 acres. [8] Since effective settlement and cultivation had begun only fourteen years prior to the British capture, this would account for the fact that just under one-tenth of the available land had been under cultivation at the time. Col. Thomas Picton, left as interim Governor by the British Commander, estimated the sugar crop for 1798 to be 10,000 hogsheads of 1,000 pounds each, [9] a considerable crop under the circumstances for such an undeveloped colony.

The capture of Trinidad gave to Britain a colony, which had extensive areas of uncultivated crown lands. The existence of such vast areas of rich, virgin soil acted as a powerful attraction to many who had an interest in the potential of the colony as a sugar producer. One of these was Picton himself, shortly to become the colony's first Governor. Keenly interested in the agricultural development of the colony, he quite consistently maintained that it was particularly suited to the cultivation of the sugar cane. [10] He believed that it was, more than anything else, a sugar colony capable of producing more sugar than all the Windward and Leeward islands together. [11] This might well have been an exaggeration on his part; but as he expanded on the subject, one can see that he had in mind very large establishments. The quantity of land which he believed should be granted to immigrants was, quite naturally, to depend on the means of the individual grantee. But he was of the view that no estate should have less than 200 acres: one hundred for sugar cane, fifty for pasture, and another fifty for provision grounds for the slaves.[12] Picton himself made very large grants of land to planters, in some cases amounting to over 1,000 acres. One of these beneficiaries, St. Hiliaire Begorrat, was to become a staunch ally and an influential figure in the colony's development. [13]

The cultivation of sugar cane raised for discussants interested in the colony two very serious issues: the first of these was capital, the second was labour. An estate of the size envisaged by Governor Picton would have required, by his own reckoning, an initial outlay of some £8,000 sterling – presumably for stock and equipment. In view of the soil exhaustion of the old British islands, it was his opinion that some of their capital might profitably have been transferred to Trinidad. Picton was particularly concerned that, if sugar were to be cultivated on a large scale in the island, then the labour force was not only insufficient but urgently needed to be supplemented.[14] The Governor therefore expressed the hope that the British government would give some encouragement to the importation of slaves. He did admit, however, the comparative ease with which cotton, coffee, and cocoa could have been produced even by white labourers – a most unlikely development under the circumstances. Added to this, Picton attested to the valuable work done by the free coloured people from Trinidad and the peons or peasant labourers from the Spanish mainland, whom, however, he considered too unreliable as a source of labour.[15] His preference of crop being what it was, he shared the commonly held view that the sugar cane could not have been cultivated without employing slaves. In support of his appeal to the British government, he observed that nine years' experience in the West Indies had allayed any fears he might have entertained about the slave system. [16]

Given his outlook, therefore, the Governor might well have inundated the new colony with slaves, had not the mere accident of time been against him. For in 1783 – the same year in which the Spanish decree, which initiated the effective settlement of the colony, was published – the Quakers had presented to the British Parliament a motion condemning the slave trade. The loss of the American colonies in the same year deprived slave-owning colonies in the West Indies of valuable trade and support against the humanitarians,[17] which might have ensured the protraction of the slave trade. In addition to this, in 1789 William Wilberforce presented a motion, followed in 1792 by resolutions, to Parliament censuring the continuance of the slave trade. Above all, in the latter year, the British government gave an undertaking to support the abolition of the trade as from January 1, 1796. Although this plan was not eventually carried out, there was a growing body of feeling both inside and outside Parliament, which was opposed to the continuance of the trade.

Slave importation into the new colony was by no means forbidden, however; in fact there was remarkable indecision as to what line was to be followed. The Prime Minister, William Pitt, was willing to promote an Order in Council prohibiting the trade in slaves to the new colonies. But before anything could be done about this, Pitt fell from power; and the new Prime Minister, Addington, refused to prohibit the importation of slaves into Trinidad.[18] This ministerial vacillation and change of attitude explains in part the increase in the slave population in the early years of British occupation. There were, of course, other contributory factors.

In 1799 Dundas, the Secretary of State for the colonies instructed Picton to receive those planters who were migrating to the colony with the approval of Lord Balcarres, Governor of Jamaica.[19] The following year four families arrived with 300 slaves, and there subsequently followed a 'corps' of 300 Africans from St. Domingue under the Count de Rouvray. All except 39 of the latter were admitted by Picton, in spite of strong objections on the part of the Cabildo and other inhabitants.[20] Later on, in 1802, Picton was asked by Lord Hobart, Secretary of State for the colonies, to receive a body of Africans being sent from the Dutch colonies. By his instructions these Africans were to be employed in public works, and were to be fed and clothed at the expense of the new colony.[21] Hobart added another instruction, with respect to persons migrating from the Dutch islands with their slaves, to the effect that the Dutch immigrants were to be given conditional grants of land until the terms of their settlement could be finalised. In further instructions, Hobart apprised Picton of the migration to Trinidad of French Royalists from Martinique, among them a Col. De Soter who had recently embarked with five or six hundred slaves.[22] Intermittently throughout the first years of British occupation the official policy was one of encouraging French Royalists to migrate to Trinidad with their slaves. As a result of such a policy there was a steady increase in the colony's slave population and of persons who both eschewed and supported republican ideology.

The sources of other importation at this time are uncertain. However, the figures for Picton's term as sole administrator of the colony reflect the extent to which such importation took place. In 1797 there were 10,009 slaves in the colony, while by 1798 the slave population had risen to 11,021. By 1799 the number of slaves had risen further to 13,311; and by 1800 to 15,810;[23] in 1801 to 15,975 and in 1802 to 19,709.[24] During the same period the figures for the rest of the population remained fairly constant, with only the free coloured and free black population showing any substantial increase. The following Table illustrates the development:

Table I:
Population of Trinidad, 1797 – 1802

Class	1797	1798	1799	1800	1801	1802
Whites	2151	2186	2128	2140	2153	2261
Free Coloureds	4476	4799	4594	4582	4909	5275
Indians	1082	1005	1143	1149	1112	1232
Slaves	10009	11021	13311	15810	15975	19709

Source: Report of Capt. Mallett for 1797. Trinidad and Tobago Historical Society publications, TTHS 876 for 1798 to 1800, and TTHS 875 for 1801 and 1802.

This table shows that while, on the whole, the total population was increasing comparatively slowly, the slave population had almost doubled. When it is considered that many slaves died during the period of seasoning, that infant mortality was high and that there was death from overwork, the figures suggest that importation was taking place at a rapid rate. As a result the economic change in the colony can be seen to bear eloquent testimony to the benefits, which such an increased slave population had brought. For example, whereas 7,970 acres had been under sugar cultivation only as recently as 1801, the area under cultivation had risen to 9,692 in 1802. Similarly, the total number of sugar mills increased from 159 in 1797 to 231 in 1802.[25] By contrast, however, coffee mills had decreased from 130 to 103 during the same period, and cotton mills from 344 to 256.[26] It was a clear indication that sugar had begun its ascendancy and that, if the alienation of land and the importation of slaves continued at the same rate, Trinidad was likely to be a threat to other neighbouring islands.

TOWARDS A CONSTITUTION AND A SLAVE POLICY

Under the Spanish regime, the administration of government and of justice was in the hands of an organization called the Cabildo, a small self-perpetuating body. After the capitulation of the colony to the British forces in 1797, the military commander, Sir Ralph Abercromby, announced the retention of Spanish laws and virtually the same judicial system.[27] In order to assert British sovereignty and also to deal with the extent of corruption in the Spanish administration, Abercromby appointed a Chief Judge in the person of the Irishman, John Nihell. Nihell was probably the best of a corrupt lot and, at that time, held the office of First Alcalde.[28] The fact that there was widespread ignorance of Spanish law did not appear to have had any influence on Abercromby's decision. Nihell was given jurisdiction in all civil and criminal matters. However, civil appeals from his Court were permitted to the King in Council for sums in excess of £500 sterling; while in criminal cases, appeals were permitted to the Governor. The new Chief Judge was not required to be extremely scrupulous in the interpretation of the Spanish law, but was to be guided virtually by common sense. [29] The Chief Judge, however, was a Commandant of Port of Spain and a planter, [30] and his only qualification for the post was limited acquaintance with the procedures which obtained under the Spaniards. This meant the immediate entrenchment of slave interests within the court system; as far as the slaves and the later amelioration programme were concerned, he was not the person best qualified to carry out the demands of the Colonial Office. The same could be said of the principal officers of the early British period, including Picton.

This retention of Spanish laws became the cause of intermittent petitions to Parliament calling for the introduction of a British constitution and laws. British merchants residing in the colony were of the view that they stood to lose if they were unable to take legal action against debtors. The process by which debt was recovered under Spanish law was long and involved, giving rise to frustration on the part of those who were accustomed to the British system. Under the Spanish administration, bankruptcy was settled at a concursus of creditors, leaving them to divide the property belonging to the debtor among themselves.[31] This procedure was unlike that which prevailed in the British colonies, in which a creditor could satisfy his own account if he were the first to proceed against the debtor. This in itself was no more just than the Spanish process, in which no creditor was likely to recover the amount due to him. In fact, the Spanish process might even be considered more acceptable in that each creditor satisfied at least a part of his debt. What probably made the retention of Spanish law unbearable to the British merchant class in the colony was the fact that the produce of an estate, and not the estate itself, was usually subject to legal process. Neither a sugar estate, nor the slaves on that estate, could be levied on for the repayment of debt, unless the debt amounted to the full value of the estate. [32] This meant that the estates of proprietors, who frequently obtained large sums on credit, were virtually immune from legal action on the part of their creditors. Merchants were therefore naturally eager to have a British constitution and laws introduced, while the Spanish and French proprietors were equally anxious to have Spanish laws retained. The system of laws which the British merchants sought would have enabled not only the estates, but also the slaves, to be sold in settlement of debts.[33]

The demand for a British Constitution and laws included the introduction of a political arrangement similar to that which obtained in the older British colonies of the West Indies. This entailed the introduction of an elected assembly based on an extremely limited franchise, the free coloureds and blacks being specifically excluded. The free coloured planters in the colony were no less resourceful than their white counterparts, and exerted themselves in presenting petitions seeking to be included in whatever political arrangement was arrived at for the future government of the new colony. This concern for the free coloureds came to light in the ill fated Commission government of 1803, in which the plight of the coloureds divided the membership of the Commission.

The contest between planters and merchants had stirred to life a variety of prejudices and ill feeling, at the same time that it failed to produce any beneficial results. The early years of the conflict were characterised by Governor Picton's opposition to the introduction of English laws, almost certainly because he had more power under the Spanish legal system. Neither the *Cabildo*, what could be called the city council, nor a group of persons calling themselves the "colonists", had shown any eagerness for the English laws or constitution. The result of that early contest was the decision, at the time of the cession, to appoint a Council of Advice to assist the Governor whenever he should call on them to do so.[34] This Council consisted of such persons as the Chief Judge, and the chief representatives of the propertied whites – all of whom were slave owners. The Council also functioned as a Court of Appeal; and so a conflict of interest was in the making when the final decision on the island's future as a plantation colony was determined.

This was the state of things when, after the failure of the experiment in Commission government, and the Chief Justiceship of George Smith, Lord Liverpool confirmed the retention of the system of government then in force in the colony. His despatch of November 27, 1810, asserted that circumstances in Trinidad were substantially different from those in the other West Indian colonies, in that the free coloured and black people formed the majority of the free population. In most other colonies, on the contrary, whites formed the majority of that free population, and it was neither just nor politic to accord to Trinidad the same type of government that the others enjoyed. As a result of this decision, Trinidad was not to become like the older colonies – that is, a colony having the capacity to make laws for its own government. It was to be a Crown colony, with its laws taking the form of Orders in Council emanating from the King in Privy Council. The colony would have no legislative authority, and was not expected to be as intractable as the older colonies with their representative system. It would not be able to frame the regulations by which the slaves were to be governed – a privilege which had been accorded settlers by the royal *Cedula* of 1783.[35] This absence of legislative authority was intended to be a way of ensuring that British policy for the colony generally, and for the slaves in particular, were followed to the letter.

The policy which the government might wish to follow in the development of the island excited great interest, as the cession of the island to Britain moved closer to becoming a reality. In some quarters there was continuing opposition to the importation of slaves, as one can see from Hobart's letter to Picton dated February 18, 1802. In this letter the Secretary of State sought to promote settlement by Europeans rather than by wholesale importation of slaves.[36] The idea was to encourage a white Protestant peasantry in the island. Less than 200 such persons were eventually settled in the island; they seem not to have attracted much interest and to have merged into the landscape. Given the existing atmosphere, in which agricultural labour was relegated to slaves by established custom, it seems from this distance very unlikely to have been successful. His view found support in a book written a few years later, while the issue of the slave trade was still unsettled, by one who thought that Scottish highlanders were sufficiently sturdy to survive the rigours of the West Indian climate. What was necessary, the writer explained, was for the government to hold out attractive terms to white persons. In his view "colonial strength consists in the number of the whites," a statement which could have meant a complete system of free white labour or something akin to the system of deficiency laws common in some islands.[37]

Among the abolitionists, any further extension of the slave trade was viewed as a course to be discouraged. In *The Crisis of the Sugar Colonies*, James Stephen, senior, argued that the sale of crown lands was likely to be construed as Government's support for the continuance of the slave trade. Opposed to the expansion of what he termed the "cart whip empire," his preference was for cultivation by means of free labour; but his commercial interest was clear when he argued that 3,000 free Negroes would purchase more British commodities than 10,000 slaves.[38] Canning, though not an abolitionist, later argued in the House of Commons that so large an amount of slaves was required to meet the needs of the colony that the trade would have had to be considerably extended, in which case he was not in favour of the extension. This, however, does not mean that there was agreement on the issue among the principal members of the government. Addington seems not to have committed himself to the suspension of the trade, and was considered suspect by the abolitionists.[39] The planters and merchants of the older colonies were themselves opposed to large scale trading in slaves to

Trinidad, but not for the same reason as the abolitionists. On the one hand they were opposed to the emergence of a new rival in the production of sugar; on the other hand, they were fearful that the lack of the British legal system would have made the recovery of debt difficult for them.[40]

Uncertainty about the future direction of the colony was brought to a head when it was decided to use Trinidad as a laboratory in colonial government. More than one issue was at stake in this decision. One of these related to the issue of the importation of slaves; the other related to the form of government which should be established in the new colony. Ever since the cession of the island seemed likely to become a reality, British inhabitants, although in a minority, had begun to agitate for a British Constitution and laws. In abolitionist circles, however, there was considerable opposition to the introduction of the old system of representative government enjoyed by the older West Indian colonies. With great justice the abolitionist view was expressed that the colonial assemblies were composed of slave owners, whose interests were at stake, and who were jealous of their authority.[41] For this reason, among others, they thought it necessary for Britain to refuse to Trinidad a form of government similar to that which existed in the other West Indian colonies.[42] What probably operated most in their minds was the fact that the older colonies, which enjoyed representative institutions, had never shown themselves amenable to the intervention of the British government in their internal affairs. And this did not augur well for persons like the abolitionists, who were inclined to prefer the imposition of the authority of the mother country.

By way of variation, discussion occasionally veered towards the introduction of "free labourers" to Trinidad. As an alternative to the European labourers, Chinese were imported because of the perception, in some quarters, that they were more industrious than the African slaves. But their introduction into the colony proved to be an unhappy episode, as planter dissatisfaction and administrative bungling led to their being quickly repatriated.[43] The colony was therefore left dependent on slaves, at the very time that the British government was in the last stages of arrangements for the suppression of the slave trade.

This was the state of the colony when, on March 25, 1807, the Act for the Abolition of the Slave Trade received the Royal assent. In theory, this Act closed the door to British participation in that trade as from January 1, 1808. But a concession was granted until March 1, 1808 for those who might have initiated purchases, to ensure that those slaves were finally landed in the West Indies. In order to benefit from the concession, they were required to give proof of hindrance by "Capture, the loss of the Vessel, by the appearance of an enemy upon the Coast, or any other unavoidable

Necessity."[44] However, this concession was seen as giving encouragement to slave importation as well as causing ruin for the capitulants.

While it is true that a primary aim of the abolitionists was to ensure the cessation of the slave trade, it can also be said that, as the abolition debates indicated, they were also concerned about the condition of slavery itself. Their position is encapsulated in the following passage:

> When the trade itself shall be abolished, when the planter shall be altogether precluded from the means of supplying his losses by fresh importations of slaves he will learn the necessity of resorting to a milder treatment and of cherishing the lives of those who remain within his power. [45]

A considerable amount of effort had been applied by the abolitionists to the task of collecting evidence concerning slave mortality during the debates on the slave trade. Consequently, they pressed the argument that high slave mortality was the result of a lack of concern on the part of the owners and managers which, in its turn, was due to the ease with which they were able to replace those they had lost. And so they argued that there could not be any improvement in the condition of the slaves unless the trade was stopped. In this connection, Prime Minister Pitt argued that deaths tended to be more numerous during the period of 'seasoning'- an already established fact – and that such deaths would be reduced when the trade was eventually brought to an end [46]

Another premise of the abolitionist campaign was that the slave population would have been able to reproduce itself after the abolition of the slave trade. The view had long been held that the death rate in the West Indies had been sufficiently low to enable the then existing birth rate to facilitate the accomplishment of an increase of the slave population.[47] But two things were regarded as obstacles to natural increase – the continuing importation of slaves and the disproportion of the sexes. Abolitionists hoped that both of these would have been corrected by the abolition of the trade. In 1791 William Pitt confidently expressed the opinion that the correction of these impediments would have seen the West Indies "revert to that natural order and course of things by which population and civilization are promoted". Both abolitionists and their opponents seem to have been agreed on one thing: there was to be no immediate emancipation of the slaves. Both parties shared the same conclusion, which was, that it would have been to the detriment of the slaves to have been set free at once. So that such ameliorative objectives as there were tended to be overshadowed by these limitations; in other words, the objectives of the abolitionists were remote rather than immediate. None of the improvements, which they considered, was to be introduced at once; but rather very gradually. Even the natural increase of the slave population was something for the distant future.[48]

The prospect of the Bill for the abolition of the slave trade passing into law was not well received by those who had property in the West Indies, and especially not by those who had recently migrated to Trinidad. Everyone seemed to be afraid of economic collapse and the likelihood of unbridled violence on the part of the slaves. Merchants and planters, whose interests in Trinidad were at stake, fought the issue for all they were worth. They appealed to the fact that the colony had only been settled in 1783, and that generous land grants had been made to prospective settlers to encourage cultivation. They noted, moreover, that between 1799 and 1802 successive Colonial Secretaries had invited into Trinidad French loyalists with their slaves, as a result of which planters had incurred considerable expense in clearing land and building factories. The encouragement thus given to them to settle did not suggest anything about the abolition of the slave trade, and its passage was seen as a slap in the face of those settlers. Hinting that the Spaniards on the mainland had issued proclamations intended to attract those who wished to migrate to that place, they suggested that an exodus from Trinidad was the most likely result of the new policy. Thus slaves who might well facilitate the development of Trinidad were likely to be lost to the colony. Their representation contained a contradiction in that one clause drew attention to the large number of slaves in the colony with revolutionary principles; yet it claimed that if it were known that the trade had been abolished, Trinidad would be exposed to the same dangers which had ravaged Ste. Domingue. Its members therefore requested a suspending clause in favour of the colony, until the proportion of African slaves to the rest of the population had been increased.[49] Why an increase of the slave population in relation to whites and free coloureds was better for the colony was never made clear; so that it appears to have been protest for its own sake.

The correspondence between the Governor in Council and Joseph Marryat ,the colony's Agent in London, reflects the anxiety of the parties affected by the Act. Marryat urged a case for compensation for those who had cleared land, which they had been unable to put to good use.[50] The correspondence from Marryat in particular was highly emotive and unlikely to assist dispassionate assessment. Thus he wrote to the Council:

> The decision of Parliament on this point will, I
> think, show whether or not justice and humanity
> are divided in equitable proportion between the
> blacks, and their fellow subjects of their own colour
> in the West Indies... [51]

The contradiction implied in the fear of insurrection on the one hand, and the desire to import more slaves on the other hand, had already been dismissed by Prime Minister Pitt as senseless.[52] It is not surprising that neither the plea for a suspending clause, nor that for compensation, was upheld.

On the other hand, the imminent passage of the Act abolishing the slave trade seems to have given rise to a rapid importation into the colony. E.L.Joseph, for instance, speaks of the "inconvenient rapidity" with which slaves were brought into the colony.[53] This would suggest that slave owners had been making every attempt to ensure that they had a large supply of labourers before the abolition Act came into effect. Thus the slave population, which in 1807 numbered 21,000, had risen to 21,895 in 1808.[54] If we allow for an overall net annual decrease of 1.5 per cent, as suggested by Curtin,[55] the latter figure should have been 20,685 without any further importation. On this basis, the actual figure for 1808 would suggest an importation of over 1,200 slaves.

TREATMENT OF SLAVES

There is no hard evidence concerning the treatment of slaves in the colony at this time. That there was little improvement in the way slaves were treated in the period subsequent to the Act of 1807 was the opinion of one who favoured the system of slavery. The planters, according to Governor Sir Ralph Woodford, had increased the labour of their slaves. The reasons for thus overworking them were: to make up for the labour shortage, which followed the prohibition of slave importation; and to correct the lack of production which had resulted from it.[56] It is not possible to say how soon after 1808 this lack of numbers or decreased production became noticeable. But such statistics as do exist indicate that there were no abnormal fluctuations either in sugar production, or in that of any other crop, between 1808 and 1815. The following table illustrates production during this period.

Table II:

Production in Trinidad, 1808 - 1815

Year	lbs sugar	lbs cocoa	lbs coffee	lbs cotton
1808	25,950,928	668,993	387,028	139,200
1809	24,856,973	719,230	264,330	134,190
1810	21,746,775	726,173	295,443	114,980
1811	18,513,302	640,732	276,243	159,136
1812	20,971,580	1,375,539	282,460	130,390
1813	22,288,145	1,029,512	540,716	184,400
1814	21,604,038	1,158,163	382,888	148,505
1815	25,075,281	1,065,808	262,289	115,150

Source: D. Hart, Trinidad and other West India Islands and Colonies.

One of the great causes of slave oppression in the West Indies was held to be the absenteeism of estate owners. Many of these had bought property and acquired wealth, after which they had withdrawn from the various colonies leaving the management of their estates to attorneys. In Trinidad, the plantations were usually under the management of resident owners due, largely, to the terms of the 1783 *Cedula* of population.[57] This should have acted as a powerful aid to the programme of amelioration; but later chapters will show that there was widespread opposition in the colony to such amelioration as was undertaken. In any case, since Trinidad was not cursed by the plague of absenteeism, a greater measure of success should have been expected in this colony than elsewhere. However, an increasing number of settlers and plantation owners were not bound by the proclamation of 1783, and the desire for wealth was great; so the colony never became a willing 'guinea-pig'. While slave owners in this island did not possess the same constitutional means to oppose the British inspired amelioration programme, they were consistently unwilling to co-operate with it. This was due in part to the implied accusation that they did not treat their slaves well – an accusation, which at all times rankled, and due in part to the fact that they did not have the opportunity to formulate the slave laws themselves, as provided by the *Cedula* of 1783.[58]

The Act for the Abolition of the Slave Trade was not in itself the beginning of amelioration, in spite of the fact that amelioration was one of the long term objectives of those who promoted it. Rather it was a first step in the process of such changes as the abolitionists contemplated. The hope of the framers of the Act was that the absence of the means of replenishing their supply of slaves would have resulted in the owners resorting to a more humane manner of treating them. Events were to prove that the ameliorative objective of the Act was difficult to attain. It would reinforce the conviction that the Act had failed to produce the desired effect — a change of policy on the part of the slave owners; and it was the abolitionists' belief in the continued traffic in slaves, which gave rise to the detailed amelioration programme which followed. That detailed programme involved a set of definite improvements required or suggested by the British government to colonies with representative legislatures; and imposed on one like Trinidad, which lacked such institutions. The programme began with the process of mandatory registration in Trinidad in 1812. Thereafter, a number of specific improvements were gradually added by various Orders in Council, until the process came to an end in 1834 with the abolition of slavery.

1. The Judicial System –
The Framework For Amelioration

The administration of law was to play a significant part in the discussion and implementation of the amelioration programme in Trinidad. Not only would it affect the slaves themselves, as regards their ability to give evidence and the quality of life it helped to facilitate, it would also affect the kind of persons who could sit as judges or serve as subordinate court officials in matters affecting slaves. In order to set this subject into perspective and to get a grasp of the process attempted by the Colonial Office, it is necessary to glance, however briefly, at the nature of slavery in the West Indies. The feature most worthy of note is the arbitrariness of the slave system. According to that system, the slave was the absolute, expendable property of the owner.[1] The slave was described as a special kind of property, and because the slave was replaceable at will, the owner was not as thoughtful in the treatment of his slaves as he should have been. In addition, access to slaves was severely circumscribed, since such access was regarded as interference with another's property. One of the implications of this was the absence of any limit to the nature and extent of the work imposed on the slave; another was the lack of any real sanctions with respect to the nature and extent of the punishments inflicted on them. Until the late eighteenth century, a person could not be prosecuted for murdering a slave of which he was owner; he could only be prosecuted for the destruction of another's property, if he were not the owner of the slave in question.[2] The harshness of the practices on the estates meant that slaves could be mutilated or killed for even minor offences, since killing a slave was not recognized as murder. Where it was regarded as a crime, since slaves could not give evidence against whites, the exclusion of their evidence meant that the murderer of a slave could escape trial as long as the only witness was a slave.

Part of the arbitrariness of the slave system lay in the fact that the owners of slaves were themselves the lawmakers in the West Indies. For that matter, they also administered the law as judges. Quite naturally, therefore, the laws served to protect the interests of the slave owners in exercising control over their slaves, rather than to ensure that right was done and wrong punished. And if those judges were not trained in law, the lot of the slave was pitiable.[3] Under the French regime in the islands, as under the Spaniards, there was a mechanism for protecting the slaves; but this did not necessarily work in the slaves' interest.[4] In the British islands, the laws passed tended to restrict many of the activities of slaves, even when those activities were innocent.[5] Laws often remained on the statute books, even though they were not being enforced.

The arbitrariness of the system extended further to personal relationships, except that plantation society in the British colonies did not quite regard the slave as a person. This was a natural result of looking at the slave as property. In that context, institutions such as marriage were not provided for at law and did not receive the support of the slave owners. As David Brion Davis said, in reviewing the subject, "marriage leads to a contractual relationship of authority and obedience, of reciprocal rights and obligations within a family, which is clearly incompatible with the concept of a master's absolute ownership of his slaves."[6] On the same basis of absolute ownership, families might be separated at the whim of their owners, and women could be exploited for sexual gratification by the owners and their friends.[7] And yet, the humanity of the slaves could not be ignored. Thinking of a human being as a thing was a contradiction; and, as the abolition campaign progressed, slave owners were forced to reckon with the simple fact that "a slave was not a piece of property, nor a half-human instrument, but a man held down by force."[8] In one way or another, the whole amelioration programme in the West Indies was a development of this thesis.

The circumstances of the island, when it was ceded to Britain in 1802, were peculiar in that the Spanish colony had a predominantly French population, and later an imposing British minority. In seeking to settle the legal framework for administering the colony, Britain would embark on a series of experiments with law and administration in an effort to find a system that was satisfactory to all parties, and one which preserved the growing pressure on the colonies to deal with slaves in a more humane manner. It was a matter of concern for officials at the Colonial Office that there should be a means of ensuring that the government's system for the management of the slaves really worked, at least judicially. It was also a matter of concern for the free coloured and black population, who were indirectly affected by the amelioration programme, to discover just how the legal system either assisted or impaired that programme and what the implications were for them.

To help set the stage, let us begin by looking at the way in which the law was administered in Trinidad, and especially its implications for slavery. The Spanish system of law and administration was in force in late eighteenth century Trinidad, even though the vast majority of the population was not Spanish. Many of the settlers were ignorant of Spanish law, the only exceptions being the Governor - by dint of administrative experience, and his assessor - a trained lawyer. In that system, justice was administered by a number of functionaries in various courts. The first courts were those of two officials called Alcaldes in Ordinary, of whom there were two. The First Alcalde demitted office after functioning in that capacity for one year, while the Second Alcalde automatically succeeded to the office of First Alcalde. In effect, therefore, only one alcalde- the Second Alcalde - needed to be elected annually by the *Cabildo* or town council to replace the one who was going out of office. The purpose of this arrangement was to ensure that there always was someone in office who was acquainted with the matters before the courts. Each Alcalde presided over an independent court, and litigants had an option of appearing before the Alcalde of their choice.[9] The trouble with this arrangement was that the alcaldes were not trained in law and need not have been literate, as the legal Report of the 1820s stated. In addition to this, the short duration of their tenure meant that new officers depended on precedents set by their predecessors or their ability to acquaint themselves rapidly with Spanish law.

A Spanish Governor also presided over a separate tribunal with the assistance of his Assessor – usually a qualified lawyer. Like the Alcaldes, the Governor had both civil and criminal jurisdiction; but in criminal cases, where capital or corporal punishment was adjudged, the sentences had to be confirmed by a tribunal called the *Audiencia* in Caracas. This body had a variety of functions, such as conducting an inquiry into the performance of any Governor who had ended his term of office, as well as confirming the sentences of death as indicated earlier. Although the Governor's tribunal was normally supreme within the colony, it was possible to appeal from his tribunal to the *Audiencia*. There were also courts of the Commandants of Quarters, and there also existed a host of minor officials whose functions were somewhat peripheral to the work of the courts.[10] The Commandants of Quarters were first introduced by the last Spanish Governor, Chacon, and their functions included responsibility for the administration of their quarters, jurisdiction as magistrates in petty cases, and the raising of militias. They could impose punishment on both slave and free, though they were limited as regards their punishment of free persons.[11]

Spanish laws tended to be liberal, slavery in their colonies appearing to be milder than elsewhere in the West Indies. Nevertheless, Spain introduced, into this relatively mild system, the *Cedula* of 1789 which was intended to remedy certain abuses which had crept into the practice of slave owners. The *Cedula* therefore provided for the participation of the slaves in religious observances and for their instruction in the Christian religion by priests in each colony; for proper allowances of food and clothing, the nature of which was to be made public; for a regulated pattern of labour both in relation to age and sex; for recreation, hospitals, maintenance for those too old to work; for the regulation of punishments to be imposed on slaves, as well as of punishments for those who injured slaves. This code was not well received in some islands, the strength of planter opposition in Cuba forcing its withdrawal from use in that island in 1791.[12]

Shortly after the conquest, the British commander, Sir Ralph Abercromby, decided to retain Spanish law as far as possible, and virtually the same judicial system. All officers in the civil and criminal jurisdictions were to retain their offices and emoluments, once they had taken the oath of allegiance to the British monarch.[13] In deciding to retain Spanish law, Abercromby would seem to have opted for the most expedient course he could adopt, with a view to ensuring the continuation of a viable system of law and order in the island. The number of British settlers was far too small for him to consider an immediate change to a British legal system; and with the vast majority of the population being French, such an arrangement was impracticable. In that context, Abercromby appointed as Chief Judge the Irishman, John Nihell, who held the office of first alcalde of the Cabildo at the time. Nihell was not trained in law, nor did he know Spanish law; in fact, there was widespread ignorance of Spanish law both on the part of the conquerors and on the part of many of the residents. This did not deter the commander, almost certainly because the arrangement was intended to be temporary, that is, until the war with Spain was concluded. Nihell was given jurisdiction in all civil and criminal matters. Civil appeals from his court were permitted to the King in Council for sums in excess of £500 sterling; while, in criminal matters, appeals were to be made to the Governor. In this regard, the court of the Governor now replaced the court of the Audiencia in Caracas and, as Millette observes, left a void in legal affairs. The supervisory role of the Audiencia, which ensured that Spanish law was adhered to, now ceased to exist. There no longer was any point of reference besides the British officials.[14] However, since Britain was at war with Spain, and given the turbulent nature of Simon Bolivar's Venezuela, the connection with Caracas obviously could not be continued. The courts of the alcaldes in ordinary were to continue as they had done before, but subject to local supervision.

The new Chief Judge was not required to be unduly scrupulous in his interpretation of the Spanish law, but was to be guided by his conscience and the need to bring outstanding matters to a head. Significantly as far as future developments were concerned, Abercromby was of the view that too strict an administration of Spanish law in an English colony would lead to confusion.[15] In that regard, his comments would prove to be prophetic. In addition to having this new office, Nihell was also a member of the Cabildo, one of the Commandants of the Quarter of Port of Spain, and a planter. This meant that, as far as the new policy for the treatment of slaves was concerned, he was not the best person to carry out the demands of the Colonial Office.

With the cession of Trinidad to Britain in 1802, a permanent settlement of the affairs of the island was called for. Given the determination not to give control to a local administration consisting mainly of slave owners, the British government continued the arrangement made by Abercromby, with the exception that it created a Council which was to have limited legislative authority within the island. The Council was to consist of not less than three nor more than five persons, its members being appointed by the Governor rather than elected by the citizenry. In a disastrous experiment shortly after the cession, the British government then decided to appoint a Commission of three persons to administer the island as well as to assist it in determining those Spanish laws which should be retained and those English laws which might be introduced. This ill fated experiment proved unsuccessful, answered none of the questions, and left matters in an indeterminate form which continued until the appointment of Chief Judge George Smith in 1809.[16]

Nihell was the only untrained person to hold the office of Chief Judge during the period under review. He was superseded by the notorious George Smith, a trained lawyer. The appointment of George Smith was an experiment fraught with danger, in that the incumbent was responsible for drafting his own commission. In so doing, Smith contracted unto himself all the powers which belonged to his own office as well as those which belonged to the *Audiencia* in Caracas. Smith was appointed simultaneously to three distinct offices, which could not be altogether reconciled. He was appointed Chief *Oidor*, an office responsible for ensuring that the acts of the Council of the Indies were duly executed. He was also appointed *Alcalde del Crimen*, which properly speaking, corresponded more closely with some functions of the office of Chief Justice. Finally, he was appointed Fiscal, which made him the Governor's adviser in law. Smith's strict enforcement of the Spanish law, including his insistence that Spanish be the language of the court, and his less than cordial relationship with Governor Hislop, helped to make his tenure an unpleasant one. In the end both Smith and Hislop left Trinidad in the same year never to return.[17] Smith was replaced some three years later by another trained British lawyer, Justice John Bigge.

The appointment of trained British lawyers as Chief Justices facilitated the introduction of certain aspects of British law, especially any legislation related to slavery. Elsa Goveia has pointed out that the British had no tradition of laws for the protection of the slaves. The problem with the British colonies stemmed from the principle of non-interference in the legislative functions of those colonies with representative institutions. The result was that the colonies evolved a body of laws which reflected the interests of the slave owning legislators. The acquisition of new colonies at the end of the Napoleonic wars posed significant challenges for the British government. In the first place, the grant of those representative institutions, which English settlers demanded, would have meant giving the colonists the right to make laws for their own government. Those persons who were lawmakers, some of whom also functioned as judges, were invariably slave owners. Apart from the liberty of the subject, there was no more inviolable right than that of holding property. And since slaves were regarded as property, though property of a special kind, preservation of the slave system was likely to be a matter of tremendous importance for them.

In the second place, Britain had already committed herself to the abolition of the slave trade. The establishment of representative institutions would have run counter to the British government's intention of closely monitoring the slave system. Not only would the government have been accused of interfering in the internal affairs of the colony, it would also have been considered guilty of interfering with the property of individuals. The humanitarians' outlook that the slave was a person also ran counter to the view prevailing in the West Indies that the slave was property. One or the other had to give way. Hence there emerged the idea of a new form of colony, one in which laws were framed in London for enforcement in the colony.[18]

THE BEGINNING OF CHANGE

As British policy regarding the slave trade and slavery progressed, occasional changes were made in the laws of the colony, although the Spanish law remained largely in force. For instance, the passage of the Act for the Abolition of the Slave Trade necessitated the establishment of a Court of Vice Admiralty. This court, when it was established in Trinidad, was presided over by the Chief Justice,[19] and its responsibilities were limited to infractions of the laws dealing with slave importation. That being the case, the Court was empowered to take cognizance of cases of smuggling into Trinidad and matters respecting forfeiture and related penalties. It was therefore this Court which was charged with trying the difficult cases of 1832 and 1833, following a Proclamation of the Governor, Sir Lewis Grant, concerning the freedom of those slaves who were deemed to have been illegally imported.[20]

The counterpart of this Court was that of Admiralty, which was concerned with the illegal export of slaves from the colony. No such court was established in Trinidad, and this presented the authorities with grave difficulties when there were perceived infractions of the law. As a result, cases of this nature had to be forwarded to Barbados, where the nearest Court of Admiralty was situated [21]. But the fact that this Court was located in Barbados gave rise to other serious problems. The Governor of Trinidad, for instance, had no authority over the officers of the Court in Barbados, and was therefore dependent on the willingness of officials in that island to comply with his requests. In 1820 this resulted in the acquittal of one offender as the Attorney General in Barbados was unwilling to prosecute.[22] The case against Jose Maria Sanda furnishes another example of the difficulty involved. Sanda was charged with piracy in 1829 for having transported a few of his slaves to South America.[23] The question of the jurisdiction of existing Courts was referred by Governor Grant to his principal law officers – the Chief Justice, the Judge of the Court of Criminal Inquiry, the Assessor, the Attorney General, and the Solicitor General. They were almost unanimous in stating that the case should be transferred to Barbados, where a Court of Admiralty was located.[24] As it turned out, the case was never tried and eventually was dismissed. What is even more serious, as far as the effectiveness of the system was concerned, was the opinion of the Solicitor General, Henry Gloster, that witnesses could not have been compelled to go to Barbados.[25] To all intents and purposes, therefore, this aspect of the Act was a dead letter, because the colony lacked the proper machinery for its administration.

The authority for the judicial structure in Trinidad for most of the period of amelioration was an Order in Council of September 16, 1822,[26] which established three Criminal Courts in the colony. These were: a Court of Criminal Inquiry, a Court for the Trial of Criminal Prosecutions, and a Court of Appeals in cases of condemnation to death. The Court of Appeal was vested in the Governor or Lt. Governor with the assistance of the members of the Council. Three members of the Council, together with the Governor, constituted a court. Appeals were to be lodged within twenty-four hours of the sentence in the lower court, and no less than three votes were required for or against the appeal.[27] This court created a major anomaly in that persons could appeal from a court consisting of trained lawyers to a "higher" court in which not a single member was a lawyer. This is because the Judge, the Attorney General or other law officer, who was a member of the Council, could not be expected to sit in the Council when it sat as a Court of Appeal.

The Court for the Trial of Criminal Prosecutions consisted of the Chief Judge as President, the Governor's Assessor, and the two Alcaldes in Ordinary. This court was to take cognizance of "all criminal offences committed in the island," with the exception of some petty offences which were the responsibility of the courts of the alcaldes. In this court, which tried both slaves and free persons, the Attorney General was named prosecutor. The Order required proceedings to be conducted in accordance with Spanish law, and subject to its provisions. Given the prevailing ignorance of Spanish law in the colony, it is not clear how this was intended to work; and therefore it constituted a recipe for disaster. The Order further provided that each of the four officers constituting the court had an equal voice in determining the outcome of the trial, the vote of three of them being required for sentences of death. Decisions of the court were final, except in the case of sentences of death when defendants had a right of appeal. The three officials in favour of conviction were to sign the sentence of the Court.[28] If no appeals were filed within twenty-four hours of the conviction and sentence, that sentence was to be carried out in three days.

The Court of Criminal Inquiry was to be presided over by a single judge. As a Court of First Instance, it was competent to receive evidence from any accuser on alleged criminal offences. Information on such offences could be brought before the Court by a Commandant, if the offence were committed outside of Port of Spain; or by the Chief of Police, if the offence were committed within the limits of the town. If there were sufficient grounds for prosecution, the duty of the judge was to pass the information to the Attorney General or other law officer for action. The latter in turn was to file a charge against the accused within eight days, and within forty-eight hours thereafter was to ascertain from the Chief Judge the date of the trial.[29] All witnesses were to attend the Court under penalties specified in the Order.[30] The Alcaldes were also authorised to preside over lesser Courts to consider petty thefts, assaults, or breaches of the peace.[31]

The whole tenor of this Order suggests that considerable emphasis was being placed on an expeditious dispatch of the business of the Courts. This was one of the objectives of George Smith during his ill-fated term of office as Chief Justice of the colony,[32] as he aimed to correct the sloth of the Spanish legal system which the British had inherited and temporarily retained. At the same time, the procedure to be followed was precisely stated: all criminal prosecutions were to be initiated in the Court of Criminal Inquiry, and all prosecutions were to be conducted by the Attorney General in the Court for the Trial of Criminal Prosecutions. In both courts, the judges exercised their discretion as to whether the evidence of slaves was to be accepted; and both judges gave evidence to the Legal Commissioners to the effect that such evidence was occasionally accepted.

As a general rule, slave evidence was not accepted by courts in the Caribbean. In Trinidad, as the new slave system evolved, changes in the law were gradually introduced. The new courts, coming at a time when the amelioration programme was at its height, raises the question: how were the slaves to be accommodated? According to the Commissioners of Legal Inquiry, the Spanish law was in force in the island; that did not admit of any doubt. The report suggested that there was no distinction in proceedings "in criminal cases between them and free persons."[33] This conclusion needs to be qualified by the evidence given to the commissioners by the two judges, which indicated that slave evidence was accepted at the discretion of the court. Neither judge had any positive opinion on the veracity of slaves, and their stereotypical assessment of them seemed to militate against their acceptance of the evidence of individual slaves in criminal cases. In fact, the commissioners also found that "The only cases in which slaves can be admitted as witnesses" in the civil court was in claims for freedom under the Order in Council of March 1812.[34] Despite appearing to be divided as to the ability of slaves to acquire   property, the judges were in fact concurring in their testimony on the subject. Lewis Johnston, the judge of the Court of Criminal Inquiry, responded negatively to a question on that head, while the Chief Justice indicated their ability to acquire property, but only for their masters.[35] What all of this means is that, because of the retention of Spanish law, the legal condition of slaves in Trinidad was really not much better than that of their counterparts in the older British colonies. Everything depended on the individual slave owner. Under the existing system in Trinidad, the British government had the authority to produce laws for the benefit of the slaves. This was the situation when a detailed programme to implement the Parliamentary resolutions of May 1823 for the amelioration of slavery was introduced in the colony, by means of an Order in Council.

The Order in Council of March 1824, when it came into effect, constituted a considerable departure in that slaves were no longer to be regarded as mere chattels. Rather, the underlying principle of that Order, as indicated by Bathurst, was that the slaves had rights defensible at law.[36] In another respect, however, it created a great difficulty in that it altered the procedures for the trial of slaves. Of major importance was the fact that it empowered the Protector of Slaves to institute proceedings, in the Court for Criminal Prosecutions, against those who ill treated slaves.[37] It did not require much ingenuity on the part of the judges to point out the double irregularity involved here. In the first place, any such proceedings should have been taken to the Court of Criminal Inquiry before being brought to the Court for the Trial of Criminal Prosecutions. In the second place, only the Attorney General, or some other law officer, was authorised to prosecute in the Court for the Trial of Criminal Prosecutions. The Protector of Slaves, in that capacity, could not institute any such trial, even though the same individual subsequently held office as Solicitor General. Lack of care in drafting the Order had created an obstacle, which, while it continued, deprived the slaves of the protection which they had every right to expect.

The Chief Justice of the time, Ashton Warner, might be considered difficult when he indicated that he did not believe that the Order referred to the Court for the Trial of Criminal Prosecutions which existed in the colony.[38] This is because of an error of nomenclature, in which the Order purported to give jurisdiction for such offences to the "Court for Criminal Prosecutions" – which was not the full title of the court in question. Even when the Governor issued a Proclamation to vest the Protector with authority to take proceedings to the Court of Criminal Inquiry, the judge of that Court declined jurisdiction in the matters brought before him. Regarding prosecution as conducted "for the purpose of enforcing penalties" under the Order in Council of 1824, he declined to take cognizance of matters brought to his court by the Protector.[39] The objections of the judges were based on the incompetence of the Protector to prosecute. On the basis of the Order in Council of September 1822, he was not qualified to prosecute and presumably could not institute an inquiry in the Court of Criminal Inquiry. During one trial the defence made an objection to the effect that the Protector of Slaves was a magistrate and could not, by the laws of the colony, exercise the functions of prosecutor. This meant that the very organs which should have facilitated the amelioration programme were entangled in a web of confusion, which the framers of the law were not sufficiently careful to have anticipated.

As a result of situations such as these, one judge considered it necessary for the Governor to set out in an explanatory Proclamation the exact procedure to be followed.[40] This proposal by Lewis Johnston, the Judge of the Court of Criminal Inquiry, was adopted by Woodford reluctantly, and was seconded by James Stephen, jr. even more reluctantly. For Stephen referred to the confirmation of the Governor's Proclamation of June 1824 in which the Protector was authorised to carry information before the Court of Criminal Inquiry as sufficient; as a result of this he considered the judge's objection unintelligible.[41] Nevertheless he recommended the confirmation of the suggested Proclamation, as an act of urgent necessity, in order that the amelioration process might not prove to be a useless formality. In other words, the judge of that Court had sufficient authority to proceed; that he did not would suggest obstruction on his part. In a later Proclamation for giving effect to the Order in Council of February 1830, the Protector was authorised to prosecute in all cases of offences by free persons against slaves. The information was to be passed to the Court of Criminal Inquiry, as provided by the Order in Council of September 16, 1822.[42]

It was the ameliorative Order in Council of March 10, 1824 which, for the first time, made any part of the estates of the colony liable to criminal proceedings. For by the 42nd clause, owners were exposed to the forfeiture of their slaves if they were found guilty of more than one criminal act against them. The danger of losing their property, which this clause entailed, caused the great negative reaction reported by Woodford to Bathurst.[43] This section of the Order in Council aimed at correcting the masters' unchecked abuse of authority over their slaves; but it would operate in an atmosphere in which even complaint was regarded as an offence.

As an example of what could happen in the case of complaints, one may cite the problem of the slaves, Marquis and Regis, who complained in 1823 of the death of another slave as a result of their master's cruelty. The *Syndic Procurador* of the Cabildo, Henry Fuller, whose responsibility it was to protect the slaves, investigated the complaint in the firm belief that the accusation was false. The certificates tendered by the doctors consulted were anything but satisfactory, but they served to acquit the master. In those circumstances, Governor Woodford considered the owner humane – the only time he spoke well of coloured slave owners, so far as the documents show. In order to indicate his aversion to false complaints, he ordered the slaves, Marquis and Regis, to receive seventy-five and one hundred lashes respectively.[44] Apart from the correspondence between himself and Fuller, and the enclosed certificates, there was no 'trial' of the slaves concerned.[45] Woodford claimed to have appealed to Spanish laws to the effect that Kings and Judges could punish such conduct on their own; and also that slave could only make accusations in a limited number of cases, such as treason, withholding tribute, the issue of false money, and the murder of his master.[46] What this indicates is that, as far as Woodford was concerned, the slaves had no right to complain against their master. This was his principal objection; whether the complaint was true or false was actually secondary at best. And hence he imposed the flogging as a deterrent to other slaves who might follow the example of the slaves in question.

A grave problem, in view of the future amelioration programme, involved the active assistance rendered to the Governor in this investigation by Henry Fuller, who was at that time *Syndic Procurador General* of the

Cabildo. This responsibility subsequently led Earl Bathurst to recommend the merger of the Protectorate of Slaves with the then existing office of *Syndic Procurador General*. From the very beginning of the investigation of the slaves' complaint, Fuller was concerned with the vindication of the slave master rather than with any real investigation of the complaint. At the same time, however, Fuller was Attorney General; and in that capacity he would have had responsibility for prosecuting misdemeanours on the part of all those responsible for breaches of the law. This, of course, depended on whether or not the Order in Council of September 1822 was being strictly observed and, quite naturally, on the extent of his identification with the slave owner. Finally, Fuller was also a plantation owner and, as such, could not be expected to be impartial in the exercise of his various duties regarding the slaves. Thus the very participation of this officer in the slave system as owner militated against the proper functioning of the amelioration programme if or when he was appointed Protector.

New Directions

This raises another crucial point with respect to the administration of justice in Trinidad at this time. The demand for impartiality on the part of the judicial officers was a matter of great concern throughout the period of debates on the slave trade and slavery. While it is true that high judicial office was put in the hands of qualified lawyers, it is equally true that such office was often put into the hands of slave owners. This is particularly worthy of note when one considers that all the Courts had slave owners among their principal officials. While the Governor did not have more than one domestic slave,[47] certainly the other officials of the Courts could not be said to be aloof from major slave interests. The Judge of the Court of Criminal Inquiry, Lewis Johnston, had 207 plantation and eight personal slaves; the Chief Judge, who presided over the Court for the Trial of Criminal Prosecutions, had 81 and five respectively; the Governor's Assessor, Antonio Gomez, had 62 and eight; the Attorney General, Henry Fuller, had 343 and eight; the Deputy Registrar of Slaves had 105 plantation slaves; the Protector had nine personal slaves; and the Alcaldes had some as well. Add to this the fact that all except one Commandant had plantation slaves, yet were appointed Assistant Protectors of Slaves in 1824, and the severity of the problem becomes more apparent.[48] This involvement in the slave system was one reason for the dismissal of prosecutions against slave owners.

As a remedy for this situation, the British government issued in June 1831 an Order in Council, in which a new arrangement was established.

The Court of Criminal Inquiry and the Court for the Trial of Criminal Prosecutions were combined and vested in the Chief Justice and two Puisne Judges, none of whom was to have any interest in slaves. And though it was permissible for them to acquire slaves by way of the settlement of any debt, they were required to get rid of such slaves within six months. Another significant change instituted by this Order was its provision for three Assessors, who were to be drawn from the membership of the Cabildo. The Assessors were authorised to sit with the Judges, with whom they had equal power and authority "in every respect," conviction being the result of a majority of those voting.[49] From the perspective of the composition and function of this court, the Order had not differed greatly from that of 1822, where, in the Court for the Trial of Criminal Prosecutions, all judges had equal votes and three positive votes were required for the death sentence to be adjudged.

These provisions would have serious repercussions in Trinidad in less than a year of the establishment of the Court. The restriction against Judges owning slaves appeared to the Governor, Sir Lewis Grant, to be an obstacle of considerable magnitude, in that all the 'respectable' barristers were known to be owners of slaves. By way of resolving this difficulty, the Governor recommended the appointment of certain English barristers to fill any vacancies created as a result of this change.[50] The restriction also meant that one of the judges at that time, Lewis Johnston, stood to lose his position because he was the owner of many slaves. Two Puisne Judges were appointed in the persons of Messrs Hanley and Bent, who served in this capacity until the end of 1832. Lewis Johnston, in the meantime, had been offered the post of Attorney General, having lost his judgeship because of his ownership of slaves. This new post was made vacant by Henry Fuller's having relinquished it, he being the owner of several slaves. The basis of the offer to Johnston, therefore, suggests considerable inconsistency in policy on the part of the governor, an inconsistency which did not escape the notice of and protest by Fuller.[51] Johnston did not accept the offer.

Johnston was not sidelined for very long; by the beginning of 1833, he was appointed one of the two Puisne Judges in the colony. To gain the appointment, he had given his cocoa and sugar estates to his daughter.[52] Antonio Gomez, the Governor's Assessor, had adopted a similar expedient in that he too had given his cocoa and sugar estates to his son and daughter;[53] so that by January 30, 1833, he had been sworn in as a Puisne Judge.[54] This meant that two of the three Judges in the colony were officers whom one could only loosely describe as not being interested in slaves. In this case, we see repeated a process identical with that which surrounded the appointment of the first Registrar of Slaves in 1813.[55] Had Henry Fuller succeeded in retaining his position as Attorney General, the tragi-comedy would have been complete. The folly of the exercise of appointing such officers would then have been as amusing as the travesty of justice would have been sad. But Fuller opted to retain his slaves and therefore forfeited his office.

With the implementation of the Order in Council of November 2, 1831, the last of the ameliorative Orders, a serious problem arose in the Court for trying offenders against that code. The immediate cause was the refusal of the two Alcaldes to take their seats in Court – in essence, a refusal to be party to what one of them described as the 'persecution' of the accused.[56] As a result of this action, the sittings of the Court were interrupted for some time. Governor Grant got straight to the heart of the matter – which was that absence would be habitual unless some means were provided of ensuring the impartiality of the assessors. And he observed that, if the assessors were compelled to attend, their judgement was likely to be influenced by their perception of the relationship between master and slave.[57] This problem created a dilemma for the Government, and the big question was: how could it be resolved? Grant recommended that the Criminal Court should be composed of three judges for misdemeanours which fell short of felony; while for a felony there should be three judges and three assessors.[58] In so doing, Grant was echoing the view of Chief Justice Scotland, who had made a similar proposal.[59] In defence of his suggestion, Grant put forward the following arguments: first, that the Cabildo was a self elected body, and that it was highly objectionable that the assessors be chosen exclusively from its membership; secondly, that it was impossible to expect the same degree of impartiality from a court consisting of three judges and three assessors as from one consisting of three judges only – except in cases as serious as homicide;[60] and thirdly, that the Assessors were not to be limited to persons of British birth.[61] The modified jury system, which Grant seemed to be advocating at this point, was a step towards what people had been demanding for many years previous to this date. It was as far as he was prepared to go in the peculiar circumstances of a colony lacking the laws which accompanied such a system. But in view of the manner in which two of the judges obtained their office, Grant's optimism was by no means securely based. His system did not provide for the impartiality of the assessors – a point which he himself had raised.

While Grant's mind was grappling with the specific circumstance of the failure of the Court to function, he omitted to come to grips with what appears to have been a crucial issue – the fact that all misdemeanours with respect to breaches of the slave code were being heard in the Supreme Court of the colony. And the objection was made in view of the fact that some cases of a similar nature, which did not involve slaves, had been heard in the Courts of the Alcaldes.[62] Taxing himself with the problem, one official at the Colonial Office recommended that the Chief Justice be given a casting vote,[63] to which another objected that it would have destroyed the essential character of the institution. The latter, James Stephen, jr., also objected to dispensing with the Assessors. Instead, he proposed that every man over twenty-one years be competent to sit as an Assessor; and that misdemeanours of a lower order be cognisable before a single judge. As a matter of caution he also recommended that care should be taken to define the penalties which might be imposed by that individual.[64]

This was virtually the same position adopted by Lord Goderich, the Secretary of State, who felt that the 'popular arm' of the judiciary should be maintained; for to dispense with it, as some suggested, would in his view have constituted an unjustifiable stigma on the colonists and would have made the slave law unpopular. He also rejected the idea of a casting vote for the President of the Court, on the ground that it would have aroused public sympathy for the convicted person. However, he hoped that, by extending the office of Assessor to the general public, to restore their confidence in the Tribunals and, at the same time, to move towards the introduction of the English jury system.[65]

The complex problem was eventually settled by an Order in Council of November 6, 1832, which provided for the trial of lesser offences before a minor court;[66] subsequently, a proclamation of February 23, 1833, provided rules for the trial of such cases.[67] These instruments settled, for the time being, some of the distressing problems of the judicial system, and also helped to correct the anomaly of a law which could not be applied because of the conflict of interests in the very officials on whom its success depended.

2. The Process of Slave Registration

As observed earlier, the passage of the Act for the Abolition of the Slave Trade was partially intended as a means of rousing the slave owners in the West Indies to take a humane interest in their slaves. From the outset the abolitionists had been aware that a very difficult task still lay ahead – that was the task of enforcing the Act. Their concern for this matter showed itself in two ways: on the one hand they exerted steady pressure on the British government with a view to getting foreign governments committed to the abolition of the trade in their own countries. On the other hand, soon after the passage of the Act for the abolition of the slave trade, some of the abolitionists formed themselves into a society which came to be known as the African Institution. This Society served as a watch-dog over British efforts for the suppression of the slave trade. But the continuance of that trade was regarded by them as a distinct possibility even before the Act was passed. And they would later allege that, in spite of great watchfulness, some seventy to eighty thousand slaves had been shipped from Africa in 1810.[1]

In that same year the abolitionists began to show concern over what was perceived as the failure of the Act to deter those who were intent upon importing slaves to the West Indies. William Wilberforce complained to Zachary Macaulay that the West Indians were not adapting themselves to the new system,[2] hinting broadly at changes to come. On June15, 1810, the possibility that the Act of 1807 was being evaded was drawn to the attention of the House of Commons by Henry Brougham, who expressed the fear that the proximity of Trinidad and Guyana to the slave markets of South America was likely to render ineffective any efforts at ensuring the abolition of the slave trade.[3] In spite of lack of support from persons like Canning, a law was passed in 1811 making slave trading a felony punishable by transportation for as many as fourteen years.[4]

At a meeting of abolitionists held in December 1810, measures were agreed on for possible action by that body. Among these were the curbing of the contraband trade to conquered territories, and the devising of a means of bringing the slaves in the West Indies "under a humane and beneficent management."[5] In a way both of these plans might be considered progenitors of the Order in Council for the registration of slaves, which came into being less than two years later. Wilberforce had actually hinted at the possibility of some definite measure when, some time previously, he had informed Macaulay that James Stephen, senior, was planning to introduce his own form of improvement using Trinidad as a model.[6] He had also mentioned an unfavourable report which he had received concerning the treatment of slaves in Trinidad.[7] And this might well have given an edge to abolitionist schemes for dealing with slavery in that colony.

One of the plans which the abolitionists had in mind was a general registration of all slaves in the West Indies. For this purpose they had planned to introduce a Registry Bill in Parliament in 1812, an action which was precipitated by James Stephen's threatened withdrawal of support for the abolitionist cause.[8] Considerable pressure was therefore brought to bear on Prime Minister Perceval, whom Wilberforce was anxious to persuade to give immediate effect to the scheme. Perceval, however, did not share the enthusiasm of the abolitionists for the project, and may not even have been convinced of its merit at that time. He therefore only reluctantly agreed to let it be tried in Trinidad, expressing his preference for a general registration in the West Indies to be deferred until one year's trial had indicated the strength or weakness of the measure.[9] The result was that Trinidad was destined to be the scene of the first experiment in amelioration, which the Colonial Office decided to implement. Because of its importance for later developments, the terms of the Order are given in some detail.

The registration of slaves was formally introduced by an Order in Council of March 26, 1812.[10] This Order, the brainchild James Stephen, senior, had as its objectives the curbing of the "illegal and clandestine importation of slaves into Trinidad", and ensuring that only those who had been duly registered were kept in a state of slavery. There was no direct evidence to support the allegation of "illegal and clandestine importation", nor did the abolitionists consider it worth their while to establish that smuggling was actually taking place. Later, however, it would become clear that a view prevailed to the extent that some 5,000 slaves had been smuggled into the colony annually in the years following the Act of 1807.[11]

TERMS OF THE ORDER

In order to monitor the process of registration, the Order in Council created the office of Registrar of Slaves, the incumbent of which was to be a "fit and proper person" for that responsibility, bearing in mind that his performance was to be of critical importance to the success of the programme. The Registrar was to perform such duties as had previously been required by Article 12 of the *Cedula* of 1789, which was believed to be in force in the island. By that Article, slave owners were required to make a return of the slaves in their possession. With the introduction of this Order, however, that provision was repealed. The Order provided that the Registrar of Slaves, before he assumed office, was to be bound by two sureties in the sum of £1,000 sterling each, while he was to deposit £2,000 sterling on his own behalf for the faithful performance of his duty. In addition he was to take an oath to the effect that he would perform his duty with integrity, neither committing nor permitting any defalcations in the registers. At the public expense, the Governor was to provide a house or suitable accommodation in the town for the offices of the Registrar. The latter was to provide two large books, one for the registration of all plantation slaves – slaves normally employed in plantation labour, the other for the registration of personal slaves – the latter group consisting of any persons engaged in domestic labour, handicrafts or trade, those employed as sailors, and even those hired for task work on the plantations.[12] This last group could not properly be called domestic labourers, and their inclusion here might well have opened the door to abuse of the system.

One of the main concerns of the abolitionists was to ensure that public officers were as free as possible from the influence of planters in the various West Indian colonies [13] Concern for the independence of this officer from such influence lay behind the requirement that the Registrar was not to be an owner or part owner of slaves, and also behind the financial provisions made for him. For the point had been made intermittently, in debates on the slave question, that slaves could not get their due as long as public officers and legislators were their masters. As a further means towards an effective execution of the amelioration programme, the Order required the Registrar to perform all his duties in person and not by deputy.[14] Here again, another principle of importance was at stake. For holders of public offices in the colonies often resided in England, leaving their deputies to perform their duties. This arrangement had never been satisfactory and, in the case of slave amelioration, would have been altogether disastrous. For the deputy, as deputies were generally, would have been ill paid; and the result was likely to be that he would have become dependent on the very persons whose performance it was the Registrar's duty to monitor. In such circumstances, the provision of a fixed salary for the Registrar was intended to be another step in ensuring for him a degree of independence from the planters.

Another intention of the Order in Council was to enable an accurate determination of the exact number and condition of all slaves in the colony, not only in 1813, but in every subsequent year. Hence the Order made provision for a comprehensive return by each slave owner, which was to indicate to which of the two classes – plantation or personal – his or her slaves belonged, and to provide detailed information concerning each slave in his or her possession. Later, it will become apparent that there were deficiencies in this arrangement. Within one month of the publication of this Order, each slave owner's return was to show for each slave: the baptismal or failing that the habitual name of the slave; whether the slave was African or creole and his or her place of origin in Africa or one of the other islands; the colour of the slave, whether negro, mulatto, or mustee; the employment – whether mechanic, artisan, or if in handicraft, the "particular art or business in which he or she is employed"; the "particular domestic service or department" in which the slave is employed. Plantation slaves were to be registered "as labourers only".[15] This latter provision was also susceptible of abuse.

These returns were to be entered into the appropriate book, and the Registrar was to inform the Governor of the conclusion of the process. The latter was to give notice to the public of the readiness of the books for verification, at which time individual owners might appear before the Governor and satisfy him that any failure to submit returns on their part was due to "unavoidable impediment" and not to wilful delay. The Governor, on being satisfied, might make a written order authorising the Registrar to receive the returns of such persons. All of this had to be completed within two months of the publication of the Order. The Registrar was then to make an Index, as well as a duplicate of both registers and the Index, before the end of the two month period.[16]

The first registration was to be followed by regular annual registrations, amending information from the former where necessary. Annual returns were to be made in the first ten days of January, and were to indicate any material alteration in the bodily stature of the slaves, to show births and deaths, any new acquisitions, and any change of ownership. The Registrar was to amend the original registers as indicated by the annual returns, "carefully compare" the latter with the former to ensure that the number and the descriptions corresponded, and he was authorised to summon owners to explain any discrepancies. No annual return was to be received after January 11 in any year. However, anyone who acquired a slave at the time of registration, could register the same at the next annual registration provided the omission was not wilful. Before March 1 each year, the Registrar was required to produce a general account or abstract of all annual returns, showing the result of the exercise, the number of births and deaths, and produce the requisite duplicates.[17]   The Order did not require owners to keep a record of their slaves and the descriptions; and it is difficult to see how the annual registration could have been conducted in the limited time unless owners kept a record.

Once the first registration had taken place, the Order declared that no African could be considered a slave,[18] nor could any business, which involved slaves or estates worked by slaves, be transacted unless the slaves had first been duly registered;[19] nor could anyone claim an African as his slave, without first producing a certificate of registration.[20] Provision was made, however, for the failure of any parties to register their slaves within the period specified by the Order. A period of three years from the default was allowed for persons with interests in slaves, who had not registered such slaves after having taken possession of them, to regularise their status; and ten years in the case of slaves born at the time of registration, to correct the error.[21] In the case of joint ownership, the failure of one party to register was not to operate to the detriment of the other party or parties. The defaulters were to be prosecuted, but the others were to be enabled to register their slaves.[22] In order to facilitate the detection of default, the Order provided for a third party to visit any estate, after giving the owner ten days' notice, and to compare the slaves on it with the description in the returns. Failure to produce a slave incurred a fine of £20 sterling. These provisions made it possible for part owners to be informed of the quantity of slaves on the estate, as well as of their physical condition, and to be able to verify the information.

According to the Order, the Registrar was required, within three months, to furnish the Chief Justice with an abstract of the slaves returned by agents.[23] The Court of the Chief Justice was authorised to appoint three persons to visit the plantations to verify or correct these returns, and to report any errors they discovered within three months thereafter. This latter procedure was intended to look after the interests of minors, married women, and persons who were mentally or physically handicapped. It was also intended to ensure that owners had every opportunity to establish their ownership of slaves, since they could not claim slaves who had not been registered when the grace period ended.

Since one intention of the Order was to enable officials to observe the treatment of slaves in the colony, certain specific information was demanded on the returns.   In the case of plantation slaves, the returns were to state the name of the plantation and the Quarter in which it was situated; the crop grown, the owner or person making the return; and finally, the previous owner, if the slave had changed hands within the seven years prior to the Order. In the case of personal slaves, the return was to state the name of the owner and the description of the slaves, as indicated earlier.[24] The purpose of all this detail was that the authorities would be informed of the manner in which each owner treated his slave, by being able to take note of any changes due to scars or mutilations, and also to note the frequency of the death of slaves on a plantation. It was believed that the publication of such information would serve as a deterrent to any planters or managers who were inclined to ill-treat their slaves.[25]

That the details were to serve as a check in case of future ill treatment or deformity can be seen from the procedure for annual registrations. In the latter, the returns were expected to indicate the existence of any physical deformity which might have resulted from accident or disease, thus altering the bodily stature of the slaves from what was indicated in previous returns. In addition, any change of owner or estate was to be recorded. So that, not only was there a means of ascertaining whether or not a slave was being cruelly or negligently treated, there was also now a means of discovering whether, in changing masters, the slaves were also moving from a better to a worse situation or vice versa. The procedure for certification of the registers and their transmission to England was prescribed for the annual registrations as it was for the original. Provided that these registers were properly kept, the information they conveyed was expected to provide an accurate index not only as to the number and ownership of slaves in the colony, but as to the manner in which they were being treated. The trouble, as we shall see, was that the registers were never accurately kept; indeed, the slave owners were less than fully co-operative.

A new departure was made when the Order dealt with the question of slave evidence. In cases of prosecutions for breaches of the Order, slaves were declared competent to give evidence where their claim to freedom might be involved.[26] Thus the Order provided that no slave was to be considered incompetent as a witness within the limits of this particular legislation. These concessions appear quite hollow, however, when it is considered that the Order allowed the state of slavery to be used as a factor in determining the credibility of the evidence of the slaves. This matter of slave evidence had come under discussion at intervals during the extensive debate on the slave trade, and some meaningful provision might have been made for it. But, as it now stood, the Order demolished with one hand what it sought to construct with the other; and the problem was not settled until much later in the amelioration process.

APPOINTMENT OF THE REGISTRAR

In transmitting this Order to Trinidad, Bathurst instructed Governor Munro to see that it was promulgated, and to appoint a suitable person to the office of Registrar of Slaves.[27] With regard to the promulgation of the Order the Trinidad Council, at its meeting on August 25, 1812, resolved "that the said Order in Council be translated into the spanish and french languages & printed for the purpose of making it more public and to have its immediate execution agreeable to His Royal Highness the Prince Regent's instructions".[28] At its meeting six days later the Minutes indicated that the resolution had been complied with, and that the Order in Council was being published that very day. The proclamation in question provided that all persons with interests in slaves shall

> respectively make, and personally deliver, upon oath, either to Henry Murray, Esquire, duly appointed, according to the said Royal ordinance or cedula, Registrar of Slaves, *or to some other person that shall be by him appointed and deputed to receive* [29]

the information required by the Order. This permission to make returns before a deputy was the first breach of the Order, and was the beginning of many irregularities.

With regard to the second of Bathurst's instructions, the Council noted that the appointment of a Registrar had been duly carried out. However, the circumstances of his appointment suggest that the candidate could by no means be described as entirely free of any interest in slaves. At the Council meeting of August 31 that year, Henry Murray was named Registrar of Slaves and sworn into office on the same day. Curiously enough, however, Bathurst had expressed to Governor Munro the British government's fear that the implementation of the scheme might be attended by some difficulties; and it was the decision of the government that, in order to overcome these, a Registrar might be sent out from England.[30] This despatch might not have reached Trinidad when Henry Murray was appointed; and, in any case, he was subsequently confirmed in the office by Bathurst.

The question which naturally arises over the Registrar concerns his participation as a slave owner in the colony; for the Order specifically required that the Registrar was neither wholly nor partially to have an interest in slaves. Murray's success in obtaining the appointment was the first ominous sign that officials in the colony were prepared to be devious in precisely those areas where the Colonial Office sought their cooperation. It also shows an inclination towards carelessness on the part of officials at the Colonial Office itself. The manner in which the appointment was made, therefore, needs to be examined in some detail. The certificates, which were used in support of Murray's candidature show that he had been a recent landowner in the colony.[31] For example, that by the Attorney General, George Knox, stated that according to the records Murray was neither directly nor indirectly owner, part owner or mortgager of any slaves. The certificate signed by the Escribano or clerk of the Cabildo showed that there was no mortgage in slaves in favour of Murray; that signed by Jno. Gloster, Deputy Registrar, presumably of Deeds, stated that no record exists of his involvement in slavery. The most significant and revealing were the certificates by Manuel Garmendia, and J. Lewis, a Counsel and Conveyancer. The first recited that '*Under date of this day*' Murray and his wife 'transferred in favour of *Mr. Richard Annesley* all the right and title which they had to a moiety of the plantation called Bellevue ...' The certificate of J. Lewis stated that Murray had sold to Annesley for £39,400.3s Currency his own and his wife's 'Estates and Plantations and all their Negro and other slaves ... which belonged to Mr. & Mrs. Murray either as part owner, owners, or Mortgagee'. As a result of this, Lewis reported Murray to be without slave connection in the colony and to be therefore eligible for the office. [32]

Apart from the fact that Murray had been a recent slave owner in the colony, there are a number of other disturbing factors in this arrangement. One of these is the fact that Richard Annesley, the purchaser of Murray's estates, was introduced to the Council as one of Murray's sureties and was accepted as such. Murray's connection with slavery could hardly have passed unnoticed by the Governor or the other members of the Council.[33] This factor was actually aggravated by the fact that the Attorney General, one of the persons who issued a certificate in his favour, was also a member of that body. In spite of the fact that the Minutes refer to Murray's having been 'introduced', all the extracts forwarded to the Colonial Office were signed by Henry Murray, Deputy Clerk of the Council. In other words, Murray was already closely associated with that body, by which he had been *appointed*. The certificates in question had been submitted to the Governor in Council; and, on the basis of these documents he was appointed Registrar. So at the very start of the process the type of person, who should have been excluded from the office, had been appointed Registrar. Murray's connection with the slave system had not been so remote as to make him the best person for the office. What is even more surprising, in the circumstances, is the fact that the appointment received the confirmation of the Secretary of State.[34] For he himself had apprised the Governor of the opinion of the ministers that it would have been better to send someone from England to assume those responsibilities. Yet a blatant violation of the principle of impartiality had apparently received his approval. This was clearly not an auspicious beginning for the programme.

The execution of the process was beset by delays from the very beginning, and was to be regularly undermined in the same way as time went on. As observed earlier, the Order in Council of March 1812 had been forwarded to the Governor with instructions to put it into force. The despatch conveying these instructions had hardly left the Colonial Office before Bathurst wrote another despatch suspending the operation of the original Order. Enclosing a supplementary Order dated July 17, 1812, the despatch declared null and void any steps which might have been taken towards enforcing the Order.[35] It meant, therefore, that within a very short space of time two despatches bearing contradictory instructions had arrived in the colony. And this circumstance should be borne in mind when considering the confusion which some persons exhibited.

As a result of the second despatch, the action taken to date was cancelled and no further action was taken until early in the following year. In the middle of February 1813 Henry Murray, who had gone to England in the meantime, returned to the colony bearing his Commission of November 6, 1812. Acting on the Governor's advice, he had gone to London to put his case successfully before the Secretary of State. Once more the Secretary of State ordered the necessary procedures to be followed. On March 6, 1813, with Patrick O'Brien and James Metivier as sureties, Murray presented his commission as Registrar and again took the oath of office.[36] He was granted a salary of £500 sterling. The Order was duly proclaimed and, on this occasion, was carried into execution. [37]

THE FIRST REGISTRATION

The original registration, which should have started in April 1812, started some time after March 1813 and was not completed until the end of that year – more than a year after the the Order first arrived in Trinidad. This first registration showed that 2,531 slave owners had submitted returns yielding a slave population of 25,717. The breakdown of this number was as follows: there were 1,882 Personal returns showing an aggregate of 8,633 slaves;, and 649 Plantation returns showing an aggregate of 17,084 slaves.[38] This total represented an increase of over 4,000 slaves since the slave population figures were last recorded in 1811. In view of the presupposition of the Order, the question naturally arises: what do these statistics really tell us? It is possible that between the arrival of the Order in August 1812, and the beginning of the registration process in March 1813, slave proprietors had taken the opportunity to increase the number of their slaves. To do justice to this conclusion, one needs first of all to have an accurate account of the number of births and deaths for the intervening period; and this we do not have.

James Stephen, senior, in his complaints about the proceedings of the Registrar, strongly suggested that there had been an increase in the slave population, as a direct result of smuggling, during the period of registration. He argued that the Registrar had received returns long after the time specified for such returns by the Order. By so doing, he alleged, the Registrar had made it possible for proprietors to register slaves they actually possessed as well as those they hoped to import. In support of his contention he referred to a number of letters he had received from the Registrar in Trinidad. One of these, written on April 12, 1813, showed that the Registrar had, by that date, received two thirds of all expected returns. Stephen alleged that the Registrar probably anticipated a total of 20,000 slaves, while at the time he was writing, returns had been received for over 25,000 slaves. Arguing that Murray would not have calculated his fees on a number smaller than the total, he felt convinced that that officer had been receiving returns subsequent to the deadline set by the Order.[39] One cannot argue with this conclusion, which will be seen to be self-evident. But one must seriously question whether the material before Stephen was sufficient to prove that smuggling had taken place. If the planters had registered those they hoped to import, a serious question would arise as to whether the Registrar had received such accurate descriptions that they exactly matched the slaves the planters eventually imported and registered. That, of course, depended first on the proof of smuggling, and the absence of that proof constitutes a major area of doubt in Stephen's argument.

Stephen further accused the `two Governors of the period of being accessories to the infraction of the Order by granting extensions at the request of the Registrar. Governor Munro's Proclamation, he observed, was granted to enable the Registrar to receive returns until August 31. Woodford's, which at the time of writing he had not yet seen, he believed to be objectionable for two reasons. One was that the Order in Council of November 2, 1813 had ratified "in the most general and unqualified manner not only the original Registration, & the authentication of the Books and Duplicates, but the *returns made* after the limited Periods."[40] The second reason involved his being "Surprised and alarmed" to discover that the said Order agreed verbatim with one he had drafted. Stephen contended that he had prepared the draft with a view to correcting irregularities which, from Murray's letters, he believed needed to be regularised; and also to "prevent the great inconvenience of any practical doubts as to the validity of the Registry, and consequently, of the legal state of the Negroes comprised in it." As there seemed to be a lack of official correspondence on the subject, he had so framed his draft as to make it dependent on the receipt of information.[41] But it was the Colonial Office and not Woodford who had used the draft; for a Governor had no authority to issue an Order in Council.

What Stephen's paper shows is that there was considerable deviation, on the part of the Registrar of Slaves, from the strict deadline set in the Order leading Bathurst to seek from Woodford an explanation of the issues raised by Stephen. By this time, Bathurst seems to have been convinced that the extensions had contravened the original intentions of the Order in Council by allowing individuals to make returns or to alter those already made. And he had drawn the conclusion, based on representations made to him, that fresh importation had taken place. The evidence he sought was: a return of those who had registered their slaves within the specified time, and the number of slaves reported by each individual; a return of those who had corrected their returns, and the extent of the alterations; and finally a return of those who were late in registering their slaves and the number of slaves registered at that time. Woodford's report was also to provide any other useful information which would facilitate a determination as to whether the extensions were justified.[42] Woodford's replies served only to show that Stephen was not correct about the possible abuse of extensions, though over 4,000 slaves had been registered in the period after the deadline. The effect of later returns on the final figures can be illustrated by the following tables:

Table III:
Returns submitted up to April 22 , 1813

Personal returns up to April 22	1,537 for 6,865 slaves
Plantation returns up to April 22	584 for 14,411 slaves
Total returns for the period	2,121 for 21,276 slaves

Table IV:
Late Returns Submitted after April 22, 1813

Personal returns April 22 to August 31	205 for 1,257 slaves
Personal returns Oct. 15 to Dec. 16	141 for 511 slaves
Plantation returns Oct. 15 to Dec. 16	53 for 2,376 slaves
Plantation returns Oct. 15 to Dec. 16	12 for 297 slaves
Total Number of defaulters	411 for 4,441 slaves.

Sources: T.D.D. 1: 26 – Woodford to Bathurst, 9 May 1814, enclosure. T.D.D. 1. 64: Woodford to Bathurst, 23 Nov. 1814, enclosure dated 28 April 1814.

In other words, the Governor's responses show that approximately one-sixth of all slaves had been registered after the deadline set by the Order, in some cases, as many as eight months late. Since a total of some 4,000 slaves had been registered late, the bulk of these in December 1813, Stephen was not correct in alleging that 25,000 slaves had been registered by September 1813. While his general thesis about the lateness of a large proportion of the returns was correct, he has presented no information to prove that there had been smuggling. What is more, none of the so-called evidence seems to have considered the real difficulty and inconvenience of travel from one part of the island to another. The period allowed for the first registration was too limited, and that for annual registrations was even more unrealistic.[43]

NEGLIGENCE

The large amount of late returns reveals quite a high proportion of negligence with respect to this first registration. What were the reasons for this neglect? In 1814 the Chief Judge was commissioned by the Governor to examine defaulters to the Order.[44] His report to the governor shows that many proprietors had not taken the Order seriously. Some of them admitted negligence, even after receiving reminders from the Registrar's office. Three of the parties examined declared that they were not aware of any urgent need to make returns, one of them acting on the belief that she could register slaves any time before the books were closed. Another proprietor considered the Order contrary to Spanish law, in that it created an already existing office, and that the duties of the Registrar were already being performed by the Commissary of Population.[45] The Spanish *Cedula* of 1789 had been repealed by the Order of March 1812 as far as it respected registration; but in all fairness, the Order was making demands for specific information, which could not have been supplied by the Commissary of Population.

One other defaulter quoted current opinion to the effect that the "Order in Council would be dispensed with, in consequence of representations sent out from hence by the inhabitants of the island."[46] And nothing was more likely to support that belief than Bathurst's arrest of the proceedings after the first promulgation of the Order, and the lapse of over six months before the process actually began again. Two proprietors, originally from South America, claimed that, because of the difficulties of language, they were unable to carry out their responsibilities.[47] That they experienced no difficulty in communicating with the Chief Judge – perhaps through an interpreter – indicates with what little seriousness they regarded the whole matter. The process began, therefore, with a strong body of feeling either unconcerned with, or opposed to, the registration.

E. L. Joseph, himself a planter resident in the colony at that time, asserted that the Order was violently opposed on its arrival in the colony, and that alarm was created. According to him, even the Cabildo pretended ignorance of any law requiring any form of registration.[48] In fact, Bathurst himself had to censure the opposition of the Cabildo, and call for their cordial cooperation in the exercise. He dismissed their objections as being based on an erroneous perception of the measure, and an 'exaggerated if not imaginary picture' of its results.[49] It is clear that opposition and negligence were evident from the very beginning; but the argument of James Stephen regarding smuggling by the planters still seems to be weak. Without other evidence it cannot be regarded as the reason for the late registration.

Periodically after the first registration, some cases arose of persons who had either not previously registered their slaves, or who had subsequently failed to do so. As late as 1826, for example, there were five cases concerning slaves who had not been previously registered, and whose registration needed to be regularised. The Father General of Minors[50] presented an application to the Registrar seeking to register three slaves on behalf of a minor. One other omission was due to the lunacy of the owner; and in another case the slave was declared free.[51] The failure of such persons to register their slaves does not appear to have elicited any comment either from the Governor or the Secretary of State; nor was there any comment on the non-registration of these slaves after such a long period in a situation clearly provided for in the Order. Similarly, in 1827, applications were made to register three slaves, one of whom was eventually set free. In the case of the other two, the applicants proved that the non-registration had been due to the refusal of the Registrar to accept their returns because of errors originating at the public offices at Barbados and Tortola, from which they had been imported.[52] Again in 1829 a slave and her child were presented for registration, after not being registered for two successive periods of registration. The reason given for the failure was that the owner had left the colony and had been impressed into the Columbian army, and that his attorney had died while he was absent.[53] The matter was referred to the Council, but there is no record of any decision on this case. All of these make it difficult to state with certainty what the slave population was.

PLURALITY OF OFFICES

Irregularities in the Registrar's appointment and in the first registration were not the only factors which adversely affected the entire process of registration. Another important factor was the plurality of offices held by the Registrar – a concern which has been alluded to earlier. In January 1814, Murray assumed the duties of Deputy Secretary of the Cabildo at a salary of £150 per year.[54] In addition to this he had a patent to "act as Clerk of the Council, Secretary, Register, and Clerk of Enrollments".[55] These being salaried appointments, Murray found himself serving several masters; and in the circumstances he could not serve them all well. His appointment was in fact challenged by James Stephen, senior, who observed that the precautions of the Order to secure the office against undue local influence had been undermined, and also that there might have resulted a conflict of loyalties with the Counsellors as his superiors. On these grounds he urged the increase of Murray's fees as Registrar in order to prevent him from being dependent on the slave owners.[56]

Such plurality of offices acted as a deterrent to Murray's performance of his duties. As early as 1815, Governor Woodford wrote as follows to the Secretary of State concerning the Registry: "If Mr. Murray's other duties enabled him to give his entire attention to that office, the salary of one clerk might probably be saved".[57] Economy was certainly neither the only, nor the main, benefit to be derived from a single-minded application of himself to the tasks of his office; reliability was another and more important one. Yet neither the Governor nor the Secretary of State did anything to remedy what the former acknowledged to be a distraction from the Registrar's duties. By 1817 Henry Murray was holding at least five public offices, which included salaries and, perhaps, fees as well. The following table represents his offices and emoluments.

Table V:
Offices held by Henry Murray, and their value

Office	Salary	
Escribano de Camara	not specified	
Dep. Sec. & Clerk of Cncl.	£1420.17.71/2 Cy.	£579.19. Stg
Registrar of Slaves	£2124. 3. 8 Cy.	£885. 1. 4
Notary Public	£42. Cy.	£17. 3
Deputy Clerk of Cabildo		£330

Source: C.O. 295/43: Woodford to Bathurst, April 2, 1817: Schedule of Public Officers of Trinidad. For the last, C.O. 295/53: Woodford to Bathurst, April 11, 1821, "Schedule of Establishment for Trinidad, 1821."

In 1819 the dockets on the estate of Pere Angeli showed Murray to be also *escribano* of the Governor's Court.[58] In view of all this, the only conclusion one can draw is that Murray held too many offices, and that these prevented him from performing his duties with the efficiency required of him by the Order. This plurality of offices also left him dependent on clerks and, as such, he could be said to be in violation of the law. The Governor was fully aware of this, as he himself referred to Murray's being unable to give his entire attention to his principal duties. But the big question was: how did this escape the attention of the Colonial Office, to the extent that no action was taken against him? Even Stephen did not place much emphasis on this particular point.

In view of the plurality of offices held by him, it is not surprising that Henry Murray suffered a bout of ill health. In 1818 he was given six months' leave of absence owing to the deterioration of his health which, in its turn, was said to have resulted from the "confinement" attaching to his many duties.[59] In so reporting to Bathurst, Woodford testified to the integrity and assiduity with which Murray had always performed his duties – presumably as Registrar. However, it is very unlikely that Murray deserved the plaudits of the Governor in view of what the latter's letter stated. Murray, whose original application for leave was based partly on his ill health and partly on the need to settle his private affairs, promised to find a deputy[60] and recommended his son for the vacancy. In October 1819 he applied for a further extension of six months,[61] and further applications followed until, in 1821, Woodford appointed as Registrar Edward Murray, who had been deputising for his father.[62] Bathurst, who had it in his power to reject the new candidate, again confirmed the appointment, but this time with a mild protest.[63] By 1829 we find that one who apparently was another member of the same family, Albert Murray, had been appointed to the post of Deputy Registrar.[64] The passage of the office of Registrar from father to son, and of the office of Deputy to another relative, made it too much of a family affair, especially since the family was a landowning one. The authorities in the colony were not complying with the spirit of the Order, and the Colonial Office either did not notice the breach or consider it signifcant.

LATE REPORTS

One of the great problems respecting the execution of the Order was the frequency with which the Registrar submitted late reports. This tendency was noticeable from the very start of the registration process. The first report to be submitted by the Registrar was forwarded to England only at the beginning of 1814. This is not surprising, given the fact that returns were being accepted up to December 1813. This delay had led to Stephen's charge that the Registrar had not observed the law with respect to the receipt of returns – a charge which had some merit, and for which successive Governors must share some responsibility. For the Registrar was only permitted to receive late returns on the written instruction of the Governor. However, by the time the first annual returns were completed in 1814, both Governor Woodford and the Registrar were complaining about the severe limitation of the time allowed for the submission of returns;[65] and both recommended that one month be allotted for annual returns instead of the ten days prescribed by the Order. The law was about to have its first amendment.

Part of the blame for the delay in getting reports ready was laid by Henry Murray at the door of the Colonial Office. In February 1815 he complained that the duplicate register, for which he had applied in September 1813, had not arrived up to the time of writing.[66] Late in 1814, a consignment of books and papers for registration had been dispatched to Trinidad from the Colonial Office.[67] If the date of Murray's order is correct, then the greater blame, in this instance, lay in London. But even when he did have the books, Murray bemoaned the fact that a considerable amount of time was being expended under difficult conditions, even with the employment of eight clerks.[68] The implication clearly was that there was not sufficient time for the process to be carried out efficiently.

When Woodford was writing to the Secretary of State in March 1815, the inhabitants of the eastern coast of the island had not yet submitted their returns for the current annual registration. Apparently in defence of the planters, he explained that there were no roads and that the possibility of being carried away by currents had deterred planters from undertaking the voyage by sea.[69] By the end of that year he was attributing the late returns to the "aversion, embarrassment and expence which the Foreigners and the illiterate colored People" experienced in preparing the simplest return.[70]

How satisfactory were these explanations? If in March returns due by January 10, had not yet been submitted, delay could not have been put down simply to unsatisfactory communication. It is much more likely that slave owners, though they had known when returns were due, had been unwilling to submit them. For even at that time it would have required less than ten weeks to travel to Port of Spain from the east coast of the island. In March 1815, 450 annual returns were still outstanding for that year.[71] Woodford's attempt to place the blame on foreigners and free coloureds cannot be accepted merely on his word; and the Registrar's letter does not make it possible to say what proportion of the defaulters actually were foreigners and illiterate free coloured people. The most that this evidence indicates is that we have two other elements of the society for whom the process might have created some difficulty, provided we can accept Woodford's condemnation of the free coloureds.

The Colonial Office made two changes in an effort to remove some of the causes of complaint. In the first place, the period for submitting annual returns was extended was extended from ten days to one month;[72] in the second place, annual returns were replaced by triennial ones.[73] By the alteration of the previous time limitations under which the Registrar had at first laboured, there should have been a more efficient implementation of the process, having regard to its purpose. But even with the extension of time, the process was never properly executed, and successive Registrars continued to complain about shortage of time to the very end.

A further complication of the problem related to the time it took to get the necessary documents transmitted to the Registrar of Colonial Slaves in England. For reasons already discussed, the original registration of slaves was not completed until 1814. The pattern of late transmissions continued in later years; for example, it was not until March 1816 that the returns for 1815 had been transmitted to England; while the abstracts for 1816 were only transmitted to England in April 1817.[74] The duplicate Plantation registers for 1815 and 1816 were transmitted only in 1818 due to the late arrival of those books from England.[75] In 1821, however, these registers had not yet been seen by officials at the Colonial Office, though they had probably arrived there.[76] The returns for 1819 were not ready by the middle of 1821 – a delay which the new Registrar attributed to his own absence and his Deputy's ill health.[77] These returns were only transmitted to London towards the end of the latter year.[78] Again, towards the end of 1822, Bathurst complained about the non-arrival of registers for that year, a delay which resulted in the inability of some persons to effect a transfer of property in one instance.[79] Up to the end of 1824 the registers for 1822 had not yet reached England; they were only transmitted in October of the former year.[80] According to the Registrar, the whole process had been completed and sworn to more than two months before the allotted time had expired; and in his explanation of the delay he stated that the method of carrying out the work had always been the same.[81] By implication, therefore, registers would always be late; and so it happened.

The registers for 1825 did not reach the Colonial Office until 1828, while those for 1828 had not yet reached that Office by the end of 1830. On the latter occasion, Lord Howick, Under-Secretary in the Colonial Office, warned Governor Grant that the Colonial Office intended to take strong action on this matter in the future. So that, unless the cause of the failure was corrected immediately, "it will be necessary to have the business of the Slave Registrar performed under some different arrangement from the existing one".[82] As an immediate step, he ordered that the Registrar was to receive no further payment until outstanding work had been brought up to date. And he warned the Governor that the warrant for the Registrar's salary was, in future, to certify the completion of all outstanding returns.[83] At that time, as in 1825, the Registrar pleaded shortage of time. The preparation of registers, he explained, had always been completed before the next ensuing registration; the 1828 registers had been completed and sworn to three months before the time allotted had expired. In addition he claimed that the complex and laborious nature of the registry had made earlier completion impossible; whereas each triennial return added to the trouble and the time that was necessary.[84] In fairness to the Colonial Office, it needs to be said here that, several years previously, Bathurst had asked Woodford to suggest a simpler yet equally effective system based on his local knowledge;[85] but nothing seems to have come of that request.

That even the tough line threatened by Lord Howick failed to produce results will be seen from a study of the state of the slave registry at the time of emancipation. The triennial returns for 1831 had not been transmitted to England until 1834 – a few months before emancipation day;[86] while those for 1834 had hardly begun to be processed. But the fault was as much that of the Colonial Office as it was that of the Registrar. A policy of economy in public affairs was pursued by that department from about 1830 onwards.[87] This policy could have found no more zealous supporter than the acting Governor in 1831, Sir Charles Smith, who objected to what he termed the duplication of offices and the exorbitance of the remuneration to the incumbents. His proposals for a solution involved the combination of the offices of Registrar and Protector and the vesting of the joint office in the Protector, while leaving the existing Registrar to act as the deputy of the Protector. Smith expected that combination to result in a lighter financial burden on the colony;[88] but he obviously did not give enough thought to the question as to whether one individual would have been able to perform both functions efficiently. His plan, however, was readily approved by the Colonial Office and put into effect. However, it did nothing to improve the functioning of the office of Registrar.

DEFECTIVE RETURNS

Another cause of the ineffectiveness of the registration system was the high incidence of defective returns, which was a matter of great concern to the Registrar. In 1815, for example, Henry Murray reported that over one hundred persons had submitted late returns; and that, of those which he had received, three quarters were defective. The reasons for this state of affairs varied and included: the change of ownership of a plantation or slave, the lack of returns for comparison; and the fact that some owners had disposed of their slaves and had left the colony without submitting returns.[89] One month after reporting this, he noted that, apart from 450 late returns, 700 owners had been required to explain errors in their returns, and that 300 slaves had changed owners.[90] According to him, a number of deficiencies appeared in the books provided by the Colonial Office, in that no provision had been made for newly born slaves, slaves imported from other British islands, or new owners of slaves whose names had not appeared in the original Indexes.[91] Not many of these points appear to be as strong as the Registrar would have us believe; a new acquisition only needed to have been entered as such. A more serious omission of which he complained was that of the lack of space for the physical description of the slaves, and for the record of any deformity.[92] Although the Schedule to the Order had indicated what information was required and the manner in which it was to be presented, the books appear not to have facilitated such entries. The defects in the registers, and the failure to enter details of the physical condition of the slaves, meant that it was well nigh impossible to determine what injuries slaves might have suffered between registrations. And hence also it would have been difficult to say whether or not slaves were being better or worse-treated.

In the period following the original registration, there seems to have been considerable inattention to the requirements of the Order where imported slaves were concerned. The result was that the total number of those registered "would never correspond with the whole number taken from the Custom House Licences, as many of the slaves so imported (between any two periods of registration) have died and consequently no mention ever made of them".[93] This report by Edward Murray is in itself a sad reflection on his father – Henry Murray – whom Woodford had praised so highly the previous year for his great performance as Registrar. The figures presented by the Registrar could not be accepted with any great degree of confidence. While these deficiencies are bad enough by themselves, the figures represent considerable discrepancy when they are compared with those of the Commissary of Population. The records in the latter's office show that, in the returns for 1818 no fewer than 1,070 slaves had been omitted from four districts; that the figures for 1820 were 2,130 in excess of the actual amount; while 143 returns, representing 868 slaves, had been omitted in 1821.[94] In a covering letter, Woodford explained that returns submitted prior to 1821 were not given under oath.[95] Whether the oath would have made much of a difference one cannot say, given the general tendency to be careless about returns; what can be said is that they inspire no more confidence than the figures previously submitted by the Registrar.

The slave figures with which we are left for the period 1813 to 1822, therefore, make interesting reading:

Table VI:
Comparative Figures of the Slave Population, 1813 – 1822

	1813	1815	1816	1819	1822
a) Registrar	25,717	24,329	25,871	23,691	23,227
b) Commissary	–	–	24,846	22,854	22,328

Sources: General state of the whole Number of Slaves returned for Registration at each Period of Registry. Return of the Population (Extract), enclosed with T.D.D. 4.520: Woodford to Bathurst, November 6, 1823.

The Commissary shows no figures for 1813 or 1815, but his figures are invariably substantially smaller than those of the Registrar; and those of the Registrar of Colonial Slaves in London did not correspond with those of the local Registrar or the Commissary. An exact comparison is not as simple as this when one looks at the statistics for slaves imported at intervals during the same period. In July 1822, one report gave the number of slaves imported between 1813 and 1821 as 3,815;[96] whereas another, gives the number as 3,239. The registration figures would obviously be incorrect as would be those of the Commissary. Remarkably both returns were produced by Edward Murray.

If the various slave returns had been accurate, they would have been of benefit to the colony in another way. A Proclamation of December 1813 required the return of all slaves between the ages of 12 and 45, specifying their occupations under oath before the Alcaldes, Commandants, or Colonial Treasurer. The latter was to distinguish personal and plantation slaves, and the returns were to correspond with those of the Registrar. Where any doubt arose with respect to the number of slaves returned by any individual, the Treasurer was to obtain an extract from the Registrar to verify his figures.[97] In order to relieve the owners of slaves, Woodford considered it expedient to use only those returns made before the Registrar in January and to make the owners liable to duty although that was due in June.[98] Although this made the accuracy of returns more crucial, there was still a measure of discrepancy between the figures of the Registrar and those of the Tax Roll which the Treasurer compiled. The following comparative Table for 1825 and 1828 exemplify the problem.

Table VII:
A Comparison of the Reports of Public Officers

Year	Commissary	Registrar	Treasurer
1825	23,117	23,685	24,471
1828	23,064	23,508	23,859

Sources: Return of the population, Jan. 1825 to Jan, 1829; Slave Returns according to the Tax Roll of the Colony, 1825 to 1829.

What is remarkable about these figures is that, in each case, the amount of slaves in the Treasurer's Tax Roll exceeded the amount shown by either the Commissary of Population or the Registrar of Slaves. Bearing in mind the fact that the Treasurer was confined to reporting slaves between the ages of 12 and 45 years of age, it is very likely that his figures were quite excessive. But a comparison of the other figures raises the question whether any of them can be considered reliable. Under the circumstances, great caution needs to be exercised.

That these figures were unreliable may be further illustrated by the following. In 1832 Henry Gloster, Protector of Slaves, was appointed Registrar of Slaves in a combination of offices which was intended to effect economy. Almost immediately he reported that the slave figures for 1828 were less than those transmitted to Goderich in 1831; that is, that the correct number of slaves in the colony should have been 23,508 instead of the figure of 24,006 shown in the reports submitted.[99] His observations on this matter pointed to even more serious irregularities. He noted, for instance, that it was impossible to tell whether the slaves had changed from being plantation slaves to domestics or *vice versa*. Slaves, who had been registered as personal, had been frequently found working on estates. A gang of 200 plantation slaves in the registry of 1828 had been transferred to the personal returns of the same owner in 1831, yet the gang continued to cultivate the same estate;, and the same was true of other gangs. Above all, Gloster complained that it was impossible to discover from the registers the precise number of slaves working on the plantations.[100] This shows that Edward Murray, working with his deputy Albert Murray, had been no more satisfactory a Registrar than his father and predecessor had been. And this inefficiency in the slave registry must be regarded as one of the factors contributing to the overall defeat of this aspect of the amelioration programme. For it was in plantation labour that cruelty was most evident; and the inability to distinguish between plantation and personal slaves meant increasing difficulty in detecting and correcting the abuses involved in employing personal slaves in plantation work. Yet there is no indication, in Gloster's reports as Protector, of any action having been taken against the slave owners in question, nor was there any indication of sanctions against the owner of the gang referred to.

This shoddiness in the keeping of the registers also meant an inability to determine the real nature of any change in the condition of slaves. The confusion of plantation and personal slaves suggests that the registers had not been carefully examined by those in authority, so that those who were abusing the system escaped notice. A large proportion of the plantation slaves were appearing in the wrong section of the registry, and the irregularity seemed to cause no concern. Wherever such cases existed, and Gloster admitted that there were many others of a similar nature, the ameliorative effects of the various Orders were likely to be rendered nugatory. This would be true in another respect. The Protector and Registrar complained that the earlier registers were filled with marginal notes under the heading "corrections", so that he was unable to carry on the registry with the triennial returns for 1834. As an alternative to the existing system, he suggested either that his assistant be allowed to correct and certify the books; or that the Principal Officer superintend the Plantation registry, while the deputy be allowed to deal with the Personal one.[101] By the time this proposal reached the Colonial Office, plans for the emancipation of slaves must have been well advanced. In any case by the end of that year it was no longer of any relevance.

This process, then, was founded on the belief that improvement in the condition of the slaves was impossible while slaves were easily replaceable; and it was established to ensure that the trade in slaves was not clandestinely carried on by demanding registration. In addition, it was aimed at correcting that abuse whereby any African was presumed to be a slave, and could be treated as such. The remedy for all these ills was seen, in abolitionist circles, to lie in registration, which was to protect the African and lead to further improvements in his condition.[102] The purpose of the process was to serve as a check on ill treatment, since it was thought that no master was likely to risk the penalties which attended falsification of the annual returns. Therefore the recording of physical change was also seen as a deterrent to potential abusers.[103] What was not sufficiently borne in mind was that the whole process depended on the extent to which those concerned applied themselves to the process. And this meant both the slave owners and the officials of the Slave Registry. For had there been proper attention to the task, the irregularities to which Henry Gloster drew attention in 1833 could not have been overlooked. The manner in which the records were kept, and the uncertainty of the figures generally, were sufficient to dispel the early Stephen's optimism.

This, then, was the first attempt at amelioration, an attempt that was plagued with the negligence or opposition of planters and the unwillingness of officials, as well as with general inefficiency. Its success in Trinidad was intended to be the basis for its implementation or otherwise in the slave colonies in the West Indies. But by 1815, a bill for the registration of colonial slaves had already been introduced into the British Parliament. This bill was short lived, having encountered stiff opposition among West Indian interests in England, as well as in the West Indies.[104] Eventually slave registration became general when an Act was passed in England declaring all commercial transactions with respect to unregistered slaves to be illegal.[105] The scheme certainly had not been successful in Trinidad, and it cannot be said that its success was responsible for its extension to other colonies.

3. Emancipated Africans and Amelioration

Slave owners in nineteenth century Trinidad were always of the view that the colony lacked the labour force necessary for its development. This was partly a legacy of the Spanish period, when neglect resulted in the colony having a quite small population and an equally small labour force. As shown earlier, the publication of the Spanish *Cedula* of Population in 1783 was followed by a period of rapid immigration and the importation of many slaves. In the five years following British occupation of the island after 1797, the slave population virtually doubled itself – a testimony to the interests of those who migrated to the island at that time. When, therefore, an end was put to the slave trade in 1808, Trinidad planters protested forcefully on the grounds of shortage of labour.[1] The new proprietors, who had migrated to the island in the expectation of enriching themselves, were somewhat sceptical that the promise of a good life had any prospect of being realised. Even though slave registration had not been efficiently administered, the Order in Council of March 1812 put serious obstacles in the way of slave importation by requiring that such slaves be first registered.[2] And the Act passed in England in 1819 to establish a registry for all colonial slaves[3] ensured a reduction if not a curtailment of the entire trade.

Sir Ralph Woodford, who had arrived in Trinidad as Governor shortly after the start of the process of registration, drew to the attention of Lord Bathurst, the Secretary of State, the effect which a lack of adequate labour could have on the colony's production. In a despatch, reminiscent of some written by Governor Picton, he urged that British settlers be encouraged to migrate to Trinidad with their families and slaves. In order to realise that objective, he asked Bathurst to present to Parliament a Bill seeking the repeal of part of the Act for the Abolition of the Slave Trade, thereby facilitating a regulated traffic between the British islands.[4] He also asked, in October 1814, that captured slaves be sent to Trinidad where living conditions were more favourable for them.[5] Intermittently thereafter despatches from both Woodford and Sir William Young, who acted as Governor for the former for two years, sought the approval of Bathurst for the importation of slaves to Trinidad.[6]

Woodford's plea to Bathurst failed of its intended effect. While generally admitting the adverse effects of shortage of labour on the colony, Bathurst represented as hopeless any attempt to import slaves on a scale sufficient to meet the assumed needs of the growing colony.[7] He promised to submit to Parliament the amending bill, which Woodford requested of him, but only on the understanding that it was to be generally applicable (presumably to all the colonies) and was to constitute a further check on the slave trade rather than being a mere means of arresting the decrease of the colony's population. A bill conceived along the latter line, he thought, was bound to fail. An extension of the trade was clearly implied in the terms of the proposed bill; and any thought of its being supported, given the passage of the Act for the Abolition of the Slave Trade, involved underestimating the strength of the abolitionists. Bathurst seems to have been against an extensive trade in slaves to Trinidad, or any similar trade with South America, though he did not rule out the migration of potential investors with their slaves. As a measure of security, he thought that slaves imported from South America should be apprenticed to their respective masters.[8] In a later despatch, presumably with the failure of Chinese immigration still fresh in his mind, he was not optimistic about experiments with free Africans or Indians. The reasons he gave were that housing and subsistence were to be regarded as pre-requisites for any free settlements, and that the heavy public expense which those services involved, would have had the effect of discouraging any such scheme. Bathurst was confident that, when the fertility of the colony became generally well known, people with capital would migrate to the colony with their slaves.[9]

We have, then, a Governor and a Secretary of State, both of whom were inclined either to favour some form of slave importation, or to regard with hesitation the settlement of free Africans. How it happened that free Africans were at that very time favourably considered for settlement in the colony is not at all clear. The idea of using free labour had been current as early as 1802,[10] and the Act of 1807 for the Abolition of the Slave Trade provided for the indentureship of captured Africans; but Woodford seems to have entertained a low estimate of them as workers. He described them as lazy or capricious; and showed a preference for the "peaceable and laborious" Indians whom he expected to remain "totally withdrawn from African Connexions or feelings."[11] So that his extraordinary interest and energy in establishing African settlements later may have been due to his ability to adapt himself exactly to the wishes of his superiors if he were so inclined. Between 1815 and 1834, three groups of emancipated Africans, broadly speaking, were settled in the colony: American refugees, disbanded soldiers from West Indian regiments, and Africans captured from slave ships.

AMERICAN REFUGEES

The American refugees were enslaved Africans who, during the American war of 1812, had escaped from their owners and had served the British in a variety of ways.[12] Many of the slaves had been encouraged to desert their owners by the protection and freedom offered to them by the British Commanders.[13] It is from these 'deserters' that Sir George Cockburn formed a corps of Colonial Marines; while another commander, Admiral Cochrane, encouraged his superiors in London to enlist the men.[14] At the end of the War, in early 1815, a considerable number of these Africans were transported to either Halifax or Bermuda, from whence some were transported to Trinidad.[15] A preliminary despatch from the Colonial Office warned the Governor of their arrival, and made the Collector of Customs responsible for such arrangements as were to be made for their maintenance.[16] A further despatch authorised him to allot portions of land to those who were unwilling to undertake agricultural labour on the estates.[17]

Between June 1815 and August 1816, four batches of these refugees arrived in Trinidad. The first batch consisted of 95 persons of whom 61 were men, 27 were women, and seven were children.[18] The second batch consisted of 58 persons, of whom there was virtually an equal number of male and female adults, as well as 29 children.[19] The third batch consisted of 66 persons, 34 of whom were men, 15 being women, while 17 were children.[20] Of the fourth batch, which reportedly consisted of 574 persons, there were 405 men, while there were only 83 women and 87 children.[21] As was the case with the Chinese immigrants of 1806, there was an extremely high proportion of males; and this did not indicate any interest in the future building of a community.

The first group of refugees was settled not far from Port of Spain, somewhere in the Caroni district – which could not have been the healthiest area even in those days. But the second and subsequent arrivals were all established in the two quarters of Naparima.[22] In general the refugees appear to have expressed a preference for land grants of their own, rather than for being apprenticed to planters.[23] Free coloureds and free blacks quite naturally did not like working on the plantations, where they were in danger of being treated like slaves. In reporting to Bathurst on his deployment of the later batches of refugees, Woodford offered a number of explanations for his decision to change the area in which he had originally decided to settle them – explanations, however, which are not without a measure of contradiction. At first he explained that, because of the number of old persons and children, he was sending the later arrivals to the Naparima district, where a certain amount of uncultivated land was available for his purpose.[24] Another explanation was that the lands granted to them should be of the best quality, and that the Caroni district could not be regarded as being of the required quality.[25] This explanation raises serious questions; for Woodford was unlikely to be such an advocate of the African that he would have been willing to offer them the best land available in the island. Yet another reason he gave was that there was "no part of the Island where they could have been placed with so much advantage to themselves or Security to the public." His experience in settling the first group, he explained, and public apprehension about the ultimate effects of Government's policy in settling so many free blacks in the colony, made him resolve to place no others near to Port of Spain.[26]

Woodford never explained what his experience with the first group of refugees was; in fact, this first group seems to pass from view altogether. But it is reasonably clear that Woodford was not so aloof from the plantocracy that he failed to share the fears, which motivated their thinking on this issue. Having served as marines, their ability to use firearms must have been an additional factor in the fear some people felt. Woodford's intention clearly was to move the refugees as far away as possible from the large servile population in the north, thereby removing, to some extent, the danger of a very large rising concerted with those in Port of Spain and its environs. How much this is so may be seen from a letter written nearly two years afterwards. In explaining his action, he wrote on that occasion:

> In the case of the Marines the numbers were so great
> as to create considerable alarm in the Colony, and it was
> after the most mature deliberation that the present
> situation was fixed upon for their Settlement; and in
> this determination His Majesty's Council, to whose
> advice I resorted on the occasion, were so much guided
> by the circumstance of being thereby enabled to place them
> under the superintendence of Mr. Mitchell as by the
> advantages presented by that part of the Country where
> the expence would be less than in any other where Land
> could be assigned to them.[27]

Not only does he seem to have yielded to popular alarm, he also committed them to the care of a man whom he knew would have kept them severely under his thumb. For not only was Mitchell commandant of the Quarter in which they were located, he was also one of the foremost supporters of the Governor in the latter's efforts to suppress the coloured population.[28]

One of Woodford's greatest fears was the tendency of the African refugees to stay together; and he sought to counteract this by settling them in carefully separated villages in the Naparima area. This arrangement was to subserve another of his main objectives: to provide a line of communication to the southern and eastern coasts, "for the Passage of Goods and Provisions from thence to the Town of San Fernando." Woodford seems to have concluded that, as long as they were engaged in clearing land, they were not to be feared.[29] Quite apart from his own aversion to free blacks and coloured people, the Governor was greatly influenced by the apprehensions of the white population. The problem was that, in settling them in Naparima, he was placing them in that part of the island where a substantial part of the free coloured population was concentrated. For this reason he strongly urged Bathurst to permit the establishment of a military contingent in that district. Bathurst approved this proposal, but only on the condition that the finances of the colony were able to support the expenditure for such a course.[30] So the principle on which the settlement of whites had been advocated earlier – that is, to keep an eye on the Africans [31] – was about to be applied to the settlement of the Americans. They were conveniently separated into villages called companies and placed under the supervision of a sergeant and corporal.

The settlement of the American refugees in the Naparima Quarter was a cause of great apprehension among certain planters, and this is clear from their reaction. Shortly after the refugees were moved to Naparima, a petition was addressed to the Governor, reportedly signed by several free coloureds and blacks among others. The protest was instigated by Lewis Johnston, a white proprietor, who was later to become a judge and one of the principal figures in the slave trials of the 1820's and 1830's. What sparked off the active opposition was the circumstance of some of the refugees meeting with some of their relatives, who were still slaves on the estate of Mr. Johnston. An investigation carried out by the Chief Judge revealed that the refugees' only concern was to purchase the freedom of those relatives whom they had encountered. Yet the Governor supported the proposal, although unsuccessfully, to make them surrender the land granted to them and hire themselves out to planters. The petitioners had complained about the settlers' monopoly of the cultivation and sale of ground provisions, and the bad consequences, which were bound to follow their occupation of a fertile area. Woodford noted among the petitioners numerous coloured persons whom he described as generally illiterate and as having been duped into signing the petition. Some of them, he claimed, had been recent slaves who came to own some of the finest estates of the colony.[32] The success of the free coloureds in acquiring property was always a source of annoyance to him, and he never neglected the opportunity to express that annoyance. Even if we agree that some of them had been so duped, we shall find that there was division within the free coloured class, as a result of which those who were more affluent did not regard the poorer ones among them as equals.[33] The free coloured planters were not altogether the victims of white duplicity; some of them acted out of self interest and later made common cause with the white slave owners.

These refugees remained in the Naparima area where they were not made welcome by the white planters, and where their settlement was supervised by the Commandant of the Quarter, Robert Mitchell. They had built good huts for themselves and the more industrious among them had cleared and planted large tracts of land. But the bulk of the emancipated Africans, whom Woodford described as Virginians, were prone to idleness[34] – a view reflecting that of the white planters who regarded the refugees as generally poor workers. For a limited period, all the refugees were provided with rations as well as with a supply of various agricultural necessities; but Woodford requested for them rewards in the form of domestic animals, such as mules and pigs;[35] tools such as pickaxes and shovels, as well as saws.[36] The Colonial Office approved the provision of articles of clothing for both men and women,[37] as well as certain rations. By the middle of 1818 the Governor reported that they had cleared and planted some 1,200 acres [38] – in less than two full years; and in 1823 he observed that lands in Naparima had been opened mainly through the settlements of the refugees.[39] As a result of their efforts, it was possible to cross the south of the island from San Fernando in the west to Mayaro in the east; his principal objective had therefore been obtained without undue trouble, by the same persons he considered prone to idleness.

Figures for the arrivals showed that only a very small number of females were sent to the colony. Comparison with schemes for European settlement in 1802 shows that, whereas the settlement of a free white peasantry evoked numerous proposals about the amount of land to be granted to each member of the family, no such concern was evinced with respect to the settlement of the emancipated Africans. The policy of the government was concerned less with a coloured peasantry, than with a coloured labour force. Hence it was that the wives of several of the refugees had been left behind at Halifax. Effectively, this was not unlike the enforced separation of slave families so prevalent in the West Indies at the time. Towards the end of 1816 Woodford recognized that the disproportion of the sexes was not in the best interests of the community, and suggested to Bathurst that apprenticed African women from the other islands, or captured female Africans be sent to Trinidad for distribution among the refugees.[40] Bathurst readily agreed to this proposal, ordering the senior naval officer at Barbados to send to Trinidad females recently captured from a French ship. From these women the Americans were to select mates who might prefer such marriages to being apprenticed as servants.[41] The choice between marriage and apprenticeship seems strange; but the disparaging way in which Bathurst spoke of their marriage seems to betray his lack of interest in a black peasantry.

By the middle of 1818 Woodford was again appealing for the families of the refugees to be sent to Trinidad from Halifax,[42] subsequently sending reminders to the Colonial Office on that subject.[43] Woodford attributed the tendency towards restlessness on the part of the refugees to the absence of their families. A minute on the second of the two last despatches recommended that the females in Halifax be offered transportation to Trinidad. Although orders were apparently given for those who wished to migrate to receive transportation, none of them seemed inclined to make use of the opportunity.[44] The reason for this was the suspicion, entertained by some of them, that the Government intended to dispose of them,[45] perhaps as slaves. Quite likely, it was the fear of reverting to slavery which acted as a deterrent, and understandably so. Transportation of refugees to the West Indies had begun in 1815 with the men, and the lapse of five or six years was enough to cast doubts over the intentions of government. By 1825 the matter was still under discussion, with no immediate prospect of a resolution.[46] In the meantime, the experiment was producing grave problems for social cohesion in that, as one respondent indicated, some of the Americans had been harrassing the wives of the slaves.

In other respects, the conduct of the refugees was generally quiet and orderly.[47] It is not easy to say exactly how they were treated, as official reports were presented by a Governor who did not support the idea of having free Africans on the whole, and who was unlikely to see much wrong in the hardships they were forced to endure. However, one writer declared that they had often been exploited by the superintendent, Mr. Robert Mitchell, for the cultivation of his wife's estates.[48] He paints for us a picture of dishonesty and treachery on Mitchell's part; and mentions the meting out of summary judgement and punishment by the Commandant.[49] This picture must naturally be assessed in the light of the controversial atmosphere in which it was written. But it is true to say that some harsh treatment was meted out to them. In fact, their lot was described as analogous to that of "mere labourers in a state of qualified slavery."[50] An anti-abolitionist writer to the press testified that their aversion to labour was overcome by a "severe application of the whip ordered by Sir Ralph Woodford."[51] In 1831 the Secretary of State ordered the dismissal of the Superintendent because of his ill treatment of the refugees, instructing the Governor to advise the refugees of their freedom to be party to any arrangements made for them.[52]

White planter prejudice against the refugees ran high in the Naparimas. Perhaps as they were "free" Africans and therefore a threat to the slave system by their very presence, assessment of them was negative and based on the idea that they should have been incorporated into the slave system. The white planters of Naparima did not have a high regard for the character of the refugees, and it is their opinion which is reflected in the Report of the local Commission set up by the Trinidad Council in 1824 to investigate the character of the coloured people. These planters testified to their drunkenness, considering them worse workers than the peons; in fact, they thought it impossible to cultivate sugar with free persons – meaning free blacks and coloured persons. Mitchell, the commandant of the quarter of North Naparima, emphasised that discipline could not be dispensed with, either for their own comfort, or for the security of the neighbourhood. He was of the view that the Americans were "cunning and artful," having no idea of the truth; that "most of the thefts have been committed by them; the Africans are more steady and quiet, and you can place more reliance on their word." With slight variations, this was the general view of the witnesses.[53] They castigated the refugees as capricious labourers, persons of bad character, dissipated and insolvent, and inclined to be predatory with respect to female slaves.[54] As such bad examples to the slaves, a writer to a local paper suggested that they be dispossessed, and located among the plantations so as to add to the labour force.[55] In other words, they were to be brought to heel by being made to work on the plantations where more labourers were needed. These criticisms against the 'free' Africans were later to be turned into arguments against the emancipation of the slaves.

REGIMENTS OF DISBANDED SOLDIERS

The second group of emancipated Africans comprised soldiers from a number of disbanded West India regiments. First among these was the 6th West India regiment in Tobago, whose members had requested to be settled in Trinidad where there were large areas of available Crown land.[56] Woodford was unwilling to accept the demobilised soldiers; and this showed itself in the catalogue of faults which he indicated as characteristic of Africans generally. He alleged, for example, that they lived on little, and worked capriciously, spending a great deal of their time in "Idleness and Debauchery". Further, according to him, they disliked agriculture, and showed a preference for "hawking and huxtering and a precarious livelihood to the Insurance of a comfortable Establishment, a Garden and Plenty."[57] Woodford proposed two modes of settlement for these soldiers. One of these was the possibility of indentureship on the plantations; but he feared that the introduction of a "privileged" class on the estates would have been prejudicial to the discipline of the slave gangs. On the other hand he thought they might be settled under officers, to whom discipline and general supervision of them could be entrusted. By way of incentive, he proposed that the officers be given grants of land, and that the ex-soldiers work for them for a few days each week.[58] Militia officers were invariably white, and the disbanded soldiers were likely to become their servants. By putting such labourers at the disposal of those officers, Woodford was establishing a regime similar to that of slavery and of benefit to that class which he thought deserved to be in control.

As a means of allaying the apprehensions of the Governor, Bathurst explained that it was the intention of the Government to settle in the islands only those who were old, wounded and pensionable. Those who were still able to serve in the forces were to be deployed as replacements in other regiments.[59] In other words, this was a programme for discarding soldiers who were no longer deemed useful, but without the appearance of so doing. Notwithstanding this assurance, after Woodford had settled 180 of the soldiers, one finds him still protesting that the pension of one bitt per day was an encouragement to their habitual idleness.[60] The truth is that Woodford was more interested in having the demobilised soldiers serving as labourers on the estates. This comes out very strongly in the nature of his requests for such soldiers: "if there be any Intention of disbanding the remaining West India Regiments, I hope Your Lordship will deign to remember the Claims of this Colony, which furnished so much labour for the defence of the Island for Six Successive Years in the late War … and grant the Island some Remuneration in the services of those Men."[61]

In the following year, Bathurst apprised Woodford of the disbanding of the 3rd West India regiment; and it appears even clearer that control of the soldiers was a paramount objective of the Governor. Thus Woodford wrote to Bathurst: "they must be kept under Controul; or they would soon become dangerous Inhabitants of these Forests". And he repeated his conviction that they should not be paid, as such pay would soon be spent or gambled away. He proposed instead a very limited ration for a period of four years and a far from specific clothing allowance. To his credit, it must be said that he requested that their families be sent as well, firm in the conviction that they would not make good settlers unless they had African women. He also felt that the lack of such women was likely to render the soldiers a source of annoyance to planters. Not that that was likely to happen, for he regarded the eastern coast as the only area in which they could profitably be settled.[62] Not only was the number of plantations there too small to be significant, but the swampy nature of a large part of the terrain meant that they would effectively be cut off from the majority of the population.

One batch of the 3rd West India regiment was settled in 1819 in the north-eastern section of the colony, about eight to ten miles south east of Arima, in an area, which the Governor reported to have five streams of water.[63] This group consisted of some 310 persons, of whom 240 were men, 41 women, and 29 children. Other persons joined later, but the preponderance of males still remained. They were allotted sixteen acres of land per family; but having settled in the wet season, they found maintenance of themselves hard going. They were placed under the supervision of a superintendent who lived in Arima, where provisions for them were stored and from which they were distributed.[64] According to Woodford, while the soil was not suited to the "more favourable sorts of Produce", it enabled its occupants to grow "considerable quantities of Rice."[65] In other words, Woodford had settled the soldiers in what was almost certainly swampy land, the nature of which was reflected in the produce he expected them to grow, if they knew how. In an age when so much was being said about the unhealthiness of the colony, putting the soldiers there was an indication of the low esteem in which he held them. It also created the conditions for dissatisfaction and frustration among them.

By late 1824, Woodford was poised to receive another 400 men from this regiment, objecting to their being disbanded before Christmas, and proposing deferral of this step to early 1825. Woodford explained that the majority of them had connections with slaves in the vicinity of Port of Spain. Why this should have been an impediment he did not explain; but it is almost certain that security was his main consideration. It was customary for the militia to be under arms during the Christmas holidays; and the fact that the amelioration Order of 1824 was then in the first six months of its operation probably served as an additional spur to security. He therefore proposed to settle them in two stages – the first in January, the second in February. [66] This group was placed about seven miles further to the east of the previous group in what the Governor described as some of the finest land in the colony. The area in question must have been Manzanilla on the east coast, an area which still does not deserve the encomiums of the

Governor. This distribution of the settlers fulfilled what he considered a very important purpose — that of completing the line of communication which he wanted to establish between Arima and the east coast.[67] The roads were never well maintained, but at least it was now possible to travel from Port of Spain to the eastern littoral during the dry season.

By 1826, between 240 and 360 soldiers were regularly resident in these settlements. As was the case with the refugees, they had cleared a considerable amount of land, and were apparently so productive that the Governor felt able to reduce their rations by half. Nevertheless, he continued to regard some of these settlers as lazy, explaining that this condition was due to their not being used to providing for themselves. This assessment can only be regarded as contradictory in the light of his previous statement about their productivity. But Woodford was not very concerned about the inconsistency of his evidence, once he attained his objective. Having apprehended some loiterers and punished them, he reported himself satisfied that he would not have to "resort to means of rigor *to enforce their residence.*"[68] Here again we may note two things which also occurred in the case of the settlers: one was the use of corporal punishment in order to ensure the conformity of the soldiers; the other was a policy of compulsory restriction of the soldiers to their place of residence. One cannot escape the impression that Woodford enjoyed his authority over the Africans and the power, which his office gave him, of inflicting pain on them. After all, he had a very negative opinion of Africans generally. But he was also obsessed with notions of security, and followed a pattern of settlement of the free blacks which he hoped would prevent their inter-mingling with others of the same class or with the slaves. It was a classic case of dividing and ruling.

What they thought of their situation cannot be properly assessed, because their views have not been recorded anywhere; and such expressions as do exist come to us from the pens of third parties. A report on the conviction of one of the settlers mentioned his preference for permanent attachment to the "Galley gang" rather than a return to Manzanilla.[69] The report itself is not very reliable and, in any event, this solitary report is not enough on which to build a case. What does seem clear is that the area referred to was anything but fine land. Woodford had exaggerated the quality of the land in order to justify his placing the Africans in a location of squalor. The officials at the Colonial Office could not have known of his deception.

CAPTURED AFRICANS

At a very early stage of his tenure, Woodford had pleaded with Bathurst that the Government should favour Trinidad with Africans taken as prizes from captured slave ships.[70] These Africans were not to be regarded as slaves, but were intended to serve as indentured labourers. The manner in which they were treated cannot be stated with any assurance, but inferences may be drawn from the way in which they were deployed. It needs to be borne in mind that, at the time that large numbers of these these prize Africans were being shipped to Trinidad, the abolition of slavery was imminent; and the concern of the planters and other slave owners was for the acquisition of more labourers. The service of persons such as these, if only for a few years, was therefore highly desirable.

While several of these had been brought into Trinidad from time to time,[71] it was only in 1831 that they had begun to arrive in significantly large numbers. The first group of 99 persons arrived in Port of Spain from St. Kitts, whose Governor thought that there were too many free Africans in Tortola and not sufficient employment for them; in addition to which, pecuniary assistance to them would have been a burden to that colony.[72] Sir Charles Smith, the acting Governor of Trinidad, was reluctant to receive them since he considered himself authorised to receive only females. He therefore lost no time in reproving his colleague in St. Kitts for the lack of notice to him, and urged him to send no more of them without the authority of the Secretary of State. Out of a desire to spare the British Treasury unnecessary expense, he accepted the first shipment, pointing out, somewhat caustically, that Trinidad "is not in need of the description of persons now received."[73] The new arrivals were taken to the Orange Grove barracks, where they were to remain under the supervision of the Collector of Customs, with the ultimate object of being apprenticed to trade,[74] an objective which Sir Charles Smith did not regard with approval. In his view, it would have been more profitable for the colony if the prize Africans were apprenticed to agricultural establishments. At the end of their period of servitude, their capacity to earn high wages would have been enhanced; "whilst putting them out only as domestics or mechanics will in the end saddle the community with an additional stock of the most worthless class in its composition."[75] This conclusion is difficult to understand if the Africans were being apprenticed to trades; but it does go to show that Smith, while generally less harsh than Woodford, did not necessarily have a higher opinion of such persons than did his predecessor.[76]

In the first of two despatches to the new Governor, Sir Lewis Grant, Goderich, the Secretary of State, agreed with Smith that the Africans in question should be employed in agriculture rather than as artisans or domestics. Enlarging on Smith's plan, however, he proposed that they should be employed as free labourers with wages, and with the freedom to seek more lucrative employments if they so desired. They were to be supervised by the Customs Officers or the Protector of Slaves, whose duty it was to ensure that justice was done to them, that wages were paid punctually, and were of a fair value. The last requirement meant that the wages paid were to be equivalent to those, which a hired slave of similar attainments would have received. He recommended as the maximum term of apprenticeship three years for adults, whereas in the case of children apprenticeship was to last until the attainment of adulthood. The males were to be distributed in such a way as to enable them to find companions; the females were to be placed in those black settlements in which there was the greatest disproportion of the sexes.[77]

Goderich's second despatch, written two months later, displayed dissatisfaction with the arrangements, which had been made. The prize Negroes were all to be apprenticed to trade, in which case he considered the arrangements improper. In the first place, it turned out that a number of public officers had benefitted from the Collector's deployment of the new arrivals. Three had been apprenticed to the acting Governor - Sir Charles Smith; Henry Gloster - the Protector of Slaves, and Antonio Gomez - a Puisne Judge, had each received four. Goderich argued that Smith, as a temporary resident, was unfit to receive such a trust; he was compromised in that he was required to prevent the neglect or violation of indentures to which he had become a party; and lastly, that neither the Collector nor the Judge of the Court of Vice Admiralty was free to control the apprentices as the law required. He also considered it objectionable that Henry Gloster, the Protector of Slaves and Antonio Gomez, one of the Puisne judges, had also been recipients of apprentices, since it was their responsibility to administer the laws for the protection of these Africans.[78] These objections point to an alarming amount of corruption in the local administration, where public officials became the beneficiaries of the services of persons they were required to protect from abuse. It was not impossible for such beneficiaries to be humane; but slave society in the West Indies was so constituted that it would have been too much to rely on the good faith of so many slave owners.

Another cause of objection according to Goderich was the fact that strange terms of indenture had been arranged by the Collector of Customs.[79] For instance, female apprentices, if they gave birth to any children, were liable to a five year extension of their indenture. On the other hand, Goderich observed that the indenture of children made it possible that, when the children's existing indentures ended, those indentures could easily have been extended. In both cases he considered the indentures invalid, as no authority had been granted by Parliament for such extensions, and recommended that they be set aside. This cancellation of course included the indentures made in favour of Smith, Gloster and Gomez. In view of a predecessor's despatch that apprenticeship should follow their inability to earn their livelihood, and as Smith had made no report on that matter, Goderich ordered that an attempt be made to see if they were able to earn their livelihood.[80] All of this reveals a remarkable degree of collusion in the evasion of the law, and merited firmer action than that taken by Bathurst.

Further shipments of prize Africans were destined to enter the colony by way of a Court of Mixed Commission located at Cuba. While the Act for the Abolition of the Slave Trade in 1807 had put an end to British participation in that trade, it neither did nor could in any way affect the activity of foreign nationals. By a Treaty of September 23, 1817, however, Britain had succeeded in securing a limitation of the Spanish slave trade as from May 30, 1820.[81] That measure was to be closely supervised and, for this purpose, the Treaty established two mixed Commissions – partly British partly Spanish. One of these was to be set up on British soil, the other on Spanish soil; and the two places selected were Sierra Leone and Cuba respectively. The functions of these Commissions were: to determine the legality of the captures made by the authority concerned, and to order such compensation as they considered justified. The Commissions were each to be composed of a Commissary Judge and a Commissioner of Arbitration, nominated by each participating country. The Africans captured and declared legal prizes were to be given certificates of manumission and awarded as free labourers to the government of the territory in which the Commission was located.[82]

It was not until the middle of 1833 that the first shipment of Africans under this new arrangement was sent to Trinidad from Havana, as a result of the capture of a Spanish slave ship called the "Negrita". The Commission at Havana had decided, for reasons to be discussed later, to send these Africans to Trinidad. This gave rise to the formulation, by the Colonial Office, of a number of conditions for the transportation of such slaves to Trinidad. These conditions were as follows:

1. That the Spanish government was to bear the cost of transportation, and the care of the Africans during the voyage.

2. That the Governor of Trinidad was to be given one month's notice of their embarkation from Havana.

3. That they were not to be sent earlier, or in greater numbers, than the Governor of Trinidad prescribed.

4. That the latter was also to determine the proportion of the sexes so as to preserve a balance among the people sent.

5. That the Africans were to receive a certificate declaring that they were free from disease, and were not incapacitated for work.

6. That children were not to be sent without one or both parents.

7. That there was to be no forced separation of families.

The Commissioners introduced two modifications to these rules to the effect that the Africans were to be "suitably" clothed, and that a medical certificate was to be issued by a practitioner appointed by the Commissioners.[83]

These proposals were clearly in the British interest; but the Spanish authorities were not caught off guard. The Intendant at Havana objected to the proposals not only because of the expence which the Spanish government was likely to incur, but also because the discretion given the Trinidad government was likely to limit severely the ability of the Spanish authorities to distribute the captured Africans. The British Commissioners noted other considerations – that the authorities at Havana had found it advantageous to employ the Africans in public works contrary to the terms of the Treaty; and that the white population was anxious for their removal. In fact the Africans had been awarded to the Cuban government, but without any stipulation as to the nature of their employment. Eventually, the matter seems to have resolved itself in favour of the British government, the Africans being transferred to Trinidad.[84]

Originally 196 Africans were captured from the "Negrita", and the Cuban health authorities had intended to send them to Sierra Leone. But, reportedly on account of the length of the voyage, the condition of the captives, and what they thought might have been an infraction of the treaty, they eventually sent them to Trinidad. Only 189 of these Africans actually arrived in Trinidad: 134 males and 55 females; no mention was made of the others. These were quarantined in barracks near Port of Spain and inoculated because there had been a cholera epidemic in Cuba at the time they were there. Lt. Governor Hill reported receiving sixty applications for their services as free labourers, while there were "innumerable" applications for their services as domestics.[85] While awaiting their allotment to applicants, the Africans were employed in clearing bush at Orange Grove, and weeding in the Government savannah.[86] When they were eventually disposed of, 120 were sent to fifteen plantations in lots of eight each to be employed as agricultural labourers. Thirty-eight others were sent as domestics to 23 "respectable" householders and, of the remainder, seven had died and 24 were yet to be disposed of. Governor Hill believed that their work in the first year was unlikely to be of any value, as they did not understand any of the languages of the "civilised world". Therefore he considered food, clothing, medical attention, and meagre wages a sufficient recompense for their labour, these provisions being increased as they progressed.[87]

The method of deployment, and the treatment which would have gone with it, suggest that these Africans were regarded as hardly better than slaves. In fact the Secretary of State, while generally approving the arrangements, saw fit to draw Hill's attention to this point. He was concerned that, in view of the impending Act abolishing slavery, their condition should bear no resemblance to slavery as that was likely to cause the government great embarrassment. Instead, he recommended that no fixed indentures be arranged and that the Africans be hired out for periods of six months at a time, with competition for labour determining the rate of wages.[88]

Two further groups arrived in the few months immediately preceding emancipation. In February 1834, 207 arrived in the colony, and the anxiety of the planters to build up their labour supply was obvious from the 938 applications made for their services. The new arrivals were divided into twenty groups of ten, each group having five males and five females. This indicates a high proportion of females, a feature which contrasts sharply with the known figures for shipments of other such persons at this time. Seven girls under ten years of age, who were too young for estate work, were placed with "respectable" families.[89]

On March 28, 1834, another 194 persons arrived by the ship "Cristina", 97 of each sex, who were reported to be mostly in good health.[90]   Yet they were not in as good health on the whole, nor as well provided with clothing, as those of the previous shipment.[91] These were allocated to estates in 30 batches of six persons each, and one of five. Eight young girls were placed once more in "respectable" families in and around Port of Spain, the remaining one having died.[92] What is noticeable is that, on the whole, local officials preferred placing them on estates rather than putting them in settlements as was the case with the other free Africans. In other words, the Trinidad officials were pandering to the desire of the planters for more labour, rather than treating the Africans as free. And as the arrangements were generally approved by the Colonial Office, that department must be included in any strictures passed on the subordinate administration.

Governor Hill expressed satisfaction with these last two groups, none of whom seems to have run away, and against whom he had received no charge of misconduct. But he complained of mis-management in the case of those who had arrived the previous July. That first group had been kept for many weeks in the same barracks as one of the black West India regiments which had been quartered near Port of Spain,[93] and so could easily have been corrupted. In approving that arrangement, he claimed to have yielded to those who had professed "practical experience"; but thereafter the various arrivals were allotted to their employers as soon as they had disembarked.[94] In his despatch of July 1, 1833, he had merely stated that the immigrants had been placed in barracks and inoculated; but perhaps they had also been kept there for seasoning. It may also have been the case that the shortage of women, as far as the soldiers were concerned, had been productive of some unpleasantness. Or it is quite likely that popular white opinion was a significant factor in determining his future action. The settlement of numerous free Africans so close to Port of Spain had resulted in Governor Woodford rethinking a similar course of action in 1816. And it was not to be supposed that a much larger number would have been overlooked, although they were only temporarily quartered there. In addition to this, the whole colony was in a very disturbed state as emancipation became imminent.

This source of labour seemed to open new possibilities for extending cultivation in the colony. With the advent of emancipation, estate proprietors fixed their eyes with increasing anxiety on the acquisition of more labourers.[95] And so it was that a body of proprietors petitioned the Governor for a further 5,000 Africans, offering to take another 10,000 if the British government was willing to sanction their apprenticeship until 1840. Hill supported the proposal to the extent that he gave his approval for the importation of no more than 1,000 of them, provided that they had been in Cuba for less than two years and were under thirty years of age.[96] In refusing to accept any who had been in Cuba for five or six years, his reason was that their best years of labour would have been past apart from which it would have meant disturbing any unions they might have formed. Even at this stage he had not thought of transporting families, as specified in the regulations for these people. He was also afraid that they might have been of doubtful character. The Secretary of State, Stanley, was of the view that Hill should exercise caution in proceeding with this matter, and requested periodic reports as to their conduct. He surmised that the Governor's fear had been based on reports which he had apparently received to the effect that the Africans had left their owners after the first six months and, as vagrants, had constituted a danger and a nuisance to the colony.[97]

Hill's assurances must have satisfied him, for there was no further query from the Colonial Office on the matter. The immigrants were subjected to the same regulations which governed the conduct of free labourers towards their employers and *vice versa*.[98] In other, words, they were brought into the same condition as slaves who were about to be emancipated, with all that the later apprenticeship entailed.

In the light of the foregoing, we must now look at the questions which Hill raised concerning the extent of his authority over these immigrants. Since the Africans had been emancipated on Spanish territory, were they to be regarded as aliens? And if they were not to be so regarded, what control did he have over them? For his part, he thought it would have been necessary to have an Order in Council sent out or a local Ordinance passed to enable him to subject the refractory among them to such "wholesome Control that should not even cast a Shade upon the Spirit of humanity and kindness with which this class of our fellow Creatures ought to be treated."[99]

The emphasis on precisely regulating the relative positions of employers and employees was one which began about 1832; and, as emancipation drew nearer, so the demand for such regulations seemed to become more exacting. In 1834 the new Secretary of State, T.S. Rice, excluded the newly released Africans from those privileges enjoyed by other free aliens. Perhaps unwittingly he had answered Hill's query of a few months previously. "As in the case of children", he had written, "so in the case of these Africans, there are certain abridgements of the rights common to all other persons, which the necessity of the case demands & justifies."[100] So again, we see that these prize Africans were being placed on a footing that was a level below and even worse than that of those to be freed by the Act for the Abolition of Slavery of 1833. These persons had not actually been enslaved. Rice, in addition to regulations already made for their transportation, required that explanations be given them of their exact situation in Trinidad and of the need for regular labour in return for maintenance and protection from injury.

By 1834, when emancipation became a formal state for those previously enslaved, these immigrants found themselves in a dubious position. In general, their situation was that of being superintended and supervised, and made to labour for the welfare of the colony; but of personal freedom, there was still very little.

4. THE INTER-ISLAND TRADE AND AMELIORATION

Very frequently during the slave trade debates, the abolitionists had stressed the existence of a connection between continued importation of slaves and the failure of slave owners to treat them well. When the Order in Council of March 1812 established in Trinidad the process of slave registration, it also left open the possibility of individuals importing slaves who had already been registered in other colonies. The clause making this provision might have been inserted when the abolitionists were thinking of a general registration of slaves in the West Indies in 1812. However, it had never been removed, though such a general registration did not materialise in that year. When the Slave Registry Bill was introduced into Parliament in 1815, it met with such stiff opposition from West Indian interests that Parliament was persuaded to leave the passage of such a system to the local legislatures. Only a few of the older colonies had passed registration acts by September 1817;[1] so that until 1819, when an Act of the British Parliament made it illegal to have any interest in unregistered slaves,[2] only a few colonies beside Trinidad had registered slaves.

The years following reveal a policy permitting the movement of slaves from various colonies to Trinidad, both by officials at the Colonial Office as well as by the local administration. Ostensibly done to relieve colonies which could not sustain such large numbers as they had, or to allow persons of quality to carry their domestic servants with them as they travelled, this dangerous experiment opened wide the door to abuse. When action was eventually taken to correct the abuse, the confusion was found to be compounded by serious administrative bungling. What follows is an attempt to explain the circumstances, as far as this is possible.

For several years, many persons showed an interest in importing slaves into Trinidad. In 1813, the disasters of civil war in Venezuela caused some proprietors there to seek asylum in Trinidad as they sought to escape the ravages of war. In due course, the Customs Officers in Trinidad seized such slaves on the grounds that they had been illegally imported. But Henry Fuller, the Attorney General and a considerable slave owner, intervened in the proceedings on the grounds that the circumstances did not warrant the prosecution of the slaves or their owners. Immediately following this development, he set out certain instructions for the future guidance of the Customs Officers in matters of a similar nature. These required that the owners be allowed to register their slaves; that they give security in the sum of £100 per slave; and that the slaves should not be sold or withheld from any investigation which might follow should they be declared illegal.[3] He did not explain those circumstances which might cause them to be declared illegal, nor did he indicate what authority he had for taking such a step. Fuller was similarly obstructive, some eleven months later, when the Customs officers made another seizure of slaves. Expressing his unwillingness to believe that the owners had any intention of evading the abolition law, he argued that the slaves were being imported under circumstances permitted by the law. Moreover, he seemed confident that the Judge of the Court of Vice-Admiralty was unlikely to pass sentences of forfeiture under the circumstances.[4] Fuller failed to indicate what was the law to which he referred, and what were those circumstances under which the law permitted the importation. Sir Ralph Woodford, the Governor, was in favour of importation, and expressed disappointment that Bathurst, when he eventually heard from him, did not sanction the reception of the slaves in question.[5] Whether Woodford himself knew the law to which Fuller referred is not indicated; not only should Bathurst and his Law Officers have been acquainted with whatever colonial law existed on that matter, but Fuller's claim was clearly called into question. As an estate owner, Fuller was in a position which reeked of conflict of interest – a conflict which he did not easily avoid in his official capacity.

The situation, then, was that both the Governor and the principal Crown lawyer were disposed to encourage a liberal policy regarding importation of slaves, and the Customs Officers seemed to be deterred from taking action against persons alleged to have offended. A return of 1818 shows that only fourteen seizures had been made between 1812 and 1814; the slaves in question were either apprenticed to planters or made to serve in the 3rd West India Regiment. One of the slaves was apprenticed to "Mr. Johnstone", later to become the Judge of the Court of Criminal Inquiry; and two others were reported to be in the Governor's care.[6] In 1819 the investigation of a slave's complaint revealed four other cases of smuggling. In one of these a slave was sold under the name of another who had been legally imported from Dominica, the owner using the Customs certificate and affidavit of the first slave for the later transaction. One of the parties involved was Phillip St. Laurent who was at the time employed as principal clerk in the Slave Registry. The other, James St. Laurent, was reported by Woodford to have imported slaves more than once from a foreign country; yet he apparently saw no reason to take action against either of them, believing such importation to be sanctioned by law, if reported to the Customs.[7] This indicates that infractions of the law were taking place within the very organs established to prevent them, and that the law was proably being mis-interpreted. And the fact that one James St. Laurent was reported to be a frequent importer of slaves,[8] which he might have sold thereafter, suggests that Phillip St. Laurent was likely to turn a blind eye to the offence as well as to facilitate the registration of any slaves so imported.

Nothing resulted from the legal action which was instituted by the authorities in Trinidad against the offenders. The matter was passed to Barbados, presumably because it was thought that the matter could only be tried in a Court of Admiralty, when it should really have been passed to the Court of Vice-Admiralty. After a delay of about nine months, the Attorney General of Barbados proposed the release of the slaves in question; and the offenders were acquitted, "but with an *obligation* on the parties *to carry back the slaves to Guadeloupe*." Governor Woodford's objection to this concerned the close involvement of one who had enjoyed a position of public trust;[9] his objection might also have been directed at the repeated advice in favour of such action by one whose duty it was to prosecute infractions of the law. The Customs Board in London was also surprised at the failure of their Trinidad counterparts to prosecute; and demanded of them that action be taken in the Court of Vice Admiralty if the slaves were still in the colony. The Board emphasized that "no slave can be brought into any British Colony from a Foreign Colony for any purpose Whatsoever, and you are to govern yourselves accordingly."[10] The directive confirms that referring the case to Barbados was not necessary, and that the colony possessed the machinery necessary for handling such cases. This is particularly important because the line adopted by the Customs, as problems arose later, shows culpable negligence in the face of clear guidance. Such official negligence not only made the law a dead letter; it also showed their willingness to evade their responsibilities.

Numerous other slaves had been imported into the colony, sometimes with the sanction of both the Governor and the Colonial Office. Between 1813 and 1824, more than 5,000 slaves were imported into the colony.[11] Bathurst considered the immigration of propertied individuals to be in the best interests of the colony, and was quite prepared to encourage their immigration with generous grants of land. It is with this in view that he permitted Lord Rolle to move 170 slaves from the Bahamas to Trinidad, instructing the Governor to give Rolle a grant of his choice.[12] Similarly, he authorised a grant of land in Naparima to Sir Alexander Cochrane some years later.[13] A burning question arises: that is, whether any of the slaves so imported before 1820 can be considered to have been legally imported. The Order in Council of March 1812 permitted duly registered slaves to be imported; but as scarcely any of the older West Indian colonies in question had a slave registry until after the Slave Registry Act of 1819, this provision of the Order could not properly be acted on. It is therefore questionable whether slaves could be legally imported according to the terms of the Order, when the islands from which they were imported had no registry. The provision therefore was sure to create severe problems in the absence of an appropriate system of registration in the older colonies.

The generosity of the Colonial Office, in facilitating importation, offered encouragement to the local administration in its attempt to attract an increasing number of slaves for the estates. Thus, when 24 slaves were imported from New Providence in the Bahamas in 1821, the Acting Governor, Col. A. W. Young, solicited for the importer exemption from the 3½ % tax chargeable on such importation. In support of his proposal, he pointed out that the colony had been deficient in its labour supply; and also that the colony's revenue was likely to benefit from the work done by the slaves.[14] Bathurst's ready approval of his action was only qualified by his recommendation that Governor Young bear in mind the necessity for a certificate of registration as required by law.[15]

Not long afterwards another Bahamian proprietor, Burton Williams, applied for land on which to settle 105 slaves with whom he intended to establish a sugar plantation and to breed cattle. Williams had previously received in the colony a grant of some 300 acres of land in the "most fertile part of the island"; but the Acting Governor recommended an additional grant of two quarrees or six acres of land per slave in a less fertile part of the island, without depriving Williams of the original grant in Savana Grande.[16] There was no other ground for this action except Williams' complaints about the cost of transporting his slaves from the Bahamas to Trinidad, and the fact that he was required to purchase Crown lands.[17] Young's recommendation met with a favourable response at the Colonial Office, though Bathurst warned him against letting Williams have too large a tract of fertile land, which in his view did not appear to be in the public interest. Bathurst authorised the second grant, but with the condition that Williams' retention of it be subject to the maintenance on it of a fixed amount of cattle.[18]

In mid-1823, Burton Williams imported a further 300 slaves from the Bahamas, craving exemption from the slave tax of $2.00 per head due on them. Acting on the advice of the Council, Woodford, who by this time had resumed office as Governor, recommended the remittance of the annual slave tax for a period of three years in the case of every importation of over fifty slaves, provided that the slaves were to be employed in agriculture. This recommendation was based on what he termed the "unexpectedly" low mortality among Williams' slaves – less than one per cent.[19] Williams, who seems to have been the greatest single importer of this period, was later reported by Woodford to have imported 324 slaves between 1821 and 1823. Of that number seven had died and, there were nineteen births.[20] Impressed with Woodford's recommendation for relief, Bathurst granted this petition as well.[21] If Williams had been granted land to the same extent as was recommended earlier by Young, a single individual would have benefited from a considerable amount of land as well as from massive exemptions from taxes.

In an effort to attract greater importation, the Trinidad Council later recommended that the exemption from the slave tax should be extended so as to be of benefit to persons importing twenty or more slaves. Other incentives offered by the Council included exemption from the 3½ % tax for one year, and from the slave tax for three years. The only condition the Council stipulated was that the owners should forfeit those benefits if they sold the slaves.[22] On this occasion, the Colonial Office did not respond favourably to the recommendation. Bathurst did not want such concessions, granted in a particular case, to become generally applicable; but he still left the door open for the consideration of such special cases as might arise later on.[23]

At no time during this period did it occur to officials, either in Trinidad or at the Colonial Office, that they were creating a situation which might later prove embarrassing. Their readiness to encourage importation seemed certain, sooner or later, to degenerate into the licence of importing without proper authority. In fact, cases of illegal importation did crop up from time to time. The scale of such illegality can be seen from the large number of slaves imported during this early period. Two sets of figures are given for the period 1812 to 1822, though they do not agree. As shown in Appendix A No. 5, between 1812 and 1821, some 3,815 slaves had been imported into Trinidad; one year later, another report gave the numbers for 1813 to 1822 as 3,239. Even at that stage the traffic was quite high. After the Consolidated Slave Trade Act of 1824, systematic illegal importation took place in such a way as to cause considerable embarrassment to public officials. Apart from this, it must ever be kept in mind that the ready supply of slaves was held by the abolitionists to have an adverse effect on efforts at amelioration. So that, when such importation was encouraged, it could be said that the right hand was not working in harmony with the left.

The Consolidated Slave Trade Act [24] came into effect on January 1, 1825. Although its intention was not to facilitate any extension of the slave trade, the actual effect of the Act was to extend it because of the misinterpretation of one of its clauses. This Act declared illegal the fitting out of slave ships – or engaging in any commercial transaction involving slaves – except under certain specific conditions. It permitted individuals to purchase slaves in any British island or territory, so long as the slaves were to be employed in the same island or territory. It also permitted the removal of slaves to any part of the same island, or from one island to another, if there were several islands within the same government. In this case, the purpose of the removal was to be declared to the Officer administering the government for the time being, the latter being authorised to issue a licence to the applicant.[25] The King in Council was empowered, until July 31, 1827, to authorise the removal of slaves from one British West Indian island to another, provided that he was assured that such removal was important for the welfare of the slaves concerned. He could also stipulate the regulations and conditions which were to govern such transfers, and take security in double the value of the slaves to be removed.[26]

Because of its importance to this chapter, the following section is spelt out in some detail. Any slave who was "really and truly the Domestic Servant of any Person residing or being in any Island, Colony, or Plantation or Territory" was free to accompany his owner, or master, or any member of the latter's family who might be travelling to another colony. Two conditions had to be satisfied in this regard: first of all, *the name and occupation of each domestic* was to be inserted in the ship's clearance in the presence of the Customs Officer at the port of embarkation. It was then that officer's duty to certify that "the Slave or Slaves so embarked or carried were reported or described to him as Domestic Servants". Secondly, the master or owner was to obtain an extract of the Slave Register showing the name and description of each slave. This document was to be presented to the Customs Officer at the port of disembarkation; and he, in turn, was to furnish the local Registrar of Slaves with a copy of that extract.[27]

Almost immediately, Woodford expressed doubts about certain parts of the Act; and it is obvious from his comments that he was not particularly disposed to support the home government's policy. For instance, he raised questions about the fifteenth clause, which required that the transporter enter a bond to observe periodic regulations for the welfare of the slaves. In his view, compliance with this requirement would have been impossible to achieve, while on the other hand, that clause was likely to serve only to "prohibit altogether the removal of the Slaves from the exhausted soil of the old colonies …" Woodford argued further that, since Trinidad and Demerara were the only colonies to which Africans could have been sent, and since it was the King who made regulations for both, there really was no necessity for bonds.[28] That obligation, he thought, would have acted as a deterrent to any conscientious individual. Apart from this Woodford considered it superfluous to require a bond for obedience to the law. The Governor was perhaps optimistic that, once the appropriate regulations had been made, compliance would have followed as a matter of course; but to be so optimistic was to ignore the pattern of planter behaviour during this period. Woodford believed that only two conditions were pre-requisite for the settlement of the slaves, and these showed a remarkable affinity to his scheme for settling the free refugees. One of these conditions was that land should be cleared, and that a house and provisions should be prepared for them. Another was that they were to be provided with medical attention and clothing, and be placed under the care of the Protector of Slaves, until they could be settled to the satisfaction of that officer.[29]

The second clause about which the Governor had some reservation was that which concerned the allotment of the slaves to various persons as apprentices. Obviously focussing on the fact that some free blacks were owners of slaves, Woodford did not think that the plan would have been satisfactory to the slaves, in that they were likely to become the servants of people a little above their own station. This observation was made in the interest of his own preference, rather than strictly in the interest of the slaves. All the slaves, as far as he was concerned, needed to be controlled; and the proposals he made for settling them reflected this conviction. Thus they were to be organised in a manner similar to that of an Indian mission, under a *Corregidor*, Curate, Schoolmaster and Doctor. They were also to be fed and clothed until they were able to support themselves; and were to plant the ground with a view to establishing a plantation to meet the cost of their settlement. If they performed to his satisfaction, they might be "promoted" to an upper class to serve as constables, while their *children* might inherit the right of free persons. One important purpose, which Woodford hoped the scheme would serve, was that of enabling the British government to study the "susceptibility" of the African for civilization.[30] It is not altogether surprising that this scheme was never implemented; Bathurst had previously discouraged the expenditure of large sums of money for any schemes of that nature,[31] and Woodford should have cherished no high hopes on that score. Nothing, therefore, came of the suggestion.

Noel Titus

Irregular importation after 1824

Importation continued, if not in a flood, then certainly at a steady rate. Between 1825 and 1829, a large number of people sought permission to transport their slaves to Trinidad. According to some reports, no fewer than 1,797 slaves would have been affected if permission had been granted, the chief sources being the Bahamas, Tortola, St. Kitts, and Barbados.[32] As an example of the anxiety to import slaves to Trinidad, the case may be cited of one Jesse Woodward, who submitted an application for a grant of land which was to be cultivated by free Africans from Antigua.[33] Bathurst ordered that these Africans be employed on seven year indentures, renewable or otherwise at the discretion of the Africans, who were also to give their consent prior to their removal. The cost of their transportation to Trinidad was to be borne by the authorities at Antigua.[34] Woodford granted to Woodward 300 acres of land made available through the renunciation of claims by two proprietors of North Naparima.[35] The grant was confirmed by Bathurst,[36] who wrote to the administrator at Antigua asking him to set the arrangements in train.

It does not appear that any free Africans were ever brought to Trinidad for work in this enterprise; Woodford had not heard from Woodward almost a year after the application was made. The unindentured Africans, fearing that they might have been treated as slaves, were unwilling to leave Antigua. Although Bathurst recommended that some of their own colour might be sent from Trinidad to Antigua to encourage them to emigrate from the latter,[37] no progress seems to have been made on that matter. While this was under consideration, Bathurst referred to Woodford an opinion of the Law Officers of the Crown to the effect that the Consolidated slave Trade Act had made it illegal "to import or to bring, or to contract for the importing or bringing into any place whatsoever slaves or other persons, as, or in order to their being dealt with as slaves."[38] This seems to suggest that the Africans could only have been brought to Trinidad as free labourers; and any action which deviated from this opinion might therefore be construed as a breach of the Act. It was a gentle warning from the Secretary of State, and it shows that Woodford could not claim ignorance of what was expected of him.

In terms of numbers, the extent of importation after this Act was not as great as before it; but considering that the Act limited movement to domestic servants in attendance on their masters, then the activity was very significant. The following table illustrates the extent of slave importation in the six years following the Act.

Table VIII:
Slaves Imported into Trinidad, 1825 – 1830

Year	Males	Females	Total
1825	236	232	468
1826	37	33	70
1827	200	101	301
1828	59	63	122
1829	86	43	129
1830	7	12	19
TOTAL			1109

Source: "Importation and Exportation of Slaves," British Parliamentary Papers, Slave Trade, Vol. 80, 132.

This return, provided by the Deputy Registrar of Slaves, Albert Murray, points to a quite remarkable traffic in domestics. Of this total, 489 came from Barbados alone, while 283 came from Tortola. The Colonial Office pursued a policy of determining how such slaves ought to be employed. Bathurst, for instance, insisted that such slaves were not to be employed in the cultivation of sugar; they were not to be removed to any other location without their consent; there was not to be any separation of their families; and lastly, females born after migration were to be freed.[39] In a similar way Bathurst's successor, Sir George Murray, had made it a point to inquire whether the removal requested by slave owners was essential to the welfare of the slaves concerned.[40]

The insistence of the two Secretaries of State on the considerations outlined above furnishes the best explanation of the illegal importation to which slave proprietors in Trinidad resorted in the mid-1820's. Their policy merely sought to implement what was set out in the Consolidated Slave Trade Act. Any strict adherence to the law, especially as it was explained by the Law Officers of the Crown, would have made it impossible for slaves to be moved to that locality where so many people wanted them – that is, to Trinidad and Guyana, where there were extensive tracts of virgin soil. Sugar and its by-products were still the major revenue earners in the West Indies; but sugar production meant plentiful and intensive labour such as the abolitionists complained of as being detrimental to the Africans. Yet the Trinidad slave owners appeared to be less concerned about the welfare of the

Africans, and instead were anxious and even determined to get the labour they needed. They therefore found an effective way around the obstacles, and were not without official support. Woodford showed himself eager to recommend waivers of the restriction with respect to their employment, as for instance in the case of Louis de le Grenade,[41] who wanted to import slaves from Grenada to work on cocoa estates he had already purchased.

Thwarted by the queries and demands of the Colonial Office, a well organised system of smuggling was successfully carried out. Taking advantage of that clause of the 1824 Act, which permitted domestics to accompany their owners while travelling, some proprietors formed the habit of purchasing slaves in Barbados and travelling with them to Trinidad as their own domestics. Once arrived in the colony, these persons invariably sold their slaves, which were frequently purchased by others for service on sugar estates. In this way a certain amount of agricultural labour was regularly provided for the plantation owners. This traffic began shortly after the publication of the Consolidated Slave Trade Act and not after Woodford had left the scene, as some writers have argued.[42]

The extent of the traffic is not easy to determine because of carelessness and incompetence in the Customs Department in Barbados. An indication of their laxity may be found in the postscript to a return of slaves shipped from Barbados to Trinidad between 1821 and 1824, in which the Customs officials wrote:

Slaves as Domestic Servants are generally carried from this Island by their Owners in the Packets, Mail Boats, or some other Government Vessels, which never Enter or Clear in this Office, consequently the Return of such Slaves cannot be made.[43]

This practice apparently continued subsequently, so that it was only in 1827 that the suspicions of acting Governor Skeete in Barbados were aroused about the nature of the traffic, when it transpired that the irregularities might have originated in the office of the Secretary. The Customs officials, the Secretary, and the Attorney General seem not to be in harmony in their reading of the law. But there is enough to suggest the circumvention of the law by persons travelling from Barbados, and of negligence by Customs officers and others. Correspondence between Aberdeen, the Collector of Customs at Barbados, and Skeete suggests that the latter might unwittingly have given countenance to the abuse of the provision concerning domestics.[44] Even where the Customs were concerned, it is possible that the term "owner" was interpreted to mean the person currently in possession of the slave – however recently. This led to abuses which should not have escaped notice. Skeete therefore referred this matter to Huskisson, Secretary of State, on the advice of the Attorney General in Barbados.[45]

Early in 1828, Skeete also drew the attention of Woodford to the possibility that the Consolidated Slave Act was being infringed.[46] Not long before that, Huskisson had written to the Governor instructing him to take action against the offenders.[47] However, Woodford was unwilling to do so, being content with the assurance given to him by the Collector of Customs in Trinidad that the law had always been complied with, and that seizure would not have been valid. Even so, as Woodford himself rightly acknowledged, the precise occupation of the slaves could only have been ascertained at the port of embarkation; and it was a duty which devolved upon the Customs officials in Barbados. Compounding the difficulty, Woodford indicated that once slaves had been legally imported, their sale was not prohibited.[48] The real question, however, was whether the slaves were legally imported; his answer would seem to be in the affirmative. Either Woodford was not aware of, or he did not stop to consider, the circumvention of the law, which his last remark about freedom to sell suggested. The regulations embodied in the despatches explicitly forbade the employment of these slaves in agriculture; so that by overlooking sales, he was closing his eyes to the contravention of the law made easy by the ability to sell slaves into agricultural occupations. Moreover, it never occurred to the Customs Officers to question whether the slaves imported were actually domestics; in this regard they differed from their counterparts in Demerara, who prosecuted importers for this offence.[49] The law required their *occupations* to be declared, which meant more than just the word "domestic". Their description as cooks, maids, butlers, and such like was what the law required. It is therefore far from true to say, as L. M. Fraser and Mrs. Gertrude Carmichael have done, that the breach of the abolition laws began after the death of Woodford.[50] The Governor condoned the breach, and the negligence of the Customs Officials facilitated it.

The irregularities seem to have arisen, not only from lax administration of the law, but also from the abuse of an old Barbados law which required persons leaving that colony to have a licence from the Governor for the removal of their slaves. It should be noted, at this point, that the fifteenth clause of the Consolidated Slave Trade Act also required a licence for the removal of slaves, but only if they were within the same government. The licence given by Skeete was merely a security for creditors – to ensure that the slaves who were being removed were not mortgaged, and to prevent their being taken beyond the reach of the creditors.[51] The Collector of Customs usually issued a certificate to anyone who was in possession of a licence from the Governor; but those who were travelling usually ignored the Customs officials if the latter refused to issue the necessary certificates.[52]

INVESTIGATION OF ILLEGAL IMPORTATION

This was the problem facing him when, immediately after his arrival as Governor in 1829, Sir Lewis Grant instituted an inquiry into the nature and extent of the evasion of the slave laws. Reminding the Secretary of State of a previous occasion when he had found it necessary to observe that the Act did not deter abuses, Grant noted that before the Act of 1825 few people travelled with two domestics, and several carried none with them.[53] The case was far different after the passage of the Act. An objection had been raised by James Stephen, junior, to a shipment of domestics from Barbados to Demerara on the same ground, which was, that the abolition laws were being evaded.[54] So that the Colonial Office should have been aware of those infringements which were already taking place and which were likely to escalate. Grant himself expressed the view that the Customs officials in Port of Spain should have been more alert, especially since the clearance certificates did not specify the occupations of the domestics. Acting promptly on his suspicions, he demanded a scrutiny of every importation of more than one slave, except where the slave had been previously moved from Trinidad as a domestic. He required particular attention to be paid to one individual who had brought six or seven slaves from Barbados, and had since returned to that island.[55]

The fact that this activity escaped the notice of the Trinidad Customs can only be regarded as surprising, for it was evasions such as these that the framers of the law had foreseen and thus empowered the Customs Officers to deal with. The ameliorative process partly depended on curbing the inflow of slaves; so that the Customs Officers had an important role to play in it. Grant sought the assistance of the Attorney General, Henry Fuller, in prosecuting fraudulent importers. But the new Governor's zeal did not blind him to the difficulty of the situation in which he was placed. In his letter soliciting Fuller's help, he wrote:

> I conceive the Laws of the country and the Public
> Functionaries are held in defiance and insulted by
> the subterfuges which there are so much grounds for
> believing have been made use of to evade the laws,
> and when the extent of importations which we already
> know was carried on in 1827 and previously is
> considered, there is no doubt that Government will
> be rather surprised that it was suffered to gain ground
> in 1828 and 1829 which I suspect it has done.[56]

This was an indictment of the Customs and other enforcement agencies, who tended to find nothing deserving of prosecution in the actions of importers.

Considerable involvement of local proprietors in illegal importation of slaves was revealed as a result of Grant's investigations. A number of prosecutions were instituted in 1829, and this action continued until the eve of emancipation. One of the early prosecutions for breach of the abolition laws was that against Charles Gibbon Hobson, a proprietor of Dominica. Hobson had applied for permission to import three hundred slaves, about forty of whom he declared his intention of liberating at once, and placing on his estate in Trinidad under ten and fifteen year indentures. This plan appeared unobjectionable to the Governor, although Grant suspected that only males physically able to survive the indentures would have been selected. His own preference was for the importation of families, in which the proportion of the sexes would have been nearly equal. Grant's suggestion to the Colonial Secretary in support of such a scheme included keeping them enslaved for ten years after the age of fifteen, allowing them Saturday and Sunday free during those ten years, and giving them fifty-two additional free days thereafter.[57] Eventually they were to be placed on the same footing as the emancipated Africans. Grant took no notice of Hobson's promise to liberate some of the slaves, a promise that was unlikely to be kept given the propensity for control on the part of the planters. His preference for them to continue in slavery for ten years after age 15 would surely have carried great weight with the slave owners.

Hobson seems not to have awaited a reply from the Governor, but imported seventeen slaves, fourteen of whom were put to work in the fields.[58] All seem to have been imported as domestics. The swiftness of Grant's response contrasted sharply with the lack of action by the Collector of Customs. No action was taken by that officer until Grant ordered him to investigate the matter, consult with the Attorney General, and take effective action. The Governor also warned him that so large a number of domestics should have aroused his suspicion;[59] the fact that it did not is one of the peculiarities of the situation. Hobson's protests of innocence were not only weak and contradictory, but somewhat incriminating. His private letter to the Governor clearly indicates that the slaves in question had been employed in plantation work on the estate of his nephew, George Hobson. He claimed to have asked the latter not to employ them in agriculture;[60] but we might be unwise to attach any importance to that claim.

Much more serious was the fact that Hobson charged both the Attorney General, Fuller, and Collector of Customs, Clogstoun, with responsibility for any error into which he or any other importers might have fallen. According to him, when he had decided to take up residence in Trinidad, he inquired of the latter how many domestics he was able to import. In reply to his inquiry, he was told that no limits had been set by the Act.[61] Strictly speaking, this reply was correct. However, the framers of the Act did not envisage that persons would assume a need either to travel with several domestics or to have a different set of domestics with each voyage, all purchased in the colony to which they were originally travelling. It should have been apparent, from the very nature of the question, that a breach of the law was likely, for the Act provided that only *bona fide* domestics in attendance on their owners might accompany the latter. Therefore, Clogstoun's reply might, with some justification, be regarded as connivance.

When the slaves were actually imported, a certificate of legal importation was issued by the Collector of Customs, who subsequently took the slaves into custody as a result of Grant's instructions rather than his own initiative. Hobson asserted that they had been seized seven weeks after he had imported and registered them. This is even more surprising since the documents presented to him should also have aroused the suspicion of the Registrar of Slaves; Hobson should have been shown as a new owner. According to Hobson, both Fuller (the Attorney General) and Clogstoun (the Collector of Customs) were fully aware of the sale of the slaves to estates; the conveyances for some of these sales had actually been prepared by Fuller. But what is more, Hobson accused the Protector of Slaves – who was also Solicitor General – of importing slaves in his wife's name. These accusations can hardly be dismissed as merely malicious; but there is no indication that they were ever investigated. There is nowhere among the records any denials by either Clogstoun or Gloster about their involvement in the illegal activity. And although Fuller disclaimed any responsibility for illegal importation, he admitted *preparing mortgages on slaves* of whose illegal importance he professed ignorance.[62] That Fuller's case was weak is evident from the fact that, if the slaves were local, he would have had a certificate of their registration at the time of the mortgages. If they had been imported, the onus was on him to obtain verification of their status. Fuller was in an even more critical position in that he was breaking the law in private practice while prosecuting as a public official.

Hobson was in due course prosecuted, the prosecutor being the Attorney General whom he had accused of connivance. The Secretary of State, Lord Goderich, in seeking information about the course of action taken by the Attorney General, sounded an ominous note when he reminded the Customs Officers of the risks involved in admitting vessels carrying slaves under suspicious circumstances.[63] Hobson's trial resulted in his conviction, in the imposition of a fine of £1,200 sterling, and in his being imprisoned until he was able to pay the debt.[64] Goderich upheld the sentence on the ground that Hobson had no intention of returning to Dominica; and also that he had purchased the slaves on the eve of his departure, taking them to a place where their value was enhanced and the price of their manumission proportionately increased. Nevertheless, having regard to the climate, and the danger, which a protracted imprisonment posed for his health, the sentence was commuted, and the portion of the penalties due to the Crown[65] was remitted. Goderich also instructed that Hobson be discharged on payment of the costs, unless he was without the means to do so.[66] What is surprising is that he did not ask for any investigation of or action against officials accused by Hobson.

In the case of the slaves imported from Barbados, an important turn of events took place when Benjamin Parkhurst arrived in the colony.[67] A former Collector of Customs in Barbados, he had been commissioned to investigate the collection of revenue in Trinidad; but he felt, as he proceeded, that he was competent to take cognisance of slave importation.[68] A number of problems confronted Parkhurst as he began his investigations. The first of these related to the fact that many slaves imported as domestics had been sold at a profit to work in agriculture. The next problem immediately confronting Parkhurst was whether the importation of slaves under the general heading "domestics" was in conformity with section 17 of the Consolidated Slave Trade Act, which required the occupation of the domestic to be inserted on the ship's clearance. Expressing the need for caution, he observed that the burden of proving evasion of the law rested on the officer at the port of embarkation. Parkhurst also expressed concern at an inconsistency in the position of the Attorney General in allowing a domestic to be transported from the island with the same vagueness on a ship's clearance. Although disposed to give the slaves the benefit of the law, if there was evasion, he recommended that no further seizures be made until instructions were received from the Colonial Office, since the error originated elsewhere.[69] Parkhurst showed an inclination to be lenient where the occupation of the domestic was the only omission, suggesting that this error be referred to the Colonial Office. He had certainly found himself in a false position in that he was investigating irregularities in which he himself might have been implicated, as others were quick to observe.[70] What is more, an altercation between himself and Fuller, who demanded a clearance for his own domestic slave, only served to make matters more difficult.

Grant saw a more important point at issue: this was, whether the slaves in question really were the domestics of those who had imported them, and whether they had been imported in accordance with the true intent of the Act. In his view, most of the slaves had been imported for profit, and he regarded the course being followed by Parkhurst as clearly wrong. Its only purpose was to prolong the evil without providing any redress for the slaves. As it turned out, importers had even confined their slaves in order to deny them any opportunity of obtaining their freedom,[71] leading Grant to insist on continuing the investigations. On the other hand the Secretary of State, mindful of the hardships attendant on so unpopular a course as the prosecution of all the importers, recommended to the acting Governor, Sir Charles Smith, the issuing of a Proclamation pardoning all those who had unwittingly broken the law, provided they manumitted the slaves within a period of six weeks.[72] Arguing that the guilty parties – the original importers – were likely to go free, while third parties – such as the mortgagers – would be denied their right of recovery, Smith expressed a preference for seizure of the slaves after trial. He accused Woodford of conniving at a traffic which should certainly have been stopped after the receipt of a despatch from Huskisson on the subject. And in an even more sweeping charge, he blamed the entire system for the non-prosecution of offenders for the innocent purchase of property brought in

> under the authority of the Governor and Customs –
> admitted into Trinidad by the King's officers –
> certified by the office of Registry to have been
> legally imported – and *passed regularly through the*
> *Slave Registry offices of Trinidad and Whitehall.*[73]

Apart from censuring Smith for his failure to act in favour of the slaves, Goderich postponed further action until the return of Grant whose support for the abolition cause was quite obvious. He expressed a lack of sympathy for the purchasers of the illegally imported slaves, whom he believed must certainly have been aware of the risks involved.[74] What he did not undertake was a response to the charges in the letter from the acting Governor, charges which clearly implicated the Colonial Office. Indeed, it is possible that the nature of those charges may have been more annoying to Goderich than Smith's failure to follow orders. Objecting to Smith's proposal that the slaves be apprenticed to their owners or be repatriated, he insisted that they should be free to choose where they wished to live once they were declared free.[75] This position was not consonant with that of the Trinidad planters, who were averse to having free Africans in the colony.

It is very difficult to say how many slaves the investigations revealed to have been illegally imported. The last Attorney General of the period under review was said to have been involved in over five hundred cases up to the eve of emancipation; and at that time several cases were still outstanding. For instance, Goderich revealed that, according to the evidence, 266 domestics had been imported from Barbados alone between 1827 and 1828. Of this number 204 had been sold, 186 retaining their status as domestics while 12 had become field labourers. The Secretary of State rightly commented that the removal of so many domestics should have aroused the suspicion of the Customs, and that the motives of the importers needed to be examined.[76] The evidence which Grant submitted to Murray showed even greater irregularities, which ought to have been noticed by the Customs, if that institution had been more alert. For instance, 228 slaves had been imported in seven vessels as follows:

Eliza Pratt	32
Mary and Nancy	14 in two voyages
Endeavour	24
Steer-me-well	61 in 7 trips in the last 7 months of 1827
Beautiful Maid	34 in 3 trips, Aug. – Nov., 1827
" "	13 in 1 trip in May 1829
Perseverance	32 since 1826
Collector	18 since 1826.

Source: T.D.D. 8. 18: Grant to Murray, July 10, 1829.

Grant portrayed this level of importation as constituting the most glaring cases of fraud, the very point Smith was making. More important than the actual numbers, these figures show that, apart from one case in 1829, all the infractions had taken place during Woodford's tenure.[77]

TOWARDS A RESOLUTION OF THE PROBLEM

On February 3, 1832, the last stage in the matter of the smuggling began when Sir Lewis Grant published the proclamation, which Sir Charles Smith had earlier declined to publish. This proclamation aimed at correcting the abuse, which had been practised by the proprietors of slaves, and the violation of the abolition laws which such abuse had entailed. It therefore declared all such slaves forfeited to the Crown and their owners liable to prosecution; but it allowed them six weeks' grace in which to manumit those slaves voluntarily.[78] For many slave proprietors this was the straw which broke the camel's back. Coming so soon after the publication in

January that year of the Order in Council of November 2, 1831, it aroused considerable opposition on their side. This Order was the last of a series of ameliorative Orders intended to improve the condition of slaves in Trinidad, and will be discussed later.

The immediate reaction to the proclamation was a series of meetings and protests by a committee of slave proprietors and other interested persons. The editor of the anti-abolitionist paper, the *Port of Spain Gazette*, denounced the proceedings as preposterous, appearing to express disbelief about a rumour of a plot to overlook the importations at first so as to emancipate a large number of slaves. He described the slaves as the refuse of Barbados – a description which does little credit to the judgement of the importers – persons who would not benefit by being manumitted. Yet, if they were manumitted, they should either be sent back to Barbados, or be apprenticed for five to seven years with their present employers.[79] As far as he was concerned, the issue was that they should not be set free.

White slave owners, who usually met to protest every new order for the amelioration of the condition of the slaves,[80] appointed a committee to present a memorial to the Governor. Their memorial made three points, and these were largely similar to those repeated in other memorials. The first point was basically concerned with security, one which ameliorative efforts never ceased to evoke. Here the Committee referred to the "consternation and alarm" with which the community received the proclamation. Admitting that a great number of slaves were involved, the Committee argued that to turn them loose on the community would have been as "dangerous and impolitic" as it would have been oppressive to the individual proprietors. And they asked the Governor to consider the possible effects of such a course on other slaves. The second point was another timeworn one – deprivation of property. Here the committee charged that owners were being deprived of property, which had been acquired in ignorance of any violation of the law. The third point was condemnatory by nature. The memorial ended on a note of unprecedented virulence in that the "memorialists" charged every administration "including that of your Excellency – Every Tribunal of Justice and every Officer of the Crown in the Colony" with compounding a felony. And, on the basis of these arguments, they asked the Governor either to revoke the proclamation or suspend its operation.[81]

Grant rejected the request for revocation or suspension on the grounds that he had no such discretion in the matter, and also that great injustice stood to be perpetrated by prolonging the sufferings of the slaves.[82] It is not to be assumed that Grant was unaware of the hardship to be suffered by those who had purchased illegally imported slaves, but he considered himself to be under an obligation to set free at all costs those who had been illegally imported.[83] By the time he replied to correspondence from Grant, Goderich was a good deal more relentless in his insistence that ignorance was no plea. As far as he was concerned, the purchasers should have been aware of the risks they were running.[84] However, he failed to show appreciation for the fact that the failure of the government to act could also have lulled all concerned into a false sense of security. This, in fact, was what happened and why many had been caught.

Not satisfied with Grant's response to their memorial, the committee sought in vain from the Collector of Customs some indication as to which slaves had been illegally imported.[85] Perhaps the silence of that officer was an indication that he considered all the slaves in the period concerned to have been illegally imported. Grant's own view was that "every person who has been introduced into Trinidad in a condition of Slavery, since the year 1824, in any other capacity than really and truly a Domestic Servant in attendance upon his Master or Owner or part of his Family ... has constituted an illegal importation."[86] There could, therefore, be very little doubt on the matter as far as he was concerned. And the Governor remained firm in his belief that it was an injustice to deny the slaves the relief offered by the proclamation.

The correspondence between the Governor and the committee exhausted the six week period of grace, during which nothing was done about freeing the slaves in question. Parkhurst, who by this time had become Collector of Customs in Trinidad, was instructed by the Governor to commence proceedings, beginning with the largest number imported at any one time. In that way the Governor intended to ensure the condemnation to the Crown of as large a number of slaves as possible from a small number of cases.[87] By the end of March 1832, 53 cases had been sent to the Attorney General for prosecution, the Collector professing that he would do nothing to retard the progress of the prosecutions. The certificates of registration issued in Barbados did not specify the occupation of the slaves, as required by the Act, and that omission had led him to believe that the slaves had been imported for sale and not for employment as domestics.[88] If the omission was clear to Parkhurst in Trinidad, it is conceivable that it should have been clear to him or his colleagues in Barbados at the time the slaves were being transported to Trinidad. The Act did not require the Customs officials to see the extract of the slave registry; nor did it envisage someone purchasing a slave in Barbados to use as a domestic on his return to Trinidad. The Act specified that the "occupation" of each "domestic" was to be entered on the ship's clearance; so that just using the term "domestic" did not fulfil that requirement. The vagueness of that description should not have been overlooked by the Customs officials in Barbados; they can be said to have failed to observe the precise terms of the Act, and were therefore culpable for their neglect. As time passed, his own investigations were rendering Parkhurst less qualified to handle the matter, an involvement in which the Colonial Office had earlier expressed disapproval.

The involvement of Parkhurst might well explain the strong opposition of the slave owners both to the investigations and to the prosecutions, which resulted from them. In a society such as that of Trinidad in the early nineteenth century, it would have been surprising if his connection with events in Barbados did not soon become common knowledge. In fact, he was accused of signing some of the irregular clearances in Barbados,[89] although a contrary view was expressed but not by Parkhurst.[90] But that he could and did sign such clearances was demonstrated when a copy of one was tendered by the committee of slave owners in one of their protests against the prosecutions.[91] Surprisingly, Parkhurst was not removed from such a sensitive position. Although the Order in Council of November 1831 had helped to create the hostile atmosphere in which the controversy took place, this administrative blunder was a significant irritant. Goderich professed satisfaction that the investigations had failed to implicate Skeete and other officials in Barbados, concluding that they had been deceived; even though he conceded that both Skeete and the Customs officials should have been more cautious when applications escalated.[92] Unfortunately, the signing of a single clearance certificate in Barbados was sufficient to raise doubts about the new role in which Parkhurst was cast.

In March 1832 Parkhurst submitted for trial 53 cases of illegal importation; the number of cases had risen to 480 by August of the same year.[93] In their first petition, the proprietors of imported slaves had suggested that a few cases be tried and that the decision on these should be held to indicate the procedure which was to be followed for all others. [94] As the trials got underway, however, they and their counsels seem to have suffered a change of heart, and sought to frustrate the proceedings.[95] In the meantime the committee petitioned Goderich for an investigation into all importations since 1825, in order to justify their right to compensation, since their importation of slaves was done with the knowledge and complicity of authorities in Barbados.[96] Considering the investigation useless, Governor Grant objected that there existed sufficient proof of the notoriety of the traffic. He also rejected the claims for compensation, as those who suffered most had already paid the price by their service and were still enslaved.[97] In the end the investigation never took place, the trials went ahead, and no compensation was ever paid.

The progress of the slave trials was overshadowed by the general opposition of the slave owners to the Order in Council of November 1831. This opposition manifested itself particularly in the attempts made to ensure that the slaves were kept out of reach of the authorities. For example, as soon as proceedings for the emancipation of the slaves had begun, some of the owners seized and hid their slaves, thus forcing the Governor to place several of them in barracks.[98] Of the two hundred seized by Parkhurst and temporarily left in their owners' custody, not one was released when they were required to appear at the start of the proceedings. All were confined, or by some other means placed beyond the reach of the Collector of Customs. In an exceptional case, one slave was actually taken from the Customs House and not returned by the attorney of the owner.[99] Parkhurst's action in leaving the slaves with their owners might be considered an unwise act; but as there was probably nowhere to accommodate such large numbers, this concession might have been the best thing under the circumstances. On the other hand, there is no record of any action being taken against the owners who thus had obstructed justice; and one is left to wonder why. The Trinidad slave owners were clearly prepared to oppose the policy of the British government, even though they did not have any assembly as recalcitrant as those in Barbados or Jamaica.

Over the years the Cabildo seemed inclined to express its support for the "inhabitants" whenever any aspect of the ameliorative programme came up for discussion. But this body appeared to become even more involved as the programme for slave amelioration took a more decisive turn. The partisanship of members of that body with the cause of the slave owners became particularly overt after Grant's proclamation with respect to the illegally imported slaves. At a meeting held in August 1832 a motion was put, and "unanimously adopted", to the effect that £300 currency be voted to assist the proprietors in their defence. Grant vetoed the motion on the ground that it was an improper appropriation of the Board's funds; in response, the members unsuccessfully sought to have the motion and the Governor's objection published in the *Port of Spain Gazette*.[100] The Secretary of State, as happened with the Order in Council of 1824, declared such matters to be foreign to the functions of the Cabildo.[101] But even before the arrival of Goderich's despatch on this matter, the Board had voted against providing any maintenance for the slaves from Barbados who were in jail awaiting trial in connection with the charge of smuggling.[102] The motion to this effect was proposed by the second alcalde, one of the two officers responsible for the interruption of slave trials under the amelioration Order of 1831. Not only did Grant upbraid the Cabildo for exceeding its legitimate functions, he felt obliged to apprise Goderich of the extent of local hostility.[103]

Even more drastic action was taken by some of the proprietors. The office of the Registrar of the Court of Vice-Admiralty was broken into, and the relevant papers stolen. Investigation of the theft led to the premises of a firm of merchants – Porter and Wilson; but the papers were said to have been irretrievably disposed of.[104] No one was arrested for the theft; nor was there any certainty as to who had thus settled "all the knotty points and legal quibbles upon which the Crown and "Conservative" lawyers had PEGGED their attacks and defences."[105] This act of defiance is reminiscent of the protest of the inhabitants of Barbados against William Shrewsbury in 1823, and shows that being a Crown colony did not make the planters any more compliant than their counterparts in other West Indian colonies. Notwithstanding the strong opposition which these actions revealed, Goderich encouraged the Governor to press on with the trials, advising him that, in view of the attendant expence, he might consider a little relaxation of his energy.[106] Grant must have regarded as an encouraging note Goderich's intimation that Parliament might soon be moving towards the final settlement of the slave question.

The slave trials, which had begun in 1832, dragged on to the very eve of emancipation. How many trials took place it is not easy to determine, in view of the absence of returns for the incumbency of Wylly as acting Attorney General. But there are ample returns for that of Stephen Rothery, who succeeded Wylly as Attorney General. In 1833, between April 23 and August 1, 319 slaves had been adjudged free;[107] while from then until January 7, 1834, a further 260 had been similarly adjudged, making a total of 579 for the eight month period.[108] There were fifty cases in progress at that time, and seven more awaiting trial, giving a very graphic picture of the extent of the infraction. No further trials were destined to take place as, with emancipation only a few months away, Stanley the new Secretary of State recommended a relaxation of the prosecutions.[109] Stanley reasoned that in 1834 all slaves would become apprentices, the same status to which the 1825 Act aimed, except that the Act of 1825 did not offer as many benefits as that of 1833. He also observed that persons likely to benefit from the prosecutions were the Judge, the Advocates, and the Customs Officer. And because of this he advised a discreet relaxation of the prosecutions, but in such a way that the officers themselves did not become aware of it.[110]

Thus emancipation dawned with the contest between slave owners and the Executive Government smouldering over, among other things, the trials instituted by Grant. These trials, obviously, were never completed as the need for them was no longer there. But the very atmosphere of the trials, and the attitudes of some of the proprietors, are good indications of the frame of mind they were in at emancipation. Moreover, emancipation found the proprietors thinking as they had always done – that there was need for more labourers, and that those labourers had to be imported. This, naturally, meant a neglect of those labourers who were readily available as the search for other labourers went on.

5. A Degraded Class

It had been deemed by the whites the order
of nature, that no amelioration should ever take
place in the circumstances of those in whose
veins the blood of Africa flowed. [1]

The free coloured and free black stratum of slave societies consisted of persons of a wide range of phenotypic differences. This stratum runs the entire gamut of distinctions of colour from pure Africans who had been manumitted from slavery by their owners, to persons who themselves or their parents were the result of various stages of miscegenation between white men and slave women, so that increasingly their African features became less pronounced. Such freedom as they enjoyed, freedom from personal enslavement, had always been possible from the earliest days of slavery in the West Indies, though the free coloureds were subject to a variety of disabilities. [2] As a result of manumission, all slave societies in the West Indies evolved a substantial middle group in the centuries of chattel slavery. However, in some circumstances this freedom became distinctly tenuous, as members of this stratum ran the risk of being re-enslaved if they were ever unable to prove their freedom. To be without one's "free paper" meant running the risk of being held and treated as a slave. [3] In the late eighteenth and early nineteenth centuries, free coloured and black persons consistently exceeded the number of the whites. The experience of free coloureds and blacks in Trinidad was affected by the operation of a number of different systems – Spanish, French and English; and we turn our attention to this briefly.

The free coloureds and free blacks constituted a large proportion of the population in Spanish colonies, often outnumbering the slaves. Under the Spanish system, the free coloured and black population increased by manumission, purchase, and racial mixture. The latter did not include the marriage of a black with a white person, which was not considered sufficient grounds for freedom.[4] Some slaves were manumitted as a means of getting rid of the aged and infirm, as Frederick Bowser has shown, and to save their owners the burden of supporting them. This practice was prohibited by the Spanish slave code of 1789,[5] but that code seems not to have been generally implemented in the Spanish colonies. Slaves were also allowed to purchase their freedom, and to demand that their value be made public, offering them the opportunity to pay that sum by instalments. This process of *coartacion*, as it was called, was supported by the Crown and given legal status.[6] The largest body of free coloureds and blacks resulted from miscegenation between white males and black or coloured females. As a result, the free coloured population in Spanish colonies in the eighteenth century illustrates the extent of the growth of such mixture. In Venezuela in 1787, a partial census showed the free coloured population to be 147,564, and the slave population 53,055. Comparative figures for Puerto Rico in 1775 showed 29,236 whites, 31,687 mulattoes, 2,823 free blacks, and 7,487 slaves.[7]

The growth of the free coloured population had negative effects on the attitudes generally adopted towards them; the Spanish attitude reflected a mixture of contempt and fear. Efforts were made to restrict their movements and to restrain them in other ways. Lines of distinction were drawn so as to permit discrimination or even a measure of segregation. Regarded as legally inferior, they were debarred from public office or the professions, occasionally given commissions in the militia, with their lives regulated in "petty and galling ways." Their women were prohibited from wearing jewels, they could not be buried in a Cathedral compound, and they were barred from most educational facilities.[8] They were also debarred from the priesthood, Pope Clement XII expressing the opinion that such persons were unworthy of "directing the spiritual life of others."[9] In fact, members of the free coloured and free black stratum were frequently relegated to functions which whites considered beneath their station, such as cleaning the streets. And marriage between themselves and whites was "subject to severe societal censure."[10] The free coloureds and free blacks were not "privileged" within the Spanish colonies.

Any serious attempt to discuss their place in Trinidad society during the late eighteenth and early nineteenth centuries must also include a brief review of their status and treatment in those French islands from which the island drew the majority of its coloured population. While it is true that they were living in a Spanish colony, the customs of the majority of the white colonists with whom they interacted, and who were not Spaniards, were likely to be more influential than the Spanish laws with which they were not really familiar. The territories to which reference is being made here are St. Domingue, and the islands of Martinique and Guadeloupe. This is largely because the majority of the free coloured and black population in Trinidad consisted of persons who had migrated from these French islands before and after 1783. The colony's new population also consisted of whites who had brought with them the same outlook which marked their manner of life in the islands from which they had come.

In these islands, the first substantial attempt to determine the status of the free coloureds and blacks was made in the *Code Noir* of 1685, the provisions of which greatly facilitated the manumission of slaves. The 9th clause, in an effort to discourage concubinage, declared a slave free by virtue of marriage to her master, declaring that any children of the union were to be freed along with the mother.[11] The extent to which such marriages were common in Martinique and Guadeloupe is not certain. The provision was strongly opposed in both colonies, with Guadeloupe calling in 1711 for a ban on the practice, and Martinique in 1703 rejecting the claims to nobility of two brothers because they had married mulattoes. Opposition to such inter-racial unions were reportedly less organised in Ste Domingue, though here too there were concerns to exclude whites in such unions from all government positions.[12]

In both sets of colonies the free coloured population grew, not only in numbers, but also in wealth. They became owners of houses in the towns, and owners of extensive tracts of land in the rural areas. While some of that property was acquired by dint of hard work on their part, a considerable proportion was due to inheritance from white fathers. Not surprisingly, white hostility in the various colonies was such that efforts were made to restrict their acquisition of property. An ordinance of 1720 forbade free coloured participation in the gold and silver trades. Six years later, a royal decree prohibited free coloureds from benefitting from bequests by white persons.[13] By the time it was issued, the practice had already become so deeply rooted that the decree could not effectively end the practice. However, the decree signalled the fact that a change was taking place in the fortunes of the free coloureds, one that was not in their best interests. The tendency to over-regulate the lives of the free coloureds was characteristic of the French islands. According to Gaspar, the free coloureds in St. Lucia attributed discrimination to the laws by which were governed, and which were based on the civil code of Martinique. They were debarred from public employment, and they could not defend themselves if they were struck by white persons.[14]

The period after the Seven Years' War witnessed concerted efforts to reduce the free coloureds to an almost servile status. By a series of legislative enactments in Martinique and Guadeloupe, the free coloureds were forbidden to practice medicine, or to assemble for feasts; they were debarred from functioning as clerks of courts, notaries, or bailiffs. While allowed to practise farming, they were required to have a licence in order to engage in any trade; and finally the free coloured population was forbidden to refer to themselves in official documents as "Monsieur" or "Madame".[15] This latter action was intended to rub salt into their social wounds by seeking to remove titles that meant something significant to them in the highly prejudiced societies in which they lived. Such severities seem not to have been common in St. Domingue, though by the 1760's there was a rising tide of discrimination in that territory. Free coloured numbers and wealth were increasing rapidly in St. Domingue, and white families were growing jealous of their fortunes.[16] Efforts at restricting them proved ineffective. Gwendolyn Hall's comment on the general atmosphere probably reflects the tremendous difficulty of attempting to reverse the growth of a propertied coloured group in Ste. Domingue:

> It is easier to prevent the growth of a wealthy and powerful group within a society than to degrade or destroy it once it has come into existence.[17]

Indeed, Hall attributes the Haitian revolution to the attempt by whites to degrade the free coloureds socially, and to dispossess them of their property. Any activity that was intended to improve their civil rights was regarded as likely to undermine the basis of the slave system.

Because there were many free coloured planters in French territories, it happened that they also became owners of slaves. Garrigus indicates that in southern St. Domingue free coloured proprietors had some of the largest plantations, as well as considerable numbers of slaves.[18] The group was by no means uniform, however, and included persons of a variety of complexions, education and wealth. While phenotypic distinctions were not necessarily officially required, as in Jamaica or customary as in Cartagena, they were not ignored by members within the group itself. Those who were well off financially and well educated, put some social distance between themselves and those who were less endowed or accomplished. They were also cognizant of the oppressive tendencies of the whites. As early as the 1780's, members of the free coloured group in Haiti had begun to petition against what one of them later called the "imperious vexations of the whites". [19]

There was therefore understandable diversity among the free coloureds with respect to the institution of slavery. They shared, to some extent, a community of interests with the white slave owners. For example, some of them were responsible for the capture of runaway slaves.[20] Some of them kept relatives in slavery, either because they were unable to pay the local emancipation tax, or because they were waiting for the repayment of sums expended on the manumission of those relatives.[21] This variety of approaches may have been responsible for such ambivalence as they demonstrated. In Ste. Domingue they were unwilling to form alliances with slaves, though they might not have been altogether impartial; in Martinique they formed alliances with the white elites. At the very time that Trinidad was being opened up to development, the free coloureds in the French territiories were already in a nascent state of protest. Those who could migrate did so because of the opportunity it afforded them of becoming substantial landowners, and because of the more liberal atmosphere. They were not deterred by the discriminatory 4th clause of the *Cedula* of 1783, which might have appeared to them a lesser burden than what they experienced in their home territory. Ironically, while they petitioned for relief for themselves, they evinced no similar concern for the plight of the slaves.

Plantation society in the British colonies was not unlike that in the French islands. Douglas Hall's comparison of slave society to an isosceles triangle with two lines parallel to the base, separating the triangle into the three classes of slave society, is very helpful to our understanding of it. The lower of the two parallel lines, marking the division between free coloureds and slaves was fluid. Free coloureds, who could not prove their freedom, could easily find themselves reverting to slavery while slaves could become free. The upper parallel, between the middle section of the triangle and the apex, was rigid. Free coloureds could not hope to reach the apex, since the graduation to that area was based purely on colour, while legal status separated free coloureds from slaves.[22] As Handler summarised, "No one … who was known to be of Negroid ancestry could become legally or socially white." [23]

At an early stage of the development of plantation society, there was a tendency towards dispossession of the free coloureds in the British islands. Recognising that their social pre-eminence rested on their control of landed property, the whites very quickly nipped in the bud any pretensions of the free coloureds. In Barbados an Act of 1721 explicitly denied them the franchise by enacting that "no person what soever … whose original extraction shall be proved to have been from a Negro" could give evidence against white persons.[24] By 1733, the free coloureds and blacks in Jamaica were debarred from political and civil office, as well as from supervisory positions on estates; and had been denied the right to vote. All of this was enacted at a time when the free coloureds were beginning to acquire large properties, qualifications for the franchise being based on the acquisition of property. In 1761, the Jamaican legislature also debarred them from purchasing land worth more than £2,000 sterling, or from inheriting a similar amount of property from a white person.[25]

Opposition to the free coloureds in the British colonies was better organised than it was in the French colonies for two reasons. On the one hand, the English colonists had the power to make laws for themselves, and were not dependent on the metropolitan legislature. On the other hand, the whites in the British colonies did not allow the free coloureds to grow in wealth to the same extent they had in the Spanish or French colonies. Most of the prohibitive measures, begun after 1763 in Martinique and Guadeloupe, had already been in force in Jamaica before 1733.

There was thus a tradition of repression in the societies of the three European nations from which Trinidad's population was drawn. The Spanish tradition was not properly developed in Trinidad because neglect had stunted the island's growth. The tradition in the French islands was one which the free coloureds might have been happy to escape, except that the white French immigrants to Trinidad seemed to have brought it with them. The tradition of the British was that which English colonists knew and supported, and which many of them sought to have established in the new colony. When Trinidad was conquered by the English in 1797, the free coloureds found themselves in an unenviable position. The Colonial Office had no policy as yet for the free coloureds and free blacks. The question to be answered was: would they be able to hold on to such privileges as they had enjoyed under the benevolent administration of Governor Chacon, or were they to experience the plight of their counterparts in the British islands? As the process of slave amelioration got underway, they could not help wondering what was at stake for them.

Between 1797 and 1802, for example, the free coloured population in Trinidad more than doubled that of the whites in any year, and constituted approximately half of the free population. They were therefore not insignificant by any means, a phenomenon continued in roughly the same proportion for many years subsequently. In addition to this, the free coloureds and blacks as a group held large tracts of land in the colony, as provided by the *Cedula* of 1783. The discriminatory fourth article of that *Cedula* ensured that they received only half of the land grant made to whites; in any case, not many of them could have managed large grants any more than some of the early Spanish settlers had. Nevertheless, between 1783 and 1812, they had acquired altogether over ten thousand acres of land,[26] except for the Picton regime during which they received none.

The free coloureds and free blacks were, in almost every West Indian island, the second largest group of the free population. They generally enjoyed little or no privilege in the society, being regarded as inferior to the white inhabitants, and were also denied political and civil rights.[27] In Trinidad, the free coloureds and free blacks represented one of three groups of free persons, the others being the whites and a small group of indigenous Indians. During the period under review, the free coloureds and blacks were unable to represent themselves publicly since they did not possess any newspapers as did their counterparts in Jamaica. Such information as we have concerning them is therefore piecemeal, emanating largely from either their sympathisers or detractors. Official reports, newspapers, and an occasional work of theirs, are the sources on which the present writer had to depend for the most part.

The plight of the free coloureds and free blacks in Trinidad came to public notice during the same period as the British policy of slave amelioration in the West Indies, though their disabilities reached far into the past. One of the defects of the policy of amelioration was that it concentrated exclusively on the condition of the slave population. The result was that the free coloureds and free blacks, who remained unnoticed for most of this period, received no direct benefit from the increasing altruism of that age. Almost unnoticed in Trinidad, various derogatory measures were introduced by British Governors whereby this class was subjected to one indignity after another. And so, the state of this group in Trinidad rapidly approximated that of their counterparts in the old British West India colonies.[28] It was one thing for the abolitionists to be clamouring for freedom for the slaves – after due preparation; it was quite another thing to understand what that freedom entailed. The latter point could well have been illustrated by the experience of the free coloureds and free blacks in West Indian plantation society, an experience which clamoured for reform. The degradation of the group, and the eventual amelioration of their condition, will form the subject of the following study.

The free coloureds and blacks in Trinidad, like many of the whites in the early nineteenth century, were persons who had been attracted to the colony by the Spanish population *Cedula* of 1783. Some of them had fled from the smaller French islands as the fortunes of war oscillated between Royalists and Republicans on the one hand, and between British and French on the other. In some of the islands the Republican cause had been championed by free coloured people and embraced by freedom-seeking slaves. The title "free coloured" therefore became associated with Republican views; and this combination proved to be a millstone around the necks of persons of that class.[29]

The population *Cedula* of 1783 contained one discriminatory Article, but it was significant in itself. The fourth Article allotted them only one half of the grant of land made to white settlers; but otherwise they were not singled out. Lack of discrimination in the clauses of the *Cedula* does not in any way mean that they were free from discriminatory regulations under the Spanish government. The disabilities to which they were generally liable in Spanish colonies included employment in the mines for any who were unemployed; prohibition, with a variety of penalties, for any who had arms in their possession; and subjection to harsh punishments for drawing arms against a Spaniard, unless they could prove self-defence.[30] They were debarred from public office, and were subject to the death penalty for harbouring runaway slaves.

While in general this was potentially true of conditions under the Spanish administration, nevertheless the operation of these harsh measures had been suspended by the *Cedula* of 1783.[31] The penultimate Article dispensed with "all the laws and customs which may be contradictory to" the articles contained in it, and all royal officers were ordered "to keep, comply with, and execute, and cause to be kept, complied with, and executed the regulation inserted in this our royal Schedule." And hence the discriminatory regulations which applied to the free coloureds and blacks in Trinidad could not have been those which preceded the *Cedula*, which even the British administration accepted as having the force of law in the colony. The intention of the new law, therefore, was to leave the formulation of regulations for this special colony to those who settled in it. And the commercial regulations are indicative of the generosity of the Spanish court itself.[32]

It is against this background that not only Chacon's, but the British Governors' policies must be assessed. Under Chacon the free coloureds and free blacks were treated so considerately that one of them looked at his regime as a golden age.[33] Some of them, it seems, were admitted to civil offices while others were given commissions in the militia. In the case of the latter there were at least three at the time of the Capitulation, one having attained the rank of captain.[34] Even so, it would appear that this class owed their privilege to the generosity of Governor Chacon, rather than to strict legal rights; and this circumstance made them vulnerable. Jean Baptiste Philippe, one of the free coloured spokesmen of the 1820's, claimed that his class was exempt from the capitation tax and personal tribute, except on slaves; but so were all settlers in the newly opened colony. What his claim really meant is that they were treated virtually as equals with the whites. This was unusual for that age; but it must be remembered that, even under the Spaniards, Trinidad was treated as an exceptional colony. The normal rules, therefore, did not apply.

Chacon we know to have been a liberal Governor, whose generosity was broad enough to embrace all the new settlers. In fact, the old Spaniards in the colony expressed dissatisfaction with his apparent favouritism towards the newcomers. But it was only his solicitude for all classes, in an effort to make Trinidad a haven for the settlers, which dictated his magnanimity towards the French, the free coloureds and blacks, and the slaves. In carrying out his humane policy, Chacon did not violate the laws of Spain as L. M .Fraser has accused him of doing.[35] It is true that for some time there had existed outmoded and invidious regulations; but their operation had been suspended. Nevertheless the fact that they once existed gave Fraser a good excuse for defending the policy of the new masters.

To say this, however, is not to deny that Chacon himself was suspicious of some of the free coloured people. In the mid-1790's, when Victor Hugues and Jules Fedon were at the height of their activity in Guadeloupe and the Windward islands respectively, and with the British uncomfortably close, he looked at their presence in Trinidad as a threat to the security of the colony. Hence, in order to ensure that the revolution did not extend to Trinidad, the Governor set up a Commission "to review and scrupulously examine the condition of all aliens entering the island, and to take their passports, documents, and papers."[36]

THE WINDS OF CHANGE

With the cession of the island to the British, a change in their circumstances soon became evident. The twelfth Article of the Capitulation secured for this class protection as regards "their liberty, person and property". That property was quite considerable, as indicated earlier; by 1824 they were proprietors of 45 sugar plantations out of 296; 21 cocoa estates out of 103; 23 coffee estates out of 55; and 32 cotton estates out of 39.[37] Members of the free coloured community claimed that the twelfth Article had been inserted by Chacon, who was particularly solicitous on their behalf, and that the provision conferred on them special privileges.[38] Fraser argues that the law respecting them had previously been interpreted leniently, but that under the English they were going to be read in their strictest sense. In other words, he inferred that the Spanish laws had fallen into abeyance under Chacon, but were now being applied. The first of the free coloured claims may contain a measure of truth; the second is not strictly accurate. The Article sought this protection for them as the document did for other inhabitants at the time of the capitulation. And it should only be interpreted as a complement to the eighth article in which the "private property of the inhabitants ... is preserved to them". One needs therefore to view with a critical eye the statements, which Jean Baptiste Philippe made in the heat of controversy. For he was challenging the opinion of a pro-British author who had argued that the Articles of Capitulation did "not guarantee to them any privileges superior to the privileges enjoyed by free coloured people in some of the British West Indies."[39] The latter writer had supported his own argument by pointing out that the twelfth Article of the Capitulation recognised only reciprocal rights of protection and subjection. In substance this writer was correct, if his point extended to the entire population; and it is here — in the interpretation put on this Article — that the origin of free coloured disabilities was to be found.

Like other sections of the community in the early British period, the free coloured people suffered greatly at the hands of Colonel Thomas Picton, the first military commander, who later became the first Governor of the new colony. His administration of justice was swift and summary;[40] and this led to a migration of the colony's population. In his purge of Trinidad Picton kept a gallows, conveniently situated, which served to remind all and sundry of the Governor's authority.

These points are worth noting because of the role in which Picton was cast by the author of the *Address to Earl Bathurst*. This writer portrayed Picton as a victim of manipulation by the white inhabitants of the colony, and claimed that he was artfully led to believe that the free coloureds were revolutionaries who needed to be repressed.[41] The charge, however, was as fanciful as the characterisation was misdirected; Picton as anyone's tool was extremely unlikely. That the French whites, who were propertied, royalist, and fearful of what had happened in Ste. Domingue, carried their colour prejudices with them to their new home is natural. That Picton would have been no more magnanimous towards the free coloureds than he was towards the slaves cannot reasonably be questioned. But the combination of the two — French influence and coloured suppression — was merely fortuitous; so that the free coloureds might have fared no better under him even without the French whites to influence the Governor. Again this is in no way to deny that the latter might have been encouraged by them to carry out a policy of repression, which he might have found to his taste, and which was characteristic of the British islands.

Picton, in fact, had very definite and negative views about the free coloured and black people. Writing to the Secretary of State in 1799, he described them as "irreclaimable Republicans" who were controlled only by the constant use of authority. He considered them formidable on account of their numbers and disposition, as well as "their known communication with the enemy"; people whom it would have been very difficult, if not impossible, to make loyal to the British Government.[42] Not only was Picton's assessment exaggerated; it would certainly have taxed his ingenuity to furnish proof of their communication with the enemy. He had drawn a conclusion both about their politics and their future loyalty, which would have served to justify any action or ill treatment of them. Such was the climate of opinion in those days that subjecting such a charge to examination would have been unusual; and opinions such as Picton's formed the basis of much of the antipathy exhibited towards them. In Picton's eyes, the French free coloureds were the worst group – a dangerous set of people whose numbers had to be gradually reduced.[43] Picton, therefore, did not need to be deceived; he already had a negative opinion of the free coloureds and blacks, and harboured a desire to be rid of them.

In the course of his brief tenure as sole Governor, Picton sought to ensure the enforced subordination of non-whites to the whites. One of his early acts was to relieve the coloured officers of their commissions in the militia and to reduce them to the ranks.[44] It may be that Picton was introducing into Trinidad society what he knew to have been the practice in other colonies of the West Indies.[45] He was, after all, a man of some experience in the West Indies, as he so readily pointed out when dealing with the slave question.[46] Another early act was the promulgation of a set of regulations for the government of the free coloureds and blacks, which put them in an invidious position vis-à-vis their white counterparts. One offensive clause of a regulation required that permission be obtained from the Commandant of a Quarter before any free coloured person could give a ball. A penalty of $25 was payable if any slaves were found participating in it.[47] This regulation reflects the kind of discrimination that was already characteristic of Martinique, and it is quite likely that Picton had had it drawn up by his friend, St. Hiliaire Begorrat. Picton never gave any reason for this regulation, and it may be inferred that his aim was to make their lot more intolerable by restricting any associations they might have had with parents who were still slaves. On the other hand his action might have been dictated by a concern for security – the fear of the coloured classes combining with slaves to revolt. At a later date Governor Woodford offered, as reasons for it, the circumstances that a free black or manumitted slave could have become a proprietor simply by acquiring some land; and that they lived in inaccessible mountain areas, to which slaves probably resorted. He therefore seemed to bypass the problem on the ground that no one who failed to apply for permission had been punished.[48] This, of course, did not remove the rather offensive nature of the regulation. But the real sting lay in the fact that no white person would ever have been required to apply for such permission, while for the free coloureds it was absolutely necessary. This difference did not arise for Woodford, and therefore he did not address it.

Another offensive regulation was that which required one free coloured person to stand guard at the house of the Commandant of any Quarter, with the latter's horse saddled and bridled.[49] Allegedly this role, which was apparently intended for those who were not propertied and for coloured artisans, was required of the planter class among the free coloureds. In addition, the function of alguacil or constable was restricted to the free coloured class as it was considered too distasteful for whites;[50] and this circumstance could hardly have commended it to those of the coloured group who were considerable owners of property. Paucity of whites,[51] as Woodford claimed, was not a very convincing reason for the restriction of the office to coloureds. What was worse for Philippe and his class was that planter caprice could so operate as to extend the oppressive regulation to propertied coloureds, who would thereby have been embarrassed.

Picton's regime was interrupted by the short-lived experiment in Commission government of 1803. For the purpose of this chapter, the significant aspect of that experiment was that it pitted against each other two men of strongly divergent views, each tenacious of his own position. Picton was concerned to suppress the free coloureds, his colleague Fullarton gave the impression of being their friend. Circumstances, therefore, made them implacable enemies. The Commission quickly collapsed and a clear policy regarding the free coloureds was not developed beyond Picton's initial actions. It is significant that no free coloured person received any grant of land during his regime, which goes to show that his antipathy may have been rooted in his opposition to their rising prosperity.

The advent of Sir Thomas Hislop as Governor, in 1804, exposed the free coloureds to even further disabilities. In his very first year in office, he issued the following order which was unprovoked and, as far as one could see, unnecessary:

> All coloured persons are enjoined to present their
> certificates of having taken the oath of Allegiance
> prescribed by law to their respective Alcaldes de
> Barrio and Commandants of Quarters and also the
> proofs of their manumission. Such persons as act
> in contravention of this order will be treated as
> dangerous and bad subjects.[52]

This order caused serious alarm among the free coloureds and blacks, and not without justification. Towards the end of the previous century free coloured people had been kidnapped from Grenada along with slaves, and had been enslaved in the colony.[53] Many of the colony's coloured inhabitants had probably been forced to flee from their original homes in the islands hit by revolution. The possibility of being reduced to a servile state did not seem very remote to those who might have been unable to present proofs of their freedom, as was the case in Guadeloupe in 1802. It was that which they were really afraid of; and the actual occurrence of such violations added to their fear.[54]

One explanation of this type of regulation is that the continued subjection of the free coloured class was seen as a means of keeping the slaves themselves in subjection. Prof. Goveia has shown that this approach had been in operation in the Leeward Islands, particularly among the French proprietors who had migrated to those islands.[55] The system of subjugation had already begun in Trinidad under Picton and was to be greatly refined under Governor Woodford, whose regime spanned the bulk of the period under review. Another possible explanation might be Hislop's attempt to identify this group with republicanism. Hislop's regime constituted the period of recovery, after the constitutional crisis involved in the infamous Commission Government of 1803; and it was also this regime which saw the culmination of one stage of the constitutional debate, after the disastrous Chief Justiceship of George Smith.[56]

At this time, in 1810, the free coloureds for the first time raised the subject of the place to be allowed them when the new constitutional arrangements were effected. They appealed to their loyalty, and their superiority in numbers in the free population, as deserving consideration.[57] But they were struggling against whites who believed that they did not deserve any more privileges than they already had. Their failure to win Governor Hislop's sympathy and the retaliatory measures to which he resorted[58] helped, if not to snuff out, at least to repress the energies of their leaders. For not only was the stigma of republicanism implied in the Governor's actions, but his request for reports from Councillors and Commandants gave to these officials an authority over the coloureds which would certainly have rankled with the latter. It was in such a context that Lord Liverpool as Colonial Secretary wrote his despatch of November 1810, [59] indicating the injustice to the coloureds of the change being sought, and settling for at least twenty-one years the constitutional future of the colony.

It should at this point be said that the majority of the free coloureds and blacks were persons of very limited resources. Some of them, newly emancipated, were tradesmen and hucksters; while others even became vagrants. It is these persons whose erratic behaviour was seized upon as typifying all free coloureds, and whose manner had been held to justify the general stigma of laziness. But their conduct was by no means characteristic of the entire class. There were some very wealthy planters among the coloured population, particularly in the Naparima district where many of them had settled. Woodford reported some of them to be among the wealthiest proprietors in the colony; [60] others had become professionals, benefitting from studies in Britain and in France. In fact, it was probably as common among the wealthy free coloureds, as it was among the whites, to educate their children in Europe.

The Governor, whose regime lasted the longest before their disabilities were removed, was Sir Ralph James Woodford, who was regarded as the greatest threat to their progress. He arrived in the colony in 1813 and remained its Governor until his death in 1828. In rather fulsome language, following the conventions of the day, the free coloureds praised the Regent's wisdom in appointing him as Governor.[61] However, it was under Woodford that their greatest difficulties were encountered, as this Governor showed no inclination to encourage what he regarded as their pretensions. The disabilities which they experienced under Woodford may, for convenience, be classed under three headings: civil, legal, and social.

CIVIL DISABILITIES

The civil disabilities of the free coloureds lay in the fact that they were excluded from any form of active participation in the government of the colony. Intermittently from 1802 to 1822 the inhabitants of Trinidad made appeals to the Crown for a system of government such as there was in the older British colonies. This consisted of an elected Assembly and a Council, with trial by jury and all the appurtenances of the British legal system. These discussions included no provision for the free coloureds as was the case in the older colonies, which formed the models for the appellants from Trinidad. The free coloureds had legitimate claims to consideration by virtue of articles V and XXVII of the 1783 *Cedula* of Population. When Joseph Marryat renewed the demands for a "British Constitution and laws" in 1822, his arguments were put down by Goulburn – the Under-Secretary at the Colonial Office - using the old abolitionist rejection of the oligarchic system of government in the West Indies. This was shown to be neither a parallel to the British situation where all subjects were free in the eyes of the law (forgetting momentarily the dehumanising child labour in the British mines), nor a means calculated to guarantee to the coloureds the privileges secured by Spanish law.[62]

Discussion of the matter was to reveal how deep seated were the prejudices of whites against the free coloureds, and how very flimsy was the basis for such prejudices. Woodford, for instance, had never been an advocate of the representative system, though his objections were not those of the abolitionists. In 1820 he had written to Earl Bathurst:

> I cannot persuade myself that if the Inhabitants were
> made aware of the consequences which (might) result
> to them from the British laws, that they would in any
> case wish for them: the protection which the Inhabi-
> tants now receive from the Laws in force in their
> persons and Property would indeed be a clear sacrifice
> for the rights which such Laws would bring. [63]

Not only was he opposed to the introduction of the representative and jury systems, he was also opposed to the participation in them of the free coloureds who, he realised, could not have been excluded from jury service. Woodford expressed the belief that the whites would have been unwilling to sit with them in such service; and the partisanship, which he anticipated was likely to arise, would have led to less justice than ever.[64] Woodford did not say on whose side the partisanship was likely to arise; but while he obviously had the coloureds in mind, the whites were already known in the West Indies to have little inclination to do justice where whites were charged with offences against coloureds or slaves. It is highly probable that Woodford was representing here his own unwillingness to accommodate mixed juries, and not merely that of the white population; for he was never kindly disposed towards the free coloured and black population. Moreover he doubted whether a jury comprising an equal number of white and coloured members would have arrived at a unanimous verdict in a case involving a mulatto prisoner. Hence he advised that consideration be given to the sudden transition from slavery to freedom in which a man might be a slave one day, free the next, and find himself on a jury with the master from whom he had purchased his freedom.[65]   There seemed to be no room in Woodford's mind for a free coloured or black person, whose freedom stretched back a decade or more.

It was therefore the free coloureds whose impartiality the Governor regarded as being in question. More than this, it is clear that Woodford was just as determined to keep the various strata of the society apart. He had cleverly and deliberately created the impression that all free coloureds were manumitted slaves; and, in so doing, had failed to do justice to the existence of the large property owning coloureds of the colony. It is this kind of misinformation which could easily have been the cause of defective Colonial Office policy. Racism was more than implicit in what he proposed, which was, that it was better to have no jury than one to which coloured members were admitted. He probably also recognized that under the prevailing system he enjoyed greater power than otherwise.

Woodford's prejudice against having the free coloureds as jurors was shared by the Judge of the Court of Criminal Inquiry, Lewis Johnston. To him it was so great a departure from "colonial policy, colonial legislation, West Indian polity, and colonial habits" that results likely to endanger the safety of Trinidad and other colonies were to be expected. He was further of the view that such a proceeding would have operated to the prejudice of "the due and impartial course of justice". As if echoing Woodford's fear that a mixed jury was likely to be partial and prejudiced, he seriously questioned the eligibility of the coloureds for jury service on the ground of the widespread illiteracy in the ranks of that class. Johnston, however, went far beyond Woodford in expressing the fear that, if they were permitted to serve on juries, they would certainly resent their exclusion from other civil rights.[66] Here Johnston was striking a significant chord, for the free coloured people were seeking a share in all the constitutional arrangements for the colony. Partial amelioration would have been the worst thing under the circumstances; but this does not necessarily support Johnston's apprehension that their resentment would have led to "strong measures on their parts for the removal of the difficulty comprising the safety of the colony."[67]

The problems raised by the two officials impressed the Commission of Legal Inquiry who, in their Report, discouraged the introduction of a jury system until the question of admitting coloured persons as jurors had been resolved. The Commissioners argued that to omit them could justifiably be regarded as a retrograde step.[68] No jury system was introduced at this time; something akin to it was established towards the middle of 1831,[69] by way of the appointment of three assessors from the Cabildo to sit with three professional judges in determining causes; but this new system became seriously fractured before it was a year old. Even so, coloured people were automatically excluded by the fact that the Cabildo, from whom the Assessors were originally drawn, was composed only of white persons.

Early in 1832 a new Legislative Council was introduced, which was composed of an equal number of official and unofficial members.[70] Naturally, there were no free coloureds among the official members; but there were no free coloureds among the unofficial members either. There was a tendency among the British residents to close ranks to the extent that an old councillor, Francisco Llanos, was challenged and forced out because he was neither of British nationality nor a Protestant.[71] No place was given to the free coloureds; nor was any voice raised against their exclusion – even by members of their own class. But again their lack of an independent organ, by means of which to make their views known, was probably the reason for this. By 1834 — or at the latest 1838 — the mass of slaves had become free; but their freedom was somewhat limited in that they were debarred from any participation in the political life of the colony.[72] By that time, the free coloured and black community was enlarged by the numbers of the apprentices who had become free in the latter year, to share the lot of those who were considered a degraded class. It would be another century before universal adult suffrage opened the doors to the generality of coloured persons.

LEGAL DISABILITIES

Perhaps the most obvious of the disabilities, which the coloured community suffered, was the result either of punishments or of statutory regulations curtailing their freedom. Members of the group complained of excessive punishments in which a man was given fifty lashes and two months' imprisonment for petty theft, subsequently being banished from the island. In another instance, it was alleged that a coloured man was given one hundred lashes for robbery even though his guilt had not been established. Yet for similar offences white persons were given far less or no punishment at all, as in the case of Francis Prestici who, for fraud and theft, was merely ordered to make restitution.[73] And it did not require the example of a white planter, unpunished for the rape of a black girl, to establish the fact that colour often played a significant part in judicial decisions. While the legal disabilities complained of related to the coloured community in general, it is seldom that a coloured person of means was the victim. On one such occasion a coloured woman, who had contracted to supply goods to a white customer, sold them when the customer refused to take them, offering as an explanation that the ship to transport them had failed to arrive on time. The indignity to which she was subjected in the process received no redress from the courts.[74]

Where the free coloureds suffered most was in the case of repressive legislation. Such legislation was not unknown in the colony prior to Governor Woodford's arrival; for there were measures forbidding them to be out of doors at night without a pass, or to walk about with a cane.[75] They were not allowed to present any petition to the courts without indicating their precise status — free people of colour. The sheer necessity of doing this seemed to attach a stigma to the description. What greatly alarmed the free coloured people even more was the publication of an Order in Council of September 16, 1822,[76] which dealt with the Criminal Courts and procedures, and contained two clauses, which their leaders considered invidious:

Noel Titus

> And for the more effectual suppression of petty thefts
> and offences, within the Town of Port of Spain, and
> the Suburbs thereof ... the Alcaldes in Ordinary, shall
> sit in open court, for the hearing and determining of
> all such petty thefts ... and all similar misdemeanours
> ... and the Alcalde shall have authority to adjudge the
> Prisoner ... to a fine not exceeding Thirty Pounds
> Current Money ... or to imprisonment ... or to work in
> chains ... or to corporal punishment.

> If however in any cases of free persons ... corporal
> punishment shall be adjudged to the offence the
> prisoner shall, on his being convicted, be committed
> to the Gaol there to await the next ensuing monthly
> Gaol Meeting of the Magistrates who may order such
> punishments by stripes, not exceeding forty in number ... [77]

Insofar as they applied to free persons, coloured inhabitants interpreted both clauses as referring only to themselves. Thus viewing the matter, they resented the discretion allowed to the Alcaldes or other magistrates of awarding corporal punishment to any offence they chose. Even more alarming was their perception of the opportunity afforded to the whites by the Order to give vent to racial feelings.[78] These minor courts were presided over by persons who were not only without training in law, but who were also elected by a planter Cabildo. The latter were all white and, as their protests on the slave amelioration laws showed, they were concerned about subordinating to their authority not only the slaves but the free coloureds as well. In addition, although the monthly magistrates' meeting may or may not have confirmed the corporal punishment ordered, the likelihood of their not awarding such punishments was very slight indeed.

Given the situation in which the law was to be applied, the alarm expressed by leading members of the coloured population was quite understandable. It was unfortunate for them that they sought legal advice from a lawyer who was not in Governor Woodford's favour, and against whom the latter had written unflatteringly to the Secretary of State. But it was only on this official, prejudiced as he was by Woodford's comments on the lawyer, that the latter's criticism of the legislation was likely to fall lightly. The lawyer criticised the apparent "solecism" of the Order whereby its application was geographically limited, instead of applying to the entire colony. With respect to the persons affected by the two obnoxious clauses, he observed that white persons had never been described as "free". Either the

100

law was to be generally applicable, or "distributive Justice" would not have been equally administered but negated. Furthermore, he called attention to the severe punishments to be applied to so simple a breach of the peace; and concluded that there was less law than discretion in the Order as a whole.[79]

In an attempted palliation of the unpleasant situation, Woodford asked each Commandant to assemble all the free coloured people in his Quarter, and to explain to them that the Order was ameliorative, the nineteenth clause being introduced for their protection. The Commandants were further asked to explain that, previous to the Order, any free person might have been corporally punished by the order of a single judge; but that under the new Order the concurrence of the entire bench was necessary.[80] The Order did indicate that such punishments were to be authorised in the Courts of the Alcaldes; but the magistrates, who were to confirm the sentences, included the same Alcaldes. So that it would have been little short of miraculous if those sentences were ever reversed. But that was the kind of law passed for the experimental colony. The strategy which the Governor pursued, in dealing with the issue, also included a meeting with the "principal persons" among the free coloured class to whom he gave his own interpretation of the law, and whom he reported to be completely satisfied with his explanation.[81]

Commenting on this section of the Order, the Commissioners of Legal Inquiry felt first, that the offensive nineteenth clause was out of place in its context. In the second place, they considered the term "misdemeanour" too strong for petty offences.[82] As a result of their Report some of the repressive laws were repealed, and the disabilities under which the free coloureds laboured thereby alleviated. But the Order of September 1822 was not among those repealed.

SOCIAL DISABILITIES

The free coloureds, no less than the slaves, were ostracised in Trinidad plantation society. They suffered in a number of ways, partly at the instigation of Governor Woodford. For one thing, he consistently refused to address a coloured person as "Mr." or "Mrs.", an example which seems to have been followed by private citizens with all the spitefulness which knowledge of official sympathy was likely to attach to such behaviour.[83] That such a thing could have been official policy has the ring of fantasy about it; but it did happen, and was only corrected on the eve of emancipation. At that time the Editor of the *Port of Spain Gazette* congratulated his "fellow colonists that the enlightened day has arrived, when it is no longer in the power of an "official" to refuse to insert "Mr" before the name of a gentleman because he was not white."[84]

As stated earlier, the free coloured class comprised some very wealthy planters, whose substance gave every indication of increasing. The accumulation of property in the hands of this class resulted, in some cases, from the bequests of white parents to their coloured progeny; and this was such an annoyance to Woodford that he believed the white community was being "threatened" by the increase of a class that was "already too numerous."[85] It was in this context that he applied to Bathurst for the enactment of a regulation, which was to limit the extent of such bequests. The Governor explained that many "foreigners" bequeathed their property to their free coloured offspring, but gave none to their own brothers and sisters. Therefore, instead of the coloureds receiving property, he proposed that money alone be given to them.[86] Had that recommendation been accepted, Woodford would have been in a strong position to ensure that the coloured beneficiaries had no opportunity to purchase land – at least, land that would have been valuable in the prevailing sugar economy. And if he were so opposed to coloured persons acquiring property, to what extent was he likely to favour a slave policy which permitted slaves to do so? Yet he also gave every appearance of being interested in furthering the cause of slave amelioration. Perhaps the accusation against foreigners was a subtle way of referring to persons who differed in their practice from what was accepted as normal in any British colony. The foreigners in question were persons who had migrated to the island since 1783, and hence were landowners of some long standing.

This matter of the acquisition of property by the free coloureds, which Woodford attempted to deal with, was bound up with two other issues of importance. One of these was Woodord's desire to reduce the disproportion of whites to coloureds, an issue not directly connected with the problem, but which was introduced by him into this discussion. Originally intending to insist on a fixed proportion of whites to coloureds on each estate, he had been deterred only by the "great *impolicy* of obliging white Persons to act as Managers, or as subordinate to them in any capacity."[87] To have renewed an Order by Picton demanding one free man to every thirty slaves would, he thought, have failed of the intended effect.[88] This latter point must be understood in the light of his objection to having whites in the paid employment of coloureds. His recommendation was the establishment of a body of colonists "who might not feel any dangerous sympathy with the People of Colour", while they might command the slaves.

Another issue, more directly concerned with the original question, involved the mixed union of whites and coloureds. His plan for a white settlement included inducing them to marry before migrating, and offering premiums for the greatest number of legitimate white children maintained and educated by their parents.[89] In all of this it does not appear that Woodford's chief concern was the uplifting of public morality. It is true that he quoted Spanish law,[90] which he claimed was directed against illicit connections. But the law in question related to the endowment of illegitimate children with one-fifth of the deceased's property, out of which the funeral expenses must previously have been paid.[91] There was no indication that this law applied to illicit mixed unions rather than to illicit white unions, or that it was a positive prohibition against mixed marriages. The only difficulty Woodford foresaw was what he was prepared to attribute to those immoral whites, whose mistaken notions of marriage served as a deterrent to regular unions among themselves.[92] And his intention was to force the latter into habits more in keeping with the religious beliefs they professed. In short, Woodford was concerned that whites marry whites, rather than coloureds.

However, the real cause of laxity with respect to family life did not rest with free coloured immorality or irreligion. It seems to have escaped Woodford's blinkered vision that the free coloureds were largely the result of white immorality. As early as 1802 a visitor to the colony observed that climate was not the reason for the failure of European health; rather he attributed it to their debauchery and intemperance. In Trinidad as elsewhere in the West Indies the European's first thought, he said, was to acquire a coloured mistress, who was sometimes provided from among the slaves of some plantation.[93] Thus

> The planter collects his circle, and that circle
> naturally spreads, so that they emulate each
> other in corrupting every new comer. [94]

In addition, proprietors showed a distinct preference for single men as managers and overseers on the various estates.[95] That this must have been a factor contributory to white immorality in Trinidad as elsewhere in the West Indies need not be argued.

Dr. Philippe, the Free Mulatto, admitted the existence of concubinage among the free coloureds, a feature he attributed to the emancipated illiterates, and which he asserted to have had its origin in wants rather than inclination. At the time he was writing, however, he believed that marriage among that group was on the increase. He accused Woodford not only of hindering coloured marriages by prohibitive fees, but also of encouraging concubinage among members of that class.[96] The Governor, on his part, claimed that he had reduced fees in favour of the free coloureds and slaves, adding that he always remitted them where the parties were poor. Writing to Bathurst, he claimed that since his arrival marriages had taken place between whites and free coloureds with his permission.[97] If that had been the case, not only would such marriages have been very rare, but they would be contrary to what other evidence would lead us to expect. Writing to Bathurst in 1817, Woodford declared: "I have never received an application for the marriage of a white person with one of color but in such an event I presume it would be proper to *decline* sanctioning the same."[98] Nothing in his attitude indicates any inclination on his part to depart from this general approach.

The representatives of the free coloureds took umbrage at another form of discrimination – the reduced medical fees for members of their class, in which they alleged that an invidious distinction was created between themselves and the whites. In other words, they implied that a degree of degradation was involved in charging the free coloureds lower fees than the whites.[99] It needs to be repeated at this point that the protesters were members of the planter class and therefore did not represent the views of the entire free coloured and black group. The conclusions, which the representatives drew, were: first, that this implied that the lives of whites were of the highest value, and those of the free coloureds and slaves proportionately lower. Secondly, that doctors would have gone where the reward was more lucrative, irrespective of the urgency of the case.[100] Worse yet, they thought that the possibility of the coloured population receiving medical attention at night was non-existent, unless the few coloured practitioners in the colony were able to cater to the needs of the vast numbers who would otherwise be without such help.

In refuting the charges, Woodford alleged that they were expressions of jealousy at not being thought as rich as the whites[101] – in spite of his having considered some of them among the wealthiest proprietors in the colony. Moreover, in observing that some white tradesmen earned twice as much as their coloured counterparts,[102] he implied the financial inability of the latter to pay. Woodford was insensitive to the real point of the free coloured objection, which was that a group stood to be neglected because surgeons were likely to go where they were better paid. Even Dr. Philippe had temporarily lost sight of the principle that a fee should be charged for a service and not for the social status of the recipient of that service. Thus Dr. Philippe intruded a contradiction into his own argument when he observed that the regulation did not distinguish those free coloureds who could pay from those who could not, but merely equalised all members of that class. Prejudice, he said, dictated the distinction in fees which made the labouring mechanic pay the same fee as the possessor of thousands because they were both coloured.[103] In so saying he was making a distinction analogous to that which he condemned; yet he seemed blissfully ignorant of the inconsistency. This internal differentiation within the free coloured group blunted the edge of their effort to gain amelioration for their class.

Distinctions between whites and coloureds extended to the admission of coloureds to the medical profession. Thus it would appear that white physicians or surgeons were granted licences to practise free of cost, while their coloured counterparts had to pay a fee for the grant of such licences.[104] On one occasion an application for a licence to practise was actually refused largely on the basis of colour. In 1821 the Medical Association, although satisfied with the qualifications of Dr. Francis Williams, refused to grant him a licence to practise on the ground that he had been born in a state of slavery.[105] The only dissentient opinion was that of Dr. Alexander Williams, the President of the Board, who made two important observations. First of all, he observed, not only had Francis Williams conformed to all the requirements, but also there was no positive law forbidding his practising. And secondly, he observed that as other free coloured persons had been admitted to practise, the rejection of Francis Williams was inconsistent as well as indicative of "unbecoming partiality."[106]

Francis Williams appealed to the Governor against what seemed to him an arrogation, by the Board, of authority not belonging to it. But any hopes he might have entertained of a reversal of their decision were quickly dashed as the acting Governor declined to take any action in the matter.[107] The acting Governor, Sir William Young, communicated to Bathurst, however, that the laws of Spain prevented persons who were not of good birth and instruction from graduating. Arguing that the deprivation was a hardship, he asserted that what mattered most was the removal of the barriers which had previously existed. In addition he observed that Woodford had allowed Dr. Philippe to practise because both his parents were free, and because the Quarter in which he practised was composed largely of coloured persons. Hence he foresaw no problem, since the matter rested with those who required the physician's services. Young completely lost sight of the fact that Francis Williams had been well instructed and that he had actually graduated from a distinguished British institution. As with Philippe, the matter might well have rested with those who required his services;[108] but the principle at stake was that he was qualified to practise medicine.

George Knox, a lawyer practising in Trinidad, supported the general view on the Spanish law; and so too did Dr. Garcia to whom, with Knox, Francis Williams had referred the matter. Garcia noted, however, that after the conquest free coloured persons were allowed to study and practise surgery in Caracas, even though they were granted no degree.[109] Knox on the other hand noted the absence, even in Spanish law, of any express prohibition against free coloured persons practising medicine because they had been born in slavery. He further observed that the rules and regulations of the Royal College of Surgeons superseded the Spanish regulations referred to. And he concluded that the inhabitants of the colony were not governed by the laws of Spanish Universities, otherwise no British diploma would have been valid.[110] It was arguable that the Spanish laws previously governing the colony were in force, except insofar as they were modified by British laws. So the case seems to have rested purely on University regulations.

This lengthy debate was brought to a close by the Secretary of State granting a temporary sanction for Francis Williams to practise. The Governor, he said, was not permitted, by his Instructions, to enforce the Spanish law where His Majesty's Government might have thought fit to depart from it. But applicants were to conform to the regulations laid down for their guidance, "save and except for those which attach to the color and birth of the person in question."[111] An important victory had been won; and it is probably something like this which made them remember with gratitude the interregnum in Woodford's tenure during which Col. Young had acted as Governor.

The return of Sir Ralph Woodford from England in 1823 brought to public notice not only the offensive 1822 Order, but also the separation of the free coloureds even in a place of worship – the new Trinity Church. "At the west end of the church, at some distance behind all the pews, and at a considerable distance from the altar, is a place, separated by a low wooden enclosure from every other part of the church and filled with plain board benches."[112] This was Philippe's description of the accommodation made in the church for such free coloureds and slaves as attended the services. No word of protest is recorded from the rector of Port of Spain, Henry Clapham. If he had protested, one wonders whether any good would have come of it, especially in the light of Woodford's use of his authority with respect to the consecration of the new church, and later, in dealing with the matter of Clapham's retirement. [113] In addition, the division was clearly made on grounds of colour; no other explanation of the situation is possible. And it is probably this association which led the wealthier ones to absent themselves from the consecration of the church rather than be corralled with the slaves, whom they detested. Woodford attempted neither to palliate nor deny the prejudices so blatantly displayed. However, in an explanation which underlined the ingrained prejudices of the man, he informed the Secretary of State that one could not expect that "white families are to be obliged to admit the general Connexion that would be created by an intermixture of seats". [114] There the matter seems to have rested, not even the Secretary of State attempting to intervene.

Some time previous to this incident, the Governor was called upon to settle a dispute over the distribution of labour for the maintenance of roads in the district of North Naparima. Whereas previously the coloured planters had been consulted on the apportionment of those duties, the Commandant of the Naparima Quarter excluded them in 1822. [115] As the discussion proceeded, it became abundantly clear that Woodford was not inclined to encourage their inclusion. He considered the majority of them unprepared by education to offer an opinion; and he did not believe that they could have been admitted to such deliberations without the kind of distinctions which contradicted the very principle on which they based their claim. [116] What the Governor did not explain was the fact that they had previously been sufficiently educated to offer such opinions as circumstances called for. Nor did he explain why the Commandant of the Quarter should take such action without first consulting those who had previously enjoyed the privilege. Referring to the rapid transition from slavery to freedom, Woodford proposed a solution which was really an option for the easy way out. Unless Bathurst was prepared to dismiss the claims of the free coloureds as unfounded, it was better to let the government apportion the labour on the roads without consulting any of the inhabitants. [117] It was a brilliant stroke, achieving what the Commandant had done without making him responsible for it; and at the same time suggesting to Bathurst that any risk resulting from the inclusion of the free coloured planters would be his responsibility.

Woodford further informed Bathurst that, in the eyes of the Spanish authorities, the free coloureds had always been regarded as a degraded class, [118] a comment which was irrelevant to the discussion and only expressive of the Governor's sentiments. These sentiments are quite unmistakeable, as the following extract shows:

> if the whites are to maintain their ascendancy, and
> Great Britain is to preserve her West India islands
> as colonies, this distinction must as it appears to
> me, be maintained. [119]

It is not surprising, therefore, that the more affluent members of the free coloured group regarded their current situation in the colony as retrogression towards slavery. And what threw their plight into sharp relief was the policy of slave amelioration, which was being implemented at the same time. Hence they appealed to the favourable results of slave amelioration as an argument for their own advancement in society. In fact, they argued that the ignorance of the uncultured coloureds ought not to be decisive in determining their fate, but that the education of the "enlightened" members ought to merit consideration.[120] The free coloureds as a whole resented their repression, and this resentment found expression in a very ominous epigram: "Resentment does not sleep; it is arrested." [121]

THE SLAVE QUESTION

As owners of slaves, free coloured proprietors were brought face to face with the problem of amelioration from another angle. On the one hand there was the very real desire on their part to be distinguished from the slaves, while they sought to benefit from the increasing altruism. At no time did both groups try to form a common front against the oppressive system. On the other hand some of them were slave owners and, as was the case with the whites, some would have been good masters and others bad. Woodford testified to his satisfaction with one owner, who had been accused of cruelty; but as the incident involved the complaint of two slaves against their master, the Governor's testimony must be treated with great caution.[122] While he was not in favour of the wealth of the free coloureds, he was even less in favour of any condemnation of planters on the sole evidence of slaves.

In 1823, when the ameliorative policy entered its most significant stage, the free coloured memorialists saw their interests as being ultimately identical with those of the whites.[123] Yet they adopted a cautious stance towards the programme, and did not participate in the deliberations which led the white slave owners to protest so vehemently. On their own behalf they prepared a memorandum which was replete with claims of loyalty to the Crown, and of their desire to do their civic duty.[124] The fact that they did not join the protest meetings of the planters requires no explanation – they simply were not invited, and so were not expected to do so. It was not until 1832 that four coloured proprietors were nominated to a Standing Committee of slave owners who kept up a regular stream of protest during that year against the Order in Council of November 1831.[125] But on that occasion they courteously yet firmly declined the invitation, only to declare their determination, by the end of the same year, to oppose it by every means in their power.[126] In other words, the free coloured leaders were now in an ambivalent position, wanting to be treated by the whites with deserving respect, and yet quite prepared to deny the basic right of the slaves to the recognition of their humanity. The view of these writers contrasted sharply with the view of another memorialist, who testified to their awareness that their fate was in some way bound up with that of the slaves.[127] Clunes, the writer of this memorial, was seeking the appointment of coloured men as Assistant Protectors of Slaves. And though it may be too much to accuse him of using this argument conveniently, nevertheless it must be admitted that there was considerable ambivalence in the policy of the group where the slave question was concerned.

The free coloureds, like the more numerous servile group, were in a situation, which demanded amelioration. Their protests, coming as they did within the period of intense activity on behalf of the slaves, did not fall on deaf ears. Before the end of 1825, Bathurst ordered Woodford to repeal some of the obnoxious legislation.[128] In doing so, Bathurst was probably influenced by the Legal Commissioners, who later reported that the free coloureds of long residence were entitled to the rights of naturalization, and to civil and military offices. In complying with his instructions, Woodford issued a Proclamation in January 1826, which not only guaranteed those rights to coloureds of long residence, but extended them to other coloureds in the colony, provided that the latter and their parents had collectively resided in the colony for twenty-one years. Another Proclamation, issued on the same date as the above, repealed a number of the repressive Ordinances.[129] But this latter Proclamation did not include the repeal of the offensive 1822 Order. As a follow-up, and in response to a specific appeal from the coloured community, the benefit of Savings banks was extended to the entire coloured community at this time.[130]

It was not until 1829 that all discriminatory regulations against the free coloureds were finally abolished. The Proclamation[131] containing such important news for one section of the community passed, however, without a single comment from the press. An Address presented by the coloured people to Governor Grant on this occasion was characteristic not only of the civility of those days, but of the facility of the free coloureds for over-statement. They described the benefits of such an act as evoking all the latent talents or virtues of the population, and as creating the most powerful incentive to "enlargement of intellect and perfection of Morals, which are the solid foundations of Public Prosperity."[132] However, when applications were made to the Governor for Commissions in the militia, the latter expressed to the Secretary of State his apprehension that the free coloureds were being unduly hasty. Fearing their "jealousy and sensitiveness", he was afraid that any recommendation to less haste would have been construed into unwillingness on his part. This much could be said in his favour: he expressed a desire to see the matter settled during his tenure;[133] but he was as conscious of social distinctions as any white in the colony.

The Secretary of State, Sir George Murray, readily admitted that, in the Order in Council of March 18, 1829, the British Government contemplated the admission of free coloureds, without discrimination, to civil and military appointments.[134] The Order had made them eligible for all of those things. However, he was of the view that, at such an early period, "eligibility" should be "sparingly" acted upon, except where no offence to the white inhabitants was likely to arise. Those whom he instructed Grant to select as officers should be those "persons who shall be most likely to conduct themselves with prudence, and to conciliate the good will of those with whom they shall be associated."[135] So that the "relief", which the new legislation brought, ended with the responsibility for maintaining good relations being placed squarely on the shoulders of the coloured officers. And this was the same as it had always been.

Appointments to civil and military offices were extremely slow in coming, not only in Trinidad, but in other parts of the Caribbean. By 1834 an anonymous writer was complaining of the paucity of such appointments. He noted that there was only one salaried officer – James Rat – who had been appointed in 1833 as clerk of the market with a house, and a salary of $400 per year. [136] All other offices, to which coloured persons had been admitted, seem to have been confined to those without remuneration. [137] And this was described as both superficial and unsatisfactory. The Secretary of State, Stanley, had approved appointments to Commissions in the militia, and in 1833 some coloured persons had been awarded such Commissions.[138] Those Commissions, according to Governor George Hill, were enthusiastically received by the coloureds and were not offensive to the whites.[139] Lack of enthusiasm on the part of the latter screams from the pen of Hill, who also reported that the Port of Spain cavalry had been made open to coloured persons, and that one of them had been made a cornet.[140]

In spite of all this, it was no salve to the humiliation suffered by the free coloureds to be told that important, if not lucrative, posts had been given to persons from their class. Nor was it strictly true that the lack of salaried positions was not connected with their colour.[141] The plain fact was that prejudices died hard; and although a statute repealed the laws by which they suffered humiliating disabilities, the law could not make people accept those whom they previously regarded as degraded. Thus the free coloureds, like the slaves, found that they had obtained relief from the prejudices and hardships which had shackled them in the past. But the freedom and the recognition which they sought were not yet theirs; it was perhaps another two or more generations before those things became realities.

6. A Chapter Of Errors

> For reasons of public policy and humanity there were
> well defined limits which a slave owner could not
> transgress, but theoretically his human slave was as
> much his as were the cattle or mules on his estate, and
> therefore the moment the Legislature declared the slave
> to have "rights" defined and maintainable at law, slavery
> was virtually at an end, although emancipation was not
> formally declared.[1]

The programme for the amelioration of the condition of slaves after 1823
– a major experiment - involved a change in perspective in which slave
owners had to make the transition from thinking of persons as "property"
to thinking of that species of "property" as persons. The change was a
significant one for those who held almost unlimited power over the persons
of the slaves. The process by which this change took place in Trinidad is
one which deserves some examination in order to determine the extent to
which it was either facilitated or undermined. The treatment of the slaves
was an issue which had engaged the attention of all slave owning nations.
In the seventeenth century the French compiled their *Code Noir*, which
regulated slavery in their colonies. In 1789 the Spanish introduced their
Cedula, which differed in several respects from the French *Code*. Although
this *Cedula* appears not to have been in general use in the Spanish colonies,
it seems to have been in operation in Trinidad as the Commissioners of
Legal Inquiry reported.[2]

This Spanish *Cedula* was remarkable for the consideration it expressed
for the slaves. It placed an obligation on all slave owners to instruct their
slaves in the Christian religion, requiring the owners to provide a priest to
say mass and to instruct them on holy days, as well as to relieve them of
work on those days. The *Cedula* required magistrates and other officials to

determine the "quantity and quality" of food and clothing to be given to the slaves according to their age and sex. The said officials were to regulate the amount of work given them in accordance with a working age ranging between seventeen and sixty years.[3]

The *Cedula* demanded separate houses for men and women, with bed linen and blankets to be provided, as well as accommodation for the sick in a house erected for that purpose. Slave owners were to maintain the aged and infirm, rather than to get rid of them because they were unable to work. They were to encourage marriage and, where the slaves were from different estates, the wife was to go to the estate of her husband.[4] Had this *Cedula* been fully implemented, it would have been in operation a little less than eight years when the British took possession of the island, and would still have been very new. Like other aspects of the Spanish law this *Cedula* was not repealed; but it was substantially replaced by the code proclaimed by Picton – the first British Governor – in 1800.

Picton's code differed from the Spanish *Cedula* in certain specific respects. His code required every proprietor to provide the slaves with "good and comfortable houses," with sleeping arrangements so organized as to prevent them sleeping on the ground. Slaves were to be allowed to enclose their houses with a fence, to protect any animals they had as well as to protect the houses from wandering animals. Slave proprietors or attorneys were to cultivate provisions for their slaves, as well as to give them each an allowance of meat or fish; and each slave over fourteen years of age was to be allowed a portion of land and given Saturday afternoons off to facilitate cultivation. Those who were unable to grant land for provision grounds were to provide stipulated rations. Provision was also made for clothing allowances; working hours were regulated, providing half an hour on mornings for breakfast and two hours at noon for dinner. The code declared illegal the infliction on slaves of more than thirty-nine lashes by way of punishment, and prohibited anyone from punishing a slave in such a way as to cause bleeding or mutilation. Slaves were not to work on Sundays or holy days except as watchmen, their time being available for instruction in the Christian religion. Female slaves having more than three children were to have a day off each week for half a year, and those with seven children were exempted from all labour; no mother was to return to work until she had "recovered from child-bed."[5] Both these codes could be described as humane, and compared with contemporary practices in the West Indies, both were several cuts above what prevailed. If either had been implemented fully, the circumstances of slaves in this colony would have been superior to those of their counterparts in the older British colonies. However, the renewal of these provisions might suggest that the spirit of the law did not find expression in the slave system of the colony.

Schemes for the amelioration of slavery were proposed from time to time by persons operating plantations or having interests in the West Indies; but it appears that little or nothing was done about them. The enforcement of ameliorative schemes, therefore, tended to originate in England where the abolitionists brought pressure to bear on successive governments, who in turn required the colonial governors to effect changes in the system. The abolitionists were convinced that slaves in the colonies were being cruelly treated, and there was ample evidence to justify their claims. The cases of Hodge and Huggins in Dominica and Tortola respectively come immediately to mind;[6] but these were extreme examples of what was only too common.

West Indian planters and members of the various assemblies repeatedly argued that their slaves were well treated in the West Indies, sometimes adding that they were better off than labourers in Britain.[7] Slave owners in Trinidad were also said to treat their slaves well,[8] though not many admitted that the character of the owner was the decisive factor as to whether they were well treated or not. As early as 1813, the Cabildo of Port of Spain found it necessary to draw public attention to the frequency with which sick slaves were found wandering through the streets of the city, and to require proprietors to look after such slaves. These were slaves, moreover, who were unable to work any more. As a result, fines were imposed on owners or agents who failed to provide food or clothing for them, causing them to wander about as beggars.[9]

In 1816, Woodford reported a less than satisfactory state of affairs on the estates of the colony, based on information supplied by the Commandants of Quarters. Slave proprietors had found a way to beat the system, by resorting to overworking their slaves as a means of compensating for their inability to import replacements. Woodford also admitted that the laws abolishing the slave trade had failed to have any ameliorative effect on the treatment of the slaves in Trinidad.[10] The following year, he urged that drivers be forbidden to carry the whip, reserving that privilege to managers only.[11] But he never indicated whether that change had made any difference to the treatment of the slaves.

As indicated earlier, during the period preceding the British policy of amelioration the Spanish slave law was, theoretically at least, the law of the colony, supplemented by Picton's code of 1800.[12] The Council admitted the need for amelioration even at that stage. In 1817 Henry Goulburn, an official of the Colonial Office, sought to promote the amelioration of the condition of slaves by way of honours to be awarded to overseers whose slaves proved to be well cared for. Recognition of their good treatment was to take the form of gold and silver medals for which overseers and managers were to compete.[13] He hoped that this experiment, if it proved beneficial, might recommend itself more generally to slave owners. Goulburn further suggested that the award be made for the increase of births among the slaves, the abolition of night work, the introduction of mechanical improvements, the regular instruction of the slaves, and regular prayers.[14] As late as 1823, when a major phase of amelioration had started, none of these things was extensively practised, although it was reported that prayers were said on French estates but seldom, if ever, on English ones.[15] Woodford's own request that bells replace the whip as a means of assembling the slaves for work earned a certain positive response; but there is no evidence to indicate any favour for his proposal that night work on estates, which had only cattle mills, be stopped.[16]

Towards a New Programme

The year 1823 may be considered a landmark in the history of amelioration in the West Indies. On January 31 that year the Anti-Slavery Society, as it was popularly called, was formed with Thomas Fowell Buxton as the Parliamentary spokesman. The purpose of the Society was to focus attention on slavery, having achieved only qualified success by the abolition of the slave trade and slave registration. The campaign against slavery was launched by Wilbeforce's *Appeal*, which made three charges. First that the West Indian laws tended to degrade slaves in that Europeans, guilty of crimes, had been "put beyond the reach of the law" because slave evidence was inadmissible in the courts.[17] Second, the *Appeal* charged that the slaves were degraded by the driving system and cruel whipping;[18] and third, that the lack of encouragement given to slave marriages resulted in immorality and degradation among that class.[19] Therefore he considered it a matter of urgency to set in motion steps preparatory to the ending of that system which only public ignorance had caused to be protracted.

In May of that same year Buxton presented to the House of Commons a motion declaring the state of slavery to be against Christian principles as well as those of the British Constitution, and demanding its gradual abolition.[20] As a means towards this end, Buxton had in mind a variety of specific improvements which were, one may say, of the nature of an abolitionist manifesto. Slaves were no longer to be chattels in the eyes of the law; they were to be attached to the soil; their evidence was to be accepted for what it was worth; no obstacle was to be placed in the way of their manumission; Sunday was to be allotted as a day for repose and religious instruction, and an alternative day granted for them to look after their provision grounds; the masters' capacity to punish was to be restrained; and a substitute was to be found for the system of driving the slaves.[21] Expressing his firm commitment to the extinction of slavery, he recommended the emancipation of all children born after an unspecified date,[22] emphasising that he did not advocate immediate emancipation, but something more protracted.

While George Canning, one of the ministers, expressed an interest in seeing the "stigma" of slavery removed from the British nation, he was nevertheless desirous of saving from any ill effects of the change those who had property in slaves. Prudence rather than philanthropy, he believed, should dictate the nation's policy. Therefore he proposed, and achieved the acceptance by the Commons of, three resolutions urging decisive yet "judicious" measures for the amelioration of the slaves in the West Indies.[23] While Buxton and Canning were agreed on promoting consideration for the well being of the persons concerned, their objectives were quite different. Buxton's aim was the eventual emancipation of the slaves; Canning, on the other hand, carefully avoided any such "rashness",[24] proposing instead a compromise with both the abolitionists and the West Indians in the House of Commons. The Government of the day was either not in favour of any significant change in the condition of the West Indian slaves or preferred not to risk offending the magnates of those assemblies.

The discussions in Parliament related to the slaves in the entire West Indies; but in seeking to implement the resolutions adopted by Parliament, the Government's attention was immediately focussed on the Crown colonies, especially Trinidad, Demerara and Berbice. This was because of the unwillingness of the Government to legislate for the old West India colonies which had legislatures of their own. Bathurst, therefore, transmitted the resolutions of Parliament to Trinidad, together with a copy of a despatch which he had written to the Governors of Demerara and Berbice. In that despatch he prohibited the flogging of female slaves in the hope that such a distinction would have served to uplift the latter, and would have invoked in them a sense of shame. The despatch also recommended that the system of driving slaves should cease, and that the whip should no longer be carried in the field as a symbol of the driver's authority.[25] The Secretary of State directed the Governor to apply these instructions as far as local circumstances permitted, instructing the Governor to apprise the slave proprietors of the imminence of an Order in Council on the subject, and to encourage them to initiate in advance those improvements, which the Government was desirous of introducing.[26]

Generally speaking, the proposals embodied in these despatches were not well received in Trinidad, anymore than they were elsewhere in the West Indies. The Commandant of Chaguanas reported the unwillingness of the planters in his Quarter either to dispense with the whip, or to forego the flogging of female slaves.[27] In Arima, a meeting of planters passed a series of resolutions on the reforms proposed by Buxton. These urged that the deprivation of the right to inflict punishment would subvert the discipline of the estates; and that to delay punishment until the day after the offence suggested that punishment was usually inflicted under uncontrolled passion – a suggestion they denied.[28] The first of these was to form a staple of planter arguments against amelioration insofar as its total effect was, in their view, concerned.

In other Quarters, similar arguments were reproduced and sometimes others added. Proprietors of North Naparima contended that to have witnesses at the punishment of the slaves was to add to the suffering of the offenders.[29] Proprietors of Pointe-a-Pierre observed that they usually treated their slaves liberally. However they emphasised that "Flogging is the most humane, prompt and efficacious mode to crush disorderly behaviour."[30] The Quarter of Tacarigua reportedly expressed "unprintable" sentiments, with which the Governor did not think he should afflict the Secretary of State.[31] And in St. Joseph, planters declared that the intention of the Government to issue an Order in Council was merely a threat of which they were not afraid. In fact, they asserted that such an Order would be useless unless they approved it.[32]

In South Naparima, the proprietors petitioned the Commandant to appeal to the Governor for a military depot in the Quarter. They voiced the fear that proceedings in the "Mother Country" would have the effect of unsettling the slaves, leading to distrust between master and slave. They believed, with some justification, that the distorted channels of information would create in the slaves uncertainty and doubt concerning their future condition and their liability to the control of their masters.[33] It is highly questionable whether a show of force was the answer to that problem, as there was no real threat of unrest. However, such was the fear of insurrection in the minds of many that it showed itself some weeks later when slaves were arrested in the Diego Martin and Carenage areas on suspicion of hatching a conspiracy to revolt. The Judge of the Court of Criminal Inquiry found no ground for prosecution and the slaves were discharged.[34] Incidents such as these, when taken together, give us a fair indication of the mind of a large proportion of the proprietors during the period. And although it cannot be said with certainty that all white proprietors opposed the proposals, the views of the various meetings certainly showed great aversion to the proposed changes. They did not necessarily represent those of the free coloured slave owners.

In the meantime the Council, while professing agreement in principle with the resolutions of Parliament, thought it necessary to point out that most of the improvements proposed by Buxton were already in force in the colony. But their claim has to be treated with caution; for although a law might be on the statute books, its enforcement was not always a matter of course. The Council disapproved of Buxton's proposals to the effect that slaves should be attached to the soil, believing any advantages to be gained from that attachment to be doubtful. They also disapproved of the proposal that slaves be allowed to purchase their freedom one day at a time – a process which they deemed impracticable. They also rejected the setting aside of Sunday for religious instruction, and the substitution of another day, unless they were compensated for the free day.[35]

Taking the discussion further, members argued from the double premise that the condition of the slaves warranted amelioration, and that such amelioration should be based on religious instruction. Any form of emancipation was to be preceded by the manumission of the females, otherwise the emancipation of the children would not be attended by the anticipated advantages. Such emancipation was, in any case, to be compensated. On the other hand, the Council asked that proprietors make certain concessions; for example, that religious instructions be made available to the slaves, and that places of worship be provided in each quarter at convenient locations. The Council further recommended that twenty six days annually be granted for slaves to work on their provision grounds; that daily labour out of crop time be thirteen hours, and in crop time sixteen hours, exclusive of meal times; and that banks be conveniently located so as to encourage thrift among the slaves.[36] Looked at in the light of the various meetings of protest by proprietors, these proposals were remarkably generous. The Council, in spite of the fact that the embers of antagonism smouldered on, seemed disposed to work out measures of amelioration for the adoption of slave proprietors. But in the little time before the Order in Council of March 1824 was proclaimed, there does not appear to have been any attempt to implement the recommendations.

While the local Council was discussing the draft of an Order in Council to give effect to the amelioration programme, an influential planter, W.H.Burnley, proposed in the Council that all complaints of masters against slaves and vice versa be published in the newspapers, giving details about the nature of the complaints and the persons involved. In support of his proposal, Burnley suggested first, that the majority of proprietors treated their slaves with "Lenity," and that that fact needed to be recorded so that the threat of exposure might act as a deterrent to cruel masters. Secondly,

Burnley felt that such a measure would have secured strict impartiality and uniformity in the decrees of the Protector and the Judge of the Court of Criminal Inquiry, which were likely to form precedents for the guidance both of their successors and of the general public.[37] A firm opponent of the amelioration programme, who thought that the slaves had too much free time, Burnley proposed that the draft Order should be open to public discussion. [38]

At first unwilling to sanction this proceeding, the objects of which had not been clearly stated, Bathurst subsequently changed his mind and approved it.[39] Taking exception to the entire discussion in the Council, he had warned the Governor, in a somewhat testy letter, that it was "highly necessary that you confine your attention to those official directions which you receive from me."[40] In instructing him to apprise the slave owners of the required improvements, he merely indicated the Government's wish to avail itself of their views, and not to purchase their consent for the execution of the measures.[41] Such was the mood of planters in Trinidad, however, that they even voiced their unwillingness to make any concession without compensation in Parliament.[42] It was a bluff used by other islands in the past, and had no hope of success at this time.

In the period between July 1823 and May 1824, certain efforts were made to improve slave conditions in the colony. Woodford recommended the adoption of task work throughout the colony, on the basis of its trial and success on some plantations,[43] and suggested that the planters take steps to institute improvements on their plantations. But in answer to the Governor's query as to an alternative to flogging as a form of punishment, twenty-seven out of thirty-three Commandants still favoured its continuance as a necessity. These Commandants gave as their reason the possible disaffection of the gangs as a result of the distinction in the treatment of the sexes.[44] But no such disaffection was recorded after the Order in Council of 1824 was put in force. A change in the market hours was introduced after several meetings and investigations on behalf of the Cabildo.[45] The market in Port of Spain was in future to be closed on Sundays at 10.00 a.m., and Thursday was agreed as an alternative market day.[46]

Here one must again refer to the role of Governor Woodford in this whole drama. Woodford gave the impression of being one whose only interest was in fostering the amelioration of the slaves; but it is questionable whether his heart was ever fully in the programme. While discouraging open discussion of the subject in Trinidad, he wrote very sympathetically to Bathurst of the planters' concern about the government's interference with their authority.[47] And towards the end of this same year, he expressed to Bishop Howley of London his hope that the British Government would speedily determine the extent of its interference in colonial affairs.[48] His sympathies lay with the planters rather than with the abolitionists or with the slaves.

THE ORDER IN COUNCIL OF 1824

During the course of 1823, Bathurst asked Woodford to prepare the draft of an Order in Council which was to give effect to the various improvements recommended by the government in England.[49] The Governor and Council applied themselves to framing one which the Governor thought was more likely to gain willing obedience "than if drawn up in strict unison with the tenor of Your Lordship's Instructions". This draft – a modification of Colonial Office demands - did not intend to prohibit the flogging of female slaves, but merely aimed at preventing indecent exposure. Woodford hazarded the opinion that unless the Order [50] was greatly modified, and it was decided to indemnify the proprietors, it was likely to become a dead letter in many quarters.[51] The Governor was probably voicing the sentiments of all those involved in the preparation of the draft Order – some of whom were members of the two principal criminal courts of the colony. And this indicates something of that influence which was likely to affect their performance when the Order was eventually put into effect.

Whether on his own behalf or that of the Council, Woodford offered certain proposals for Bathurst's consideration. With an eye to a more effective performance, he proposed, first of all, that Commandants be given a salary in proportion to the population of their Quarters; and that slaves should be obliged to complain to these officers, seeking the Protector of Slaves only in extreme cases. He added that small Quarters should be united to form districts, in each of which there were to be a Church and School, and houses for the Commandant, Clergyman and Schoolmaster, along with a prison and depot for the militia. He further proposed that the *Syndic Procurador* – the officer of the Cabildo charged with responsibility for protecting slave interests – be authorised to visit estates every two years to investigate the treatment of the slaves, and to visit prisons with the prior permission of the courts; that all estates with more than six slaves should keep a journal which might be periodically inspected by the Commandant; and finally, that the clothing of slaves should be regulated by " sealed patterns", the delivery of which clothing was to be certified by the Commandants.[52] Only the first and, with some variation, the fourth were implemented between 1824 and 1829. A variation of the last was implemented after 1831, the others not at all.

A detailed programme for the improvement of the condition of slaves was set out in an Order in Council dated March 10, 1824,[53] which is summarised here. This Order established an office of Protector of Slaves, whose functions included some which were formerly performed by the *Syndic Procurador* of the Cabildo. The person appointed to this office was prohibited from having any interest in slaves or slave plantations within the island. The Protector of Slaves was deemed a magistrate and vested with all the powers of a Commandant of Quarter, except that his authority was not limited to a single Quarter, but extended throughout the colony. The Protector was to be informed of all proceedings involving slaves, at which time he was to act on the latter's behalf. However, because the Protector was also required to take cognizance of slave complaints and institute litigation on their behalf, the Order had created the anomaly of a magistrate who could also be prosecutor or defence counsel as the circumstances demanded. This problem entirely escaped the attention of the framers of the law, and offered its opponents an opening for evasion. By way of assistance for the Protector of Slaves, all Commandants of Quarters were constituted Assistant Protectors in their respective Quarters.[54] However, the Order contained no restrictions as to their ownership of slaves.

The Order next contained provisions for the abolition of Sunday markets, and restrictions on Sunday labour with a view to allowing the slaves to perform only domestic duties for their owners and such duties as were necessary to take care of their livestock. It abolished the use of any whip or cat in the field, and limited the flogging of males to twenty-five lashes in any one day. With respect to the latter, it required that punishment be inflicted only after the lapse of twenty-four hours, ordering that it be administered in the presence of free persons as witnesses. These restrictions did not apply to punishments inflicted by order of the courts.[55] The Order in Council also provided for the recording of all punishments in a Plantation Record Book to be provided for the purpose.

Slaves were free to marry once they had the written permission of their owners or managers, and a licence from the Protector of Slaves, or the Commandant of their Quarter. The Order made it legal for slaves to purchase their freedom or the freedom of any relative. Where differences arose about the value of any slave, the Protector and the owner each should appoint an appraiser and the Chief Justice an umpire to determine the value of the slave. Manumissions by private contract were to continue as previously, except that the Protector was required to ascertain whether the person manumitting a slave had the legal right to do so. The Order further provided for slaves to acquire and dispose of property, as well as for encouraging habits of thrift by the establishment of Savings Banks;[56] and it specifically prohibited the separation of the families of slaves by sale.[57] Under certain limited circumstances, slaves were permitted to give evidence in the courts. Religious ministers and teachers were authorized to issue certificates to the commandants to the effect that the slaves named on them were sufficiently instructed to understand the obligation of an oath. But as they were debarred from giving evidence in civil actions against their owners or in capital offences against whites, the concession was largely contradictory of the ameliorative intention. For if only slaves witnessed the murder of another slave by a white man, this clause served to ensure that there could not be any trial. Finally, the Order provided for the trial of misdemeanours in the "Court for Criminal Prosecutions," with penalties ranging from fines to forfeiture of ownership of any ill-treated slaves.

The principle underlying this Order, according to Bathurst, was that although he was the property of his master the slave had "a right to the protection of his master in return for his service, and the law must secure him that protection."[58] And the events of the period 1824 to 1834 might be considered a means of enforcing this proposition, the issue being to adjust the notion of the slave as mere property to that of the slave as human being. The proposal in the Trinidad draft that the Protector periodically visit estates was excluded from the Order, partly because it was thought that such visits would encourage trivial complaints, and partly because such visits might have led owners to terrorise their slaves so as to cover up complaints worth investigating.[59]

For the smooth implementation of this new programme, Bathurst recommended the combination of the office of Protector of Slaves with that of the *Syndic Procurador* General of the Cabildo, and that the number of Commandants of Quarters should be reduced. In order to ensure their co-operation, he recommended not only a salary of £150 per year, but also the appointment of only those who were likely to facilitate the process of amelioration and the dismissal of those who were opposed to it.[60] Finally, Bathurst informed the Governor that military reinforcements were on the way to Trinidad, and that more were available in the event of disturbance. A company of infantry had already arrived in the colony by the time Bathurst's despatches had reached Woodford.[61]

This Order signified, in the opinion of some contemporary writers, the "commencement of one of the most important political experiments ever attempted".[62] In fact, this was only the latest in a series of experiments tried in the colony by the British Government. The slave policy enunciated during the debate of 1802 on the abolition of the slave trade, and the slave registration of 1812, were all experiments. This latest experiment – the 1824 Order – was instituted in Trinidad for two reasons: In the first place, there was no autonomous legislative body in Trinidad as in the older British colonies, and consequently there could not be any question of the British Government superseding it.[63] Whether that made any real difference to the outcome of the experiment will become clear from what follows. In the second place, the Trinidad situation was thought to be much closer to the ideal at which the Order aimed, than that existing anywhere else in the West Indies,[64] since the Spanish slave code in force in this island provided the pattern for the elaborate programme being introduced.

The initial reaction to the Order was a mixture of fierce opposition and alarm, as slave owners expressed fears either that their crops would be ruined or that servile insurrection was imminent. Petitions and protests from interested persons were addressed to the Governor. That from the Cabildo maintained that the provisions of the Order would be injurious to the welfare of the slaves, incompatible with the colony's safety, a source of ruin to the master, and "subversive of the most sacred rights of private property." The petitioners informed the Governor that he had authority to suspend Royal Orders injurious to the colony's prosperity "until a Representation can be made to His Majesty and his final determination expressed." The Cabildo also asked for the repeal of certain clauses, claiming compensation on behalf of slave owners for any losses they might incur if the government did not accept and act on their advice.[65] In this petition they were invoking a legal principle that applied in Spanish custom, heedless of the fact that that principle did not apply in English law. In any case, few of the members had any Spanish connection.

The members of the Council also made a representation to the Governor along similar lines. Their argument was that the Order did not improve the condition of the slaves, but was likely to cause a relaxation of discipline and prevent any improvement of moral character. In addition to causing ruin to slave owners, they feared an insurrection of such a magnitude as might be beyond the power of the militia to suppress.[66] In the first of two memoranda, the free inhabitants echoed the fears of the previous petitioners. They resented having a slave code prepared by persons who represented neither their feelings nor their interests, and who imposed the code contrary to their wishes. In addition, they found the 36th clause – which permitted slave evidence – hazardous to the lives of the coloured people, [67] presumably because slaves were not prohibited from giving evidence against coloured persons in capital cases.

In a second memorandum, the free inhabitants listed some twenty-two concerns which they had with the Order, and for which they requested responses from the Governor. Some of the issues were clearly intended to be obstreperous, but others needed review. For instance, they were concerned that the Protector of Slaves was to function both as a magistrate and as a defender of the slaves, and sought clarification as to his authority and its limitations. They questioned some groups of clauses, in which one seemed to contradict another. They questioned whether an old slave could manumit a much younger slave, an act which they considered reprehensible, and sought to be enlightened about the principles which should guide manumission. They expressed unhappiness with clause 34, which required the Protector to ensure that the slave being manumitted gratuitously would be cared for until age 14, or for life if over fifty. They were concerned that clause 36, which dealt with slave evidence, appeared to be contrary to local practice based on the Order in Council of September 16, 1822.[68] If attention had been paid to these issues, some of the later difficulties might have been corrected before implementation of the Order had gone too far. There seems to have been a common error running through two of the representations: that the Order originated in England. The Council might well have protested changes to their original draft; the Cabildo and the free inhabitants might not have been aware of the provenance of the document. However, there is nothing to indicate that Woodford made any attempt to correct their error in this regard.

In spite of the dire prognostications, however, the Order in Council was duly promulgated and the Governor applied himself to the task of providing for its being put into execution. It is not to be thought that Woodford dissociated himself from the sentiments of the white slave owners. On the contrary he seems to have shared those views to the extent that he often championed the cause of the latter to the Colonial Office. Thus he represented to Bathurst the risk to which planters were exposed by what he termed an "uncertain measure"; and called for some compensation to be awarded them in order to encourage them in a course which he felt endangered them and their families.[69] Even before the Order was a year old, he was expressing to Bishop Howley in London his regret that the Order was passed as it stood.[70] And in a later correspondence to the same prelate he wrote:

> It is however to be wished that Parliament would declare
> their readiness to make compensation where Injury is
> sustained. This would calm all apprehensions. [71]

Woodford's heart, therefore, could not be said to be in this measure which it was his responsibility to see carried out.

OPERATION OF THE ORDER

As a means towards the execution of the Order, the Governor was required to appoint a Protector of Slaves. Judged by Bathurst's recommendation that the office be combined with that of the *Syndic Procurador* of the Cabildo, the obvious choice seemed to be Henry Fuller, then incumbent of the latter office. But Fuller, who was the owner of three plantations and over two hundred plantation slaves, as well as being Attorney General, was unwilling to part with this property and was therefore disqualified for the post.[72] The Governor therefore appointed as Protector Henry Gloster, a barrister who had been practising in the colony. The new official, who was the son of the Chief Justice of Dominica at that time, was a man whom Woodford considered to be well suited for the task and also acceptable to the planters. Woodford suggested that this office be combined with that of Registrar.[73] Within a short time Gloster was elected *Syndic Procurador* of the Cabildo, and less than a year later he was appointed to the office of Solicitor General.[74] In a short period Gloster had become the incumbent of three salaried positions, a multiplicity of offices which had the potential of preventing him from devoting his undivided attention to his duties as Protector of Slaves. In this respect his position was no different from that of the first Registrar of Slaves, Henry Murray; yet his appointment was approved and no notice was taken later of his additional offices.

The situation in which Henry Fuller was placed was one which might have affected a number of public officials. At that time, there was no clear policy about their ownership of slaves, except that the Registrar and Protector of Slaves were debarred from that kind of investment. We find, therefore, that a number of officials, who had responsibility for the administration of various aspects of the slave laws, were the owners of large numbers of slaves. The following extract from a return of 1826 illustrates the point:

Table IX:
Slave holding by Public Officers

Names	Office	Plantation	Personal
H. Fuller	Att. Gen.	343	8
A. Warner	Chief Judge	81	5
L. F. C. Johnston	Judge, Criminal Inquiry	207	8
A. Gomez	Assessor	62	8

Source: Return of Public Functionaries in the Island of Trinidad who are Proprietors of Slaves, October 3, 1826. T.D.D. 6. 64: Woodford to Bathurst, October 3, 1826.

The Governor and the Protector were also listed as having one and eight personal slaves respectively; and all the Commandants of Quarters save one had plantation slaves – approximately 3,288 between them.[75] As the Order did not debar Assistant Protectors from being possessors of plantation slaves, it is very unlikely that the honorarium of £150 per year was enough to secure their impartiality. For that matter, there was no guarantee that the Judges' impartiality would not have been impaired, even momentarily, by their seeing things through the eyes of planters and slave owners. And these were the officials who had a significant role to play in the protection of slaves against abuses by their owners.

Our task now is to examine the operation of the Order in Council during the period 1824 to 1829, the period during which Canning's policy of "authoritative admonition" acted as a guideline to the older colonies, and after which change in the process was enforced. During this period, only two slaves were certified as competent to give evidence in the courts of the colony. Woodford confessed to an uncertainty on his part as to the manner in which the certificates were to be issued. He expected those slaves, who adhered to the Roman Catholic persuasion, to receive theirs from the Bishop of that Church; and he assumed that those belonging to the Church of England would receive theirs at the annual visitation of the Bishop of Barbados. His major concern, however, was with the missionaries – those who did not belong to either of the two groups just mentioned. And he therefore sought advice from Bathurst as to whether a certificate from them was acceptable.[76] There is no record of any reply; but the rejection of the Barbados Slave Law of 1826, because it excluded dissenting ministers as incompetent to give certificates, suggests the direction in which the Colonial Office wished to go.

Woodford's real problem concerned the dearth of persons he considered acceptable as ministers. His attitude to dissenters was generally negative, and specifically hostile where the Methodists were concerned. It is difficult, however, to understand his proposal that the Bishop of the Anglican Church be the one to issue certificates, unless he was intent on severely restricting the number of certificates. For the Bishop, resident in Barbados, could only visit Trinidad irregularly and for short periods. One must also question his restriction of the issuance of certificates to the Roman Catholic bishop, when there were several clergy of that denomination in the island. His difficulties are even more inexplicable when it is noted that the Order extended the right to issue certificates to clergy of the Church of England, the Church of Scotland, every priest of the Roman Catholic Church, and "every other person being a public teacher of religion within the said island."

In March 1826, Woodford issued a Proclamation making slave witnesses acceptable without qualification, and declaring the certificates of competency to be unnecessary. This Proclamation also prohibited slaves from giving evidence in any lawsuits involving their masters, or in capital offences against whites.[77] At the same time, the proclamation permitted slaves to give evidence in cases against persons of colour who were not their owners. Woodford had contravened the terms of the Order in Council, which required the slaves to show that they had understood the meaning of an oath. It could also be said that, by this Proclamation, he had actually extended the restrictions against the acceptance of slave evidence. In appearing to be generous, he had actually at the same time followed the system of colour prejudice in the older British colonies by allowing slave evidence against coloured persons only.

In response to a query from Bathurst, the Governor claimed to have taken steps to remove a conflict which seems to have arisen between this Order and that of September 1822, by which "Persons not free but otherwise competent under the law of England" were allowed to give evidence in the courts. He sought to remove from the courts the discretion of accepting or rejecting slave evidence.[78] Woodford had support from other quarters in that neither of the two judges in the colony at the time regarded slave evidence as reliable; and such evidence as they gave seems to have been confined to manumission cases. One of the judges, Lewis Johnston, explained that slaves were seldom careful to distinguish what they heard from what they saw; and that knowledge of the character, manners, and habits of the slave population was a pre-requisite to the evaluation of their evidence.[79] The Chief Judge expressed the view that slave evidence was seldom reliable because of the slaves' lack of integrity. It was in this atmosphere that Woodford sought to relieve the pressures on the slaves while removing, in the meantime, the obligation on the courts to receive the evidence of persons certified to them as competent witnesses Small wonder, then, that the proclamation was disallowed, Bathurst insisting that only those who produced no certificates were to be the objects of the courts' discretion.[80]

The necessity of having certificates issued by duly qualified persons placed a great responsibility on the clergy of the Roman Catholic Church and those of the Church of England. When this Order was introduced, there was a great shortage of clergy of the latter body, as the Governor observed to the Secretary of State from time to time.[81] In fact, there was a real crisis in the Anglican Church in Trinidad in that Henry Clapham, who in 1823 had been in the island for twenty-six years, could not extend his services due to age and infirmity. Woodford appealed for an active and willing clergyman to replace Clapham, who seemed not to have been keen to undertake the demands made on him. But before the end of 1827, there were ten curates of the Roman Catholic Church, one rector of Port of Spain for the Church of England,[82] and a number of other religious teachers who were also qualified to give such certificates. In the light of this, it is surprising that the Commissioners of Legal Inquiry reported that there was no provision for the instruction of the slaves. In 1824 the Roman Catholic Church reported having 14,845 baptised slaves and the Church of England 1,498.[83] From among these slaves, it is surprising that there could only be such a small number capable of giving evidence. Were the slaves so dense that they could not understand the meaning of an oath? Or were the clergy and teachers reluctant to help them acquire the necessary certificates? The only clue we have for resolving this problem lies in Woodford's remark that the "Clergy of the Church of Rome will not lightly or easily grant" the necessary certificates.[84] But even this is not a sufficient explanation of the general attitude of the two major Christian churches. Clapham, the rector of Port of Spain, was unable to undertake the task of instructing the slaves in view of his ripe age; and by the time the Order was put into operation, he had retired from active duty.[85]

★★★★★★★

During the life of this Order, there were no more than four marriages, three of which took place in 1826.[86] Paucity of ministers was by no means the main reason for the lack of marriages among the slaves. Two very general explanations have been suggested for this deficiency of marriage among slaves in the West Indies: one relates to the uncertainty, inherent in concubinage, which served as a deterrent to would-be disobedient wives.[87] In other words, as long as the man kept putting off marriage, the female partner would be kept in a state of subservience; but once she was married she was likely to assert herself. A second explanation is that the slaves were unwilling to contract marriage, but were determined to resist not only compulsion to marry, but interference with their customs.[88] It is quite possible that the real deterrent to marriage lay in the continuing uncertainty of estate life, in which it was possible for slave families to be separated by sale, thus making married life a burden for the slaves concerned. A further reason for their unwillingness to marry probably lay in the lack of example which the slaves saw in their managers and others of that class, among whom there was considerable promiscuity involving female slaves. It is quite reasonable to assume that the general atmosphere of promiscuity and immorality contributed to the breakdown of marriage and family relationships.[89] A further consideration is whether the slaves resisted Christian marriage because it represented something quite alien to their polygamous way of life. Among Christian Churches generally, it was customary to deny membership to those slaves who had several wives. Bishop Coleridge is on record as recommending that clergy ignore the older men and focus their teaching against polygamy on the youths.[90] We need to resist a facile assumption that the Churches were negligent in responding to this provision, and allow for the possibility that the slaves might not have wanted so radical a change as monogamy entailed.

★★★★★★★

Another major aspect of this programme concerned the manumission of slaves, which could be effected privately and gratuitously by the owner, or be purchased by the slave. Between June 24, 1824 and December 24, 1827, there were 588 manumissions as against 377 for the previous two and a half years. The following comparative table illustrates the difference:

Table X:
Slave Manumissions, 1821 – 1827.

Period	By Will	Gratuitously	By Purchase	Total
Jan. 1821 – June 1824	44	166	167	377
June 1824 – Dec. 1827	24	155	409	588

Source: Return of Manumissions between 1821 and June 1824; Statement of the number of Slaves manumitted in the Island of Trinidad from June 1824 to December 24, 1827; enclosed with C.O. 295/77: Woodford to Huskisson, March 7, 1828.

The number of personal slaves manumitted since the Order was more than double the number of plantation slaves manumitted during the same period – 418 as against 170. This would indicate that freedom was more difficult to obtain in the case of plantation slaves than in the case of personal slaves. And that in itself is an indication of a desire to maintain the supply of estate labourers. Whereas before 1824 over 55% of the slaves were manumitted without payment, the rate of these had fallen to just over 30% after 1824. Before the Order private manumissions exceeded, though only slightly, those by purchase; whereas in the succeeding period, manumissions by purchase greatly exceeded those effected privately. For example, approximately 69% of manumissions since 1824 were by purchase, as against 44% of manumissions before 1824. This would suggest that the slaves took advantage of the facility granted them to purchase their manumissions, by procuring the funds to do so; it may also indicate a measure of resistance on the part of the slave owners.

The provision for the purchase of manumission was not executed without challenges. While it is true that the average price per slave up to December 1827 was £62.13.1¾ sterling, there were several occasions when the price demanded was far in excess of this sum. And the frequency with which arbitrations were called for seems to suggest that evaluations were made prohibitive in order to restrict the easy acquisition of this benefit. An early problem, over the manumission of a slave, Judy Dinzy, called for some modification in the procedures being used. Judy was the slave of a free black man, Charles Alexander, whom her father had manumitted in the presence of the Protector of Slaves after merely giving the owner a promise to pay for her within four months. A lengthy dispute as to the precise course to be followed was sparked off when the aggrieved owner, Alexander, complained to the Attorney General some time later. The latter argued that the father's promisory note did not constitute a transfer of property, and that the Protector of Slaves would have been well advised to investigate whether or not the slave was registered as the property of John Dinzy, or whether she was mortgaged. He observed that the Order was not intended to support fraudulent manumissions, but rather to improve the condition of the slaves.[91] Disagreeing with the Protector's distinction between the course to be followed with respect to private manumissions, he quoted a precedent of the colony's courts to the effect that "the Sale or Transfer of a slave, otherwise than by an Act or Bill of Sale was not legal". Therefore he advised that the Protector consult all persons concerned in an effort to avoid fraud.[92]

The Protector, on his part, argued that the intention of the 33rd clause of the Order was to secure for the slave a valid and meaningful freedom for money paid by the purchaser. As Protector, he explained, he was required by the Order to ascertain the title of the owner or reputed owner, and to ensure that that person was capable of granting a valid manumission in order to secure the rights of the slaves whose money was being paid. Voluntary manumissions, he contended, could not fall under the definition of a contract;[93] neither did clause 33 apply to it. With regard to those slaves who were manumitted gratuitously, he interpreted his and the Commandants' duty as limited to ensuring that the owners were not getting rid of persons who were unable to earn their subsistence. In view of this difference of opinion, he asked that the matter be referred to the Secretary of State without whose instructions he was unable to follow the course suggested by the Attorney-General.[94]

This time-consuming process absorbed approximately eight months and ended with Bathurst upholding the Attorney-General's opinion. If the person effecting the manumission was not the owner, the slave remained a slave; while a deed of manumission, issued without previous investigation, would only lead to serious embarrassment.[95] Gloster's way of handling the problem would clearly not have operated in the best interests of the slaves. It was also disturbing because, as Solicitor General, he should have had as clear a grasp of the law as did the Attorney General. This lengthy discussion resulted in a set of directives, issued by the Secretary of State, to the effect that the Protector or Commandant was to obtain a certificate of ownership from the Registrar of Slaves and a statement from the Registrar of Deeds stating that there was no mortgage on the slave in question. Manumission could only be effected if there were no part owners whose consent had not been granted.[96]

One principle had now been established as a result of the correspondence. However, manumission posed other problems which soon engaged attention. In 1824, the Protector of Slaves suggested to the Governor an alteration in the system of appraising slaves for manumission. Arguing that the method set out in the Order was somewhat tedious, he recommended that his own valuation be used unless the owner or other party objected. If the latter's evaluation was higher, an average of the two figures could be taken and applied.[97] This method would have got rid of the intervention of the Chief Judge and the need for an umpire; but it would have been unsatisfactory in that an owner could have obtained a very high price if he wished merely by demanding a much higher price than the Protector offered. This was precisely what eventually took place, as Gloster himself reported in 1826, when two vastly differing appraisals were submitted for the same slave.[98] Fortunately for the slaves, the Colonial Office did not sanction this procedure.

As indicated earlier, the average evaluation for manumissions up to the end of 1827 was £62.13.1¾ sterling as compared with £70.10.7 ¾ for the period 1821 to 1824. Woodford offered two explanations for the difference: first, that the lower price resulted from the comparatively low price for children. The second was that the Consolidated Slave Trade Act had prevented the removal of plantation slaves from the old colonies, thus giving rise to the depreciation.[99] One would have expected that shortage would drive the price upward. Appraisals were based on a simple rule, recommended by Bathurst, which was that the slaves were to be assessed on their moral and intellectual accomplishments, as well as on their appearance and strength.[100] As a further guide to all concerned in such matters, Woodford provided that, where there was a dispute about the value of a slave, the cost of the appraisal should be shared equally by the owner and the slave.[101] This in effect would have increased the demand made on the slave and was manifestly unfair.

Extremely high prices were occasionally demanded in the period after 1824, with £162.10 for a personal slave in June 1825, and £169 for a plantation slave in December 1825 being outstanding examples.[102] However, the case of Pamela Munro in 1826 brought the exorbitance to light, and indicated the extent to which the process could be, and was, subverted. The appraisers of the slave claimed to have been guided by two factors: first, that manumitted slaves frequently abandoned their erstwhile owners; and secondly, that it was impossible to obtain free labourers for any term because they worked capriciously. Therefore, considering that she was a domestic slave in the prime of life, healthy, "in possession of many Valuable Qualities, so that her services could not be replaced by the hire of any other Slaves in the colony at a less sum than six round dollars per month"; and considering that she had been fed and clothed, they fixed the valuation at 1200 "Round Mexican Dollars."[103] At just over $4.00 to the pound sterling, the slave would have had to pay approximately £261 sterling, the highest sum demanded since the institution of the Order.[104] One of the appraisers, W.H.Burnley, was a staunch opponent of the amelioration programme. It is therefore very likely that this unreasonably high appraisal was an act of protest on his part, just as he tried to prevent the manumission of another slave on grounds not provided in the Order. Moreover, the amount fixed was three times that paid for the same slave a short time previously.[105]

The failure of the Governor to take any action was based on the absence of any provision in the Order for this eventuality, so that such gross injustice could not be corrected. The Chief Judge interpreted his role in this exercise as being limited by the Order to the appointment of an umpire, and to the issuing of the necessary certificates when all the conditions for manumission had been complied with.[106] That being the case, he concluded that he was not authorised to take cognizance of exorbitant appraisals, which meant that slaves had no appeal against them. For his part, Bathurst contended that the appraisers had wrongly interpreted and applied principles intended solely for Demerara.[107] Woodford's explanation was that the reduction in the number of estates, the difficulty of obtaining slaves or free labour had all affected the value of the slave;[108] and it was to deal with this situation that he had given those directions. But whereas Bathurst was unable to reverse the valuation, which he himself considered exorbitant, he made no attempt to provide a means whereby a repetition of the same problem could have been forestalled. So that, in spite of the limitations to which the Chief Judge had pointed, the procedure remained exactly as it had previously been. The Protector did not believe he could intervene, in spite of his doubts about the principles employed by the appraisers; they had acted ostensibly in accordance with the Order. His report, however, revealed that appraisals were rising steadily even though the market price of slaves was not on the increase[109] – an irregularity which was not checked.

By 1829 Sir George Murray, who had succeeded Bathurst as Colonial Secretary, criticised the high price of manumissions and pointed to even greater irregularities in the execution of this aspect of the programme. In three different cases the slaves had been valued at exactly the same price – £216.13.4 – by the umpire, while the valuations of the appraisers suggested that the slaves were of different values. The law was therefore rendered a dead letter since none of the slaves had been able to pay the sum that was thus fixed. In all three cases, he noticed that the umpire was the same individual. One of the slaves had belonged to the Chief Justice,[110] whose responsibility it was to appoint the umpire. Governor Grant's explanation that the Chief Justice was in England when the umpire for his slave had been named hardly mattered, since the acting Chief Justice was not prevented from naming an umpire who had found favour with the actual incumbent of the office. In response to Murray's suggestion, however, he promised to submit the draft of an Order to prevent the Chief Justice from naming the umpire when he was a party to the transaction.[111] There is no record of any Order to that effect.

A unique problem arose in the case of another female slave, Judy Brush, who sought to purchase her freedom. W. H. Burnley, part owner of the slave, urged the rejection of the petition on the strange argument that a slave could not be manumitted solely on his or her ability to pay the required sum. He further argued that the clauses covering the subject presupposed that only an honest and industrious slave could be manumitted, and that Bathurst had made moral qualities and attainments decisive in appraisals. The Chief Justice, though declaring that he had no express authority to reject the petition, nevertheless claimed discretionary power to refuse to entertain the petition until the slave had returned to her master and made up for the offence she had supposedly committed.[112] This decision was a curious one. Burnley had exaggerated when he alleged that Bathurst had made moral qualities decisive for manumission; what Bathurst had actually stated was: "The value of a Slave, of course, depends both on his strength and on his acquirements, and an appraisement which was not formed in reference to both would be manifestly unjust to the owner."[113] In other words, the price and not the act of manumission was to be determined by the qualities indicated. Burnley's interpretation was not challenged, even by the Chief Justice, and the argument served its purpose; but there was nothing in the Order to support Burnley's plea that only an honest and industrious slave could have been manumitted. The Chief Justice granted Burnley's plea on this occasion; however, when the petition of the slave was renewed in October of the same year – 1825- it was favourably considered, much to Burnley's annoyance.[114]

★★★★★★★

An important part of the programme of amelioration was the prohibition of the flogging of female slaves, and the substitution of other forms of punishment. Prior to the Order of 1824, punishment involved their being placed on the tread wheel in Port of Spain, if they lived sufficiently close to the town; but owners of estates further removed from the town could not make use of that device.[115] In a proclamation of June 23, 1824, Woodford authorised certain forms of punishment from which he seems to have taken malicious pleasure. These included a maximum of three days' solitary confinement, with or without work; confinement in stocks – field stocks, house stocks, and bed stocks; hand cuffs; distinguishing dresses, with or without the stocks; distinguishing marks made of tin and hanging from the necks.[116] By a later Proclamation Woodford directed that female slaves under ten years of age were to be punished as free girls of a corresponding age – almost certainly by flogging. However, only those punishments listed in the Proclamation of June 1824 were to be recorded,[117] a provision which seemed to open the door for abuse.

★★★★★★★

Cases of criminal prosecutions against slaves were few – less than forty being recorded in the Protector's reports. The majority of these cases were for assault – eight altogether; five were for running away, and three for theft. Punishments varied from twenty lashes for the theft of a small sum, to 100 lashes and twelve months' hard labour for assault. On the other hand, for running away, a slave was sentenced to wear iron clogs of not less than ten pounds for a period not specified in the sentence.[118] A greater number of slave offences were tried in the inferior courts of the colony – the courts of the Alcaldes in Ordinary. The frequency with which these cases took place led to allegations that the new law had deprived the master of his power and jurisdiction over his slaves; so that offences had to be carried before the courts. They also led to allegations that crimes were increasing among the slave population as a result of the relaxed discipline under the new law, and also among the free coloureds, who were thought to be gradually losing their respect for the whites.[119] The author of these allegations viewed with concern the deprivation of the owner's right to use his property for his own profit; and saw this as destroying the slave's relations with his master, as well as "removing that check by which alone his vicious propensities can be restrained and his crimes effectually punished."[120] It had been Bathurst's contention that the slave, though he was his master's property, nevertheless had rights. What the writer was doing here – and there is little doubt that he had the approval of large sectors of the community – was showing that the slave was still regarded as absolute property. But the amelioration programme was based on the notion that the slave was a person; and the difference between these two points of view created the conflict.

The situation appears to have been unlike that represented by this correspondent – the Editor of the paper. This writer indicated that many of the trials were connected with crimes committed previous to the Order.[121] Quite interestingly, his successor as editor quoted statistics to show that crime had been on the decrease. The following table illustrates the point of the latter:

Table XI:
Slave Trials as compiled by the Newspaper

June to December 1824	11	January to June 1826	6
January to June 1825	9	July to December 1826	4
July to December 1825	9	January to June 1827	4

Causes before the Alcaldes

March to December 1823	54 (ten months)
January to December 1824	89
January to December 1825	126
January to December 1826	53
January to December 1827	33

Source: Port of Spain Gazette, August 1, 1827.

Except for the year 1825 in the latter table, there was an overall tendency towards decrease; and this, the writer concluded, was an indication of improvement in their morals.[122] It must be admitted that matters, which were previously dealt with by the slave owners, by this time had come under the jurisdiction of the courts; so that the argument for increase seems even weaker.

Prosecutions against free people for misdemeanours were not frequent, numbering no more than about ten. This does not necessarily mean that there were few breaches of the Order. It may simply mean that few breaches were brought to the attention of the Protector of Slaves; for reports depended on the slaves, who were always exposed to reprisal should they fail to prove their point. As a result some serious cases failed to reach a conclusion. The majority of the cases were for simple assault, or for assault with some other crime.[123] Only in three cases were the accused found guilty – one of them was sentenced to six months' imprisonment and ordered to pay costs; another was fined £6 sterling with an alternative of thirty days' imprisonment; while the third was fined £10 sterling.[124] In a particular case, one of assault and rape, the only person who could give evidence was the slave herself; but as she did not possess a certificate of competence, she could give no evidence in the matter and the accused was discharged.[125] The aspect of amelioration, which the clause was designed to achieve, ended for that slave in failure. In another case of assault, the prosecution's witness was twice absent; and as there was no other witness, the accused was discharged on the second sitting of the court.[126]

This was not the only way in which the ameliorative programme met with failure in the courts. The case against the manager of the "Resource" estate in 1827 illustrates another instance of such failure. Lamphier, the manager, had authorised the flogging of a ten year old girl, Marie Noel. In accordance with clause 6 of the Proclamation of June 1824, the matter was referred to the Court of Criminal Inquiry as a breach of the amelioration Order of 1824. But the Judge of that court dismissed the case on the ground that his court had no jurisdiction in the offence.[127]   Lewis Johnston, the judge, insisted that the 6th clause of the Proclamation did not supply the lack of jurisdiction of his court; and that the Order in Council of March 1824 had deviated from established judicial procedure. In support of his contention he referred to a dispatch from Bathurst in which the latter had insisted that the trials were to be conducted in the Court for the Trial of Criminal Prosecutions. By way of a remedy, he requested of the Governor a proclamation to clarify doubts and to invest the Judge of the Court of Criminal Inquiry with the authority necessary in this matter.[128] Woodford saw no need for the proclamation, and only unwillingly issued one.[129]

★★★★★★★

With respect to the encouragement of thrift among the slaves, a proclamation was issued in July 1824 for the establishment of eight Savings Banks in Trinidad. One of these was located in Port of Spain, and others in St. Joseph, San Fernando, Arima, Carenage, Cuba, La Brea, and Icacos. That in Port of Spain was under the management of the *Corregidor* of the town, and all the others by Commandants of the respective Quarters.[130] The establishment of these banks was commended by an observer as a benefit and convenience, which even the white population did not enjoy. However, the writer also expressed the view that the slaves were not sufficiently enlightened to understand money matters. She alleged that they were suspicious of strangers, and preferred to keep their money themselves.[131]

The reports of the Protector of Slaves on the banks indicate that the slaves made considerable use of these facilities. The very earliest report showed a deposit of £351.8 currency in the first six month period, and deposits up to the end of 1828 were usually quite substantial. Though the reports do not state the purposes for which money was usually withdrawn, it is highly probable that such withdrawals were for the purpose of purchasing manumissions. The following table illustrates the performance:

Table XII:
Performance of Savings Banks

Period	Deposit	Withdrawals	Balance
24 June to 30 September 1824	$679.8		$679.8
October to December 1824	(£11.10)		(£351.8)
January to March 1826	394.2	$100.0	$999.9
April to June 1826	3.6½	37.2	966.3½
December		1337.5¼	
December 1826 to March 1827	770.4½	913.8¼	1194.1¼
March to June 1827	345.6	1078.7	486.2½
June to September 1827	67.7		553.9½
September to December 1827	262.0	266.9	349.0½
January to March 1828	1353.8½	177.2½	1725.6½
March to June 1828	643.0	962.5	1406.1½
June to September 1828	1121.4½	818.2	1709.4
September to December 1828	78.7½	112.0	1676.1½

Source: Reports of the Protector of Slaves for 1824 – 1828 (C.O. 300/19 - 24)

****

Our next area of concern is that respecting Sunday labour, which was prohibited by the Order in Council. Woodford, in one of his early dispatches, had questioned this clause on the ground that it would cause serious loss to the planters. He had interpreted the clause to mean that slaves were not compelled to work on that day, but that they were free to hire themselves out.[132] Bathurst, on the other hand, emphasised that the purpose of the clause was to prohibit all labour on Sundays except that performed voluntarily by the slaves on their own grounds. He believed that to allow them to hire themselves out would have caused such evasions of the law as to defeat the objectives of the Government in securing Sunday as a day of relaxation from labour, and for religious improvement."[133]

In August 1824, therefore, Woodford sent a circular to the Commandants of Quarters directing that slaves were not to hire themselves out on Sundays, but were to work on their own grounds. However, he directed that a reasonable number be kept on estates to deal with casualties. In addition, he permitted proprietors to demand the attendance of slaves for domestic work, for keeping the peace, or for security, authorising them to punish those slaves who did not work.[134] Bathurst took strong objection to this last directive, recommending instead the loss of their plots if they did not attend to them. As a further clarification of the issue of the observance of Sunday and labour, this dispatch stated that where the owner substituted provision grounds for maintenance, he had no claim to the services of the slave on Sundays, nor did he have any claim for compensation either for that day or for part of any other day substituted;. but he authorised the work of watchmen and domestics on Sundays.[135] The directives of the Secretary of State were embodied in a proclamation limiting the slaves' hiring of themselves to their masters, or to other people with the permission of their owners, and the Protector of Slaves was given the responsibility of fixing the minimum wages payable for such services.[136] However, it was not until the middle of the following year, 1825, that a table of wages was published,[137] the slaves in the meantime being left to such generosity as their employers felt moved to display.

★★★★★★★★

The last aspect of the Order deserving our consideration is that which concerned forfeiture for misdemeanours. This provision had apparently been viewed with the greatest alarm by the planters in the colony. Woodford considered the penal clauses – clauses 41 and 42 – extremely severe,[138] and the latter clause particularly so. Clause 41 provided that anyone convicted of a breach of the Order was laible to a fine of between £50 and £500 sterling, or six months' imprisonment, or both. If convicted of cruelty, the slaves of that individual were forfeited to the Crown. Clause 42 provided that anyone who was twice convicted of cruelty, was to be "absolutely incapable in the law" of being the owner or proprietor, overseer, or superintendent of slaves within the island, and the slaves were forfeited to the Crown. Woodford considered such a course of action prejudicial to the family of the slave owner, one which showed no consideration for his creditors.[139]

In order to soften the blow, Bathurst advised that forfeiture should be at the discretion of the Court, enforceable only in extreme cases, and was not to be enforced until the whole case had been referred to the Crown.[140] This would have meant another series of delays, which could have militated against a smooth and satisfactory operation of the Order, and a further burden on the slaves in question. The Chief Justice objected to Bathurst's proposal that the 42nd clause of the Order be left to the discretion of the Court. Any person, he explained, was competent to prosecute; the matter was not left to the Crown prosecutor. He further denied the assertion of Lord Bathurst which recognised the possibility of appeals against forfeiture.[141] No case of forfeiture was recorded by the Protector, and one can only wonder whether slave owners were so cooperative or exemplary that the need never arose.

★★★★★★★★★

This first period of amelioration ended with only limited success. As the matters before the courts revealed, there was great contradiction in the laws themselves which called frequently for clarification and correction. As the Governor was slow to act on the issue of criminal prosecutions, a vital area of the programme was left dependent on a single individual – the Judge of the Court of Criminal Inquiry. The differences of opinion between the officers of the courts and the Protector of Slaves – as in the case of manumissions – created an atmosphere of uncertainty, which would have left both owners and slaves skeptical about the measures in question. In addition, the frequent need for amendments of the Order and for explanations and directions by the Secretary of State, further undermined the confidence of the population in the process.

As the months preceding the arrival of the Order and the events connected with its proclamation showed, there was considerable hostility towards it among the slave owners of the colony. And this hostility, though it was seldom overt,[142] was nevertheless fed by an anti-abolitionist newspaper editor. His closing words to the public, as he gave up his occupation, provide an example of the diet of vituperation usually offered to the public, and which fortunately, was never carried much further:

> We would wish every man in the Colony to know that
> he lives under the undefined power of an arbitrary

> Government, claiming and exercising the right of
> taxation without representation … [143]

But the constitutional issue was not taken up by planters in the colony. Their argument rested on the provisions of the Articles of Capitulation as the protests showed. As yet, therefore, a great deal remained to be done; and the slave owners could not be depended on to acquiesce in doing it.

7. Towards A Firmer Ameliorative Policy

The Order in Council of 1824, as we saw in the preceding chapter, stumbled on many a rock in Trinidad. Government officials were not inclined to support a scheme which possessed so many avenues for evasion. And, as several of them were planters or slave owners, opposition to the Order was always possible. Thus far, no great exertion was required by the opponents of the Order to ensure its lack of complete success. The grandiose expectations of the apologists of the amelioration programme remained to a large extent unrealised.

Of great importance for the final process in the West Indies was the attitude of slave owners in the old West Indian colonies. Canning's policy of "authoritative admonition" had proved to be a failure in the face of steady opposition from the colonial legislatures. Not only had these colonies failed to initiate any schemes of amelioration satisfactory to officials at the Colonial Office in London, but such acts as they passed were often rejected and returned to them for satisfactory amendments. Dissatisfaction had gone so far that, by 1830, sympathy for the West Indian cause was already on the decline.[1]

Dissatisfaction on the part of the British Government, influenced no doubt by abolitionists within the Colonial Office, showed itself in a change of policy between 1830 and 1834. The ameliorative policy in this period was aimed at correcting the mistakes which had marred the operation of the 1824 Order; and it did this by making the requirements more detailed and less open to misinterpretation. Thus a new Order in Council of February 2, 1830,[2] made certain important alterations to that of 1824, with the intention of promoting amelioration more aggressively. It required that neither the Protector nor his assistant was to have any interest in slaves or in land cultivated by them, and that they were not to have slaves as domestics unless they first satisfied the Governor that no free persons were available.

This restriction implied that the provision for the Commandants to serve as Assistant Protectors no longer obtained, since nearly all of them owned plantation slaves. Neither the protector nor his assistant was to function thereafter as a magistrate; instead, their role was limited to prosecuting on behalf of, or defending, slaves.

This Order provided that slaves were only to be employed on Sundays for domestic work, cattle rearing, or works of necessity; this last category was to be defined by the Governor. Prior notice of such works of necessity, and the attendant circumstances, were to be reported to the Protector of Slaves or his assistant; but in cases of emergency, the report was to be made not more than forty-eight hours afterwards. As a guide to appraisers for the purpose of manumission, the Order required that such appraisers consider the quality and skill of the slaves, and any other factors they considered useful. Strangely enough, the Order forbade the collecting of the cost of manumission among the relatives of the slaves in question, though previous correspondence from Bathurst had clearly indicated that one relative was competent to give another the means of purchasing his or her manumission.[3] In addition to this, the Order authorised the Governor to fix the rate of appraisals – a provision, which was intended to remove the exorbitance characteristic of appraisals between 1824 and 1829. The acceptability of slave evidence was rendered hollow by the discretion allowed judges and magistrates to refer to their servile condition in assessing the value of their evidence. This discretion was based on the commonly held view, even among judges, that slave evidence was not to be trusted. The provision was, therefore, a change from Bathurst's insistence that, once a certificate had been presented showing that the slaves understood the meaning of an oath, such slaves were acceptable witnesses. There was one very valuable addition: slaves were no longer to be punished for failing to establish a complaint, unless it could be proven that they had acted out of malice.[4]

By this time the colony had as Governor one who seemed to be more amenable to the amelioration process. In order to ensure an easy application of the Order, the Secretary of State, Sir George Murray, instructed the Governor, Sir Lewis Grant, to define precisely the works of necessity for which slave labour was likely to be required on Sundays. Murray authorised him to make some concession, given the fact that the manufacture of sugar required steady work over a long period. But the concession was of limited duration; the additional work required the consent of the slaves, and was to be remunerated by the employer. Murray further demanded that the Governor determine the courts in which offences against the Order were to be tried, as well as the role of the Protector of Slaves in defence of, and in prosecution on behalf of, the slaves. He also demanded that the Protector exert himself, as far as his health allowed, on the slaves' behalf, stipulating that he was not to receive any salary until he had submitted his report.[5] The inclusion of this last instruction might be considered at least an indication of the frustration of the Colonial Office. The whole product clearly shows that a more vigorous application of the slave laws was contemplated, and that the officials would be subjected to greater scrutiny than before.[6]

The new Order in Council did not take into account the issues of food and clothing, as the Secretary of State had indicated that a more comprehensive code was in the offing. As it turned out, a new code was ready within eighteen months of this one arriving in the colony. This may well explain why there was so little opposition to the Order of 1830. Before proceeding to the next Order in Council, the Secretary of State sought information from the Governor, concerning the quantity of work usually performed by slaves, perhaps because of allegations that the slaves were being overworked. He also requested another statement indicating the quality and quantity of food and clothing provided for the slaves – adults as well as children, males as well as females.[7]

The Protector's report showed the daily labour of plantation slaves to be as follows:

Cutting fuel wood	1 cord, 5' x 6' or 4' x 8', 3' in length.
Draining land	drains 12" wide x 12" deep, or 14" x 14". 160 to 300 running feet.
Lining land	land prepared and pickets furnished. 2 men and 2 boys: 2000 to 2500 pickets per day.[8]
Round ridging	bed 20' wide and cleared: about 100' to 150".
Holing and Embanking	ground already ridged: 130 to 300 holes; if not ridged: 70 to 230. Holes 24" x 18".
Planting canes	after holing: 250 to 400 holes.
Cutting canes	20 to 25 mules' loads, or four or five cart loads; enough to fill 300 gallons.
Weeding	with hoe: 130 to 300 holes
Stripping canes	(beds 25' wide) – 150' to 500', or 190 to 600 holes.[9]

The Protector's report also showed that the daily task started at 6.00 in the morning and finished between 1.30 and 3.00 in the afternoon. Those who were not doing tasks finished at sunset, except for "throwing grass"[10] which required an extra thirty minutes. The mothers of toddlers started work at 7.30 in the morning, while mothers of nursing infants started at 9.00. During crop time, the slaves were allowed half an hour for breakfast and another half an hour for dinner. Out of crop time, the slaves were allowed one and two hours respectively for the same meals. Night work, which usually ended at 7.00 or 8.00 in the evening, extended to 10.00 or 11.00 if the weather was bad or the fuel damp. Work gangs in the boiling house rotated every other night, but all others changed daily.

To each slave was given 3½ pounds of salt fish per head per week, and between four and six quarts of "farrinaceous" food. Heads of gangs[11] received double this amount, while children under fourteen years of age received half. Out of crop time the slaves were given one glass of rum daily; but during crop or the rainy season, they were given three drams of rum.[12] As regards clothing, the allowances were for each slave were as follows:

MALES	FEMALES
2 shirts, 2 trousers	1 Oznaburgh & 1 woollen petticoat
1 cloth jacket or wrapper	1 woollen wrapper, 2 shifts
1 hat, 1 woollen bonnet or cap	1 hat, 1 Kilmarnock cap
1 blanket every two years	1 blanket every two years

Heads of gangs received double this amount; and presents were given to well- behaved slaves.[13]

It is clear, from the report of the Protector, that the food was inadequate, of poor quality, and that it would need to be supplemented. One also needs to bear in mind that what the law prescribed was not necessarily implemented. This is as true of clothing as of food. Since there is nothing to the contrary, and in the light of later provisions, the clothing allowance also seems inadequate for a whole year. But these provisions were based on assumptions about the needs of the slaves; and to slave owners, those needs were always minimal. The amount of work seems to have been much too great and for too long a period on the whole, except for task work which must have required monumental effort to complete in the allotted time. And one cannot help concluding that the task for women with infants constituted a severe hardship.

By the Order in Council of February 2, 1830, the Governor was empowered to make regulations for Sunday labour, as well as for the punishment of slaves. The proclamation, which Governor Grant issued on April 22, 1830, was so defective, on this and other points, that the Secretary of State demanded the framing of a new proclamation. For instance, Murray observed that the proclamation did not precisely define "works of necessity", nor stipulate any hours for the drying of coffee or cocoa. He questioned whether the latter duties, together with the casking of sugar, might not be safely postponed. With respect to punishment, he refused to sanction bed stocks at night for women as injurious to their health, or the confining of women for one hour at midday which, he believed, encroached on the period of daily rest. Of the fourteen sections of the Proclamation, some six sections were found to be defective in whole or in part, and therefore needing to be amended. The conclusion he reached was that the Governor had not only exceeded his authority, but had deviated from the Order in Council in allowing magistrates to add to the punishments which might be inflicted by owners. Apart from this he regarded as unsatisfactory the eighth and ninth clauses which seemed to allow the magistrates unlimited authority.[14] Grant's proclamation in fact seems to have been an accommodation to the views of the slave owners, and might even have been drawn up by officials with planting interests. As will be seen later, a similar proclamation was rejected under the 1831 Order. A later proclamation dated February 1831 indicated the times of Sunday labour and the amounts to be paid to the slaves.[15]

A recurrent complaint of slave owners, and one of the matters on which positive action was proposed during this period, concerned the problem of runaway slaves. The manner in which Governor Grant sought to curb the evil of *marronage,* as it was called, was to issue a circular authorising the Commandants of Quarters to undertake expeditions in search of possible maroons. The Governor imposed a number of restrictions, some of which would not have prevented planter violence. For example, no expedition was to be undertaken unless at least three slaves were being sought. Violence was to be avoided as far as possible, and the slaves were only to be fired on if they offered serious resistance. Their camps, huts, and cultivation were to be completely destroyed. The ringleaders, if captured, were to be committed to stand trial; while less culpable slaves might be punished by the Commandants themselves.[16] This circular posed a number of problems. In Trinidad society, as it was in 1830, unwillingness to return to the estates or hesitation on the part of the slaves might easily have been interpreted as serious resistance. The slaves need not have resorted to the use of force. Moreover, the action suggested would not only have eradicated such maroon camps as were encountered; it would have aggravated those tensions and disorders which would have accompanied slave raids in search of food. Apart from these, the circular omitted to state the punishment for *marronage*; so that punishments inflicted by the Commandants might well have conflicted with the spirit and intent of the ameliorative process. Fortunately, there is no record of any expedition being undertaken, suggesting that Grant's proposals might never have been put to the test.

ADMINISTRATION OF THE LAW

As had happened before, the operation of the judicial system posed serious problems with respect to certain aspects of the programme, in that influential members of the courts frustrated the process. In April 1830, one Francisco Benites was charged with the whipping of a female slave, but the judges were divided as to whether the offence was a misdemeanour. Those who opposed its being considered a misdemeanour, based their opinion on the fact that the slave was neither owned nor employed by Benites, and that the assault did not originate in any matter concerning slavery. As a result, a fine of £5 was imposed on Benites, who was convicted of simple assault.[17] Four months later, there was a similar case before the courts. On this occasion also the judges were divided, but with this difference – they were uncertain whether the law applied to domestic slaves.[18] The Secretary of State, Sir George Murray, deprecated the proceedings in both cases, declaring the latter to be unsupported by the Order in Council, but in the case of the former he lacked sufficient information to justify any firm conclusion. However he advised the Governor to adopt such measures as were likely to prevent the recurrence of such misconceptions.[19]

On the other hand a dispute arose as to the type of cases in which the Protector was required to prosecute. The Judge of the Court of Criminal Inquiry was of the opinion that the Attorney General was the one to prosecute for serious offences, while the Protector was to prosecute for misdemeanours. The Chief Justice and the Attorney General disagreed with this opinion. The problem here was that none of the ameliorative orders had defined the Protector's roles clearly enough. As a result, the framers of the Order in Council had created the difficulty which others were experiencing in administering the law. The Governor thought that the Protector of Slaves should prosecute in cases involving slaves against free people; while in cases in which both plaintiff and defendant were slaves, the Attorney General should prosecute and the Protector defend.[20] Here was a matter which needed urgent attention; for as long as the dispute lasted, trials were likely to be aborted.

Almost a year elapsed, however, before a reply was received from the Colonial Office in response to a request for clarification; and this delay, a recurrent feature of the period, could be considered one of the factors contributing to the deficient operation of the amelioration process as a whole. The Secretary of State proposed a procedure whereby the Protector was to appear on the slave's behalf, in all civil or criminal cases, whether the slave was plaintiff or defendant. "The Protector should be rather the friendly Agent than the professional Advocate of the slave," not superseding the Attorney General or the other officers of justice in the exercise of their duties. But in cases of slave versus slave, the accused was to have the Protector's assistance in criminal cases; while in civil cases, the Protector was to act as mediator in order to prevent the slave expending his property in the cost of litigation. If he were unsuccessful, the Protector was to help the one who most deserved his services.[21] On the face of it, this was the same position expressed by the Governor; but the dispatch did not have the force of law and, as long as it remained an opinion, the local courts were under no obligation to adhere to that procedure.

Clearly, then, a change in the administration of the law was necessary if the slaves were to have the real benefit of the amelioration process. A certain measure of change did result from an Order in Council of June 20, 1831,[22] whereby the Courts of Criminal Prosecutions and of First Instance were reconstituted to form one court comprising three judges, none of whom was to be a slave holder. In this new Court, the three judges were to be associated with three assessors, chosen from the Cabildo of Port of Spain. Complete equality accorded all the judges, and the requirement of a majority vote for convictions, caused the undoing of this Court after the promulgation of the Order in Council of November 1831.[23]

The two existing Puisne Judges had, as indicated in chapter 1, conveyed their property to relatives and had thereby gained the confirmation of their appointments. In so confirming them, Secretary of State Goderich had undermined the effectiveness of the administration of the slave law. Neither of them could have been considered an uninterested person; and since there were no similar restrictions against the assessors owning slaves, the arrangement was fraught with danger. Here was a court, composed largely of slave owners or persons interested in slaves, yet charged with responsibility for administering a slave code heavily weighted in favour of the slaves. It may be that the officials at the Colonial Office had thought that slave owners would have taken a greater interest in their slaves' welfare by this time; but the amelioration programme turned out to be unpalatable to them, since they continued to regard it as an interference with their authority vis-a-vis their property.

The ownership of slaves by public officials, and by officers administering the slave law was nothing new,[24] and it resulted in an inability to give impartial attention to slave amelioration. In 1831 the records of the Registrar of Slaves disclosed no fewer than forty-one public officials in possession of slaves. Of these the most outstanding were: the Governor's Assessor, Antonio Gomez, with 85 plantation slaves; the Governor's Secretary with 65; the Acting Chief Judge, Lewis Johnston, with 84; the Attorney General, Henry Fuller, with 343; the Colonial Treasurer, Henry St. Hill, with 71; Francisco Llanos, Defender of the Absent and later a Puisne Judge, with 12; and the Jail Physician, Thomas Neilson, with 102. All other public officers owned between 1 and 44 personal slaves, either individually or in partnership with others.[25] All of these would have been personally concerned with the "due subordination" of the slaves towards their masters; and the extent of their involvement in slavery quite naturally would have had some bearing on the extent of their impartiality.

★★★★★

An important change, involving the restructuring of the Protector's office, was proposed in 1831 and eventually carried into effect in 1833. In a dispatch, which loudly proclaimed his ignorance of the geography of the colony, Goderich suggested that the Protector make a circuit of the island every fortnight in order to investigate complaints made to him.[26] The proposal failed to get the support of the Protector of Slaves, who saw shortage of time and the inaccessibility of some parts of the island as presenting considerable difficulties. Nevertheless, he was sufficiently accommodating to recommend, as an alternative, the division of the island into seven circuits. The frequency of his visits was to vary from once every two months – for those circuits which were easily accessible, to once every six months – for more remote areas.[27]

The plan did not commend itself to the Council. The two chief speakers during debates on this matter – Henry Fuller and William Burnley – saw the change as an unnecessary one. Burnley observed that the Governor had no authority to appoint a Deputy or Acting Protector, and that the Order required the Protector to perform his duties in person and not by a deputy. He made the further observation that the Protector was the only one authorised to prosecute on behalf of slaves, to which must be added the office of Solicitor General; and concluded that that officer could not perform all these duties while going on a circuit.[28] It is obvious that Burnley had forgotten, or perhaps had chosen to forget, that a similar breach of the same principles had taken place during the tenure of some of the same Council members, including himself. For between 1819 and 1821, the Registrar of Slaves was away on sick leave and his functions were performed by his son, Edward Murray, whom the Governor had appointed to act as Registrar. But the real fear was not the possible contravention of the Order in Council; it was more likely the result of the Protector's investigations.

Fuller showed greater concern for keeping the slaves to their tasks. Reminding the Council that the Protector's presence was necessary in cases of disputed manumissions, he argued that owners would be deprived of the slaves' services if the Protector were to go on circuit. On the other hand, he contended that slaves going from the rural districts to complain, and not finding the Protector, were likely to be considered runaways because they would not have received a pass from him. Passing on to the problem which really seemed to disturb him, Fuller then pointed out that such circuits would encourage complaints, and that the investigations which resulted from them were certain to be time consuming. Not only would the circuits have been expensive, they would have rendered the latest Order in Council a dead letter. In what way this would have happened Fuller did not explain; and we can only conclude, from the tenor of his arguments, that his only objective was to frustrate whatever benefits the Colonial Secretary intended the slaves to obtain from the proposal. Yet Fuller was one of those officials on whose shoulders rested a great deal of the responsibility for the success of the ameliorative programme.

The conclusions reached by the Council at the end of the debate leave no doubt as to their unwillingness to adopt the proposed plan. They clearly rejected even the modified plan which Gloster, a member of the same Council, had recommended. The resolutions of the Council stated: that it was inadvisable for the Protector to leave the seat of Government and the majority of the slave population; that the appointment of a Deputy Protector was absolutely necessary; that travelling expenses were likely to be a burden on the colony's Treasury; and finally, that when he was reminded of the existence of Assistant Protectors, Goderich would withdraw his plan.[29] How far Gloster had been won over by the rest of the Council it is not easy to say; but his participation in such a discussion was not likely to leave his impartiality unimpaired. It was only by the Order of November 1831 that Goderich's proposals were eventually introduced.

The acting Governor at the time, Sir Charles Smith, had his own plan in which the offices of Protector and Registrar of Slaves were to be combined. Aiming at economy, Sir Charles was of the view that the combination of these offices would have resulted in an overall reduction of the colony's excessive expenditure, which he attributed to the duplication and overpayment of public officers. In this combination of offices, the Protector was to function as the principal officer and the Registrar as his Deputy. The principal was to perform all the duties formerly divided between the two officers, thus freeing the Deputy to undertake the tours proposed by Goderich. Smith made allowances for only three circuits, with the frequency of the tours varying from monthly to half-yearly. The existing expenses for the two officers amounted to £2,423. 6. 6½; whereas, consequent on the combination, the expenses amounted to £2,576.13.4, an excess of merely £153. 6. 9½. The saving, in terms of fees to the Registrar, would have been one third of £1900.[30] In his view all that was necessary to give effect to this plan was an Order in Council uniting both offices, and giving the Governor the authority to make subsidiary rules. The offices were eventually united in 1832, Goderich reducing the overall cost to £2560.[31]

Long before the Colonial Office dealt with this matter, the Order in Council of November 1831 arrived in Trinidad. In responding to a variety of objections raised, Goderich conceded that the arguments of Fuller and Burnley, if they were based on legal grounds and on knowledge of the island, were unanswerable. He turned the tables on them, however, when he pointed out that the plan had originated in the planters' complaints about the inconvenience and loss which resulted from the slaves' having to travel to Port of Spain in order to make reports to the Protector. In the new proposals contained in the Order, he envisaged a Protector resident in Port of Spain with, at least, one Assistant in the south.[32] This latter officer was to do the circuits at very little expense; slaves in the vicinity of Port of Spain could report to the Protector who, in a few days' time, could reach those a little further away. Those slaves who were resident in Toco or Mayaro could be visited by either officer with equally little expense.[33] Expensive or otherwise, the Trinidad planters of 1832 were not disposed to facilitate the amelioration programme; and, as we shall see, the prevailing hostility and confusion did not permit the Protector to perform his duties properly.

THE LAST SLAVE AMELIORATION ORDER

Nine days before Goderich's letter was written, a new Order in Council was published in the colony.[34] This new code was to bring into the open an opposition on the part of the slave owners which was far more virulent than was the case with the earlier ameliorative Orders. This "121-pronged scourge," as it was called,[35] was by far the most comprehensive of the Orders aimed at ameliorating slavery; and, in its provisions, previous regulations were strengthened and newer, tougher ones introduced. For example, under the new code, neither the Protector nor any member of his family was to hire slaves as domestics, unless it was impossible for them to acquire the services of free persons. The Protector was authorised to visit any plantation or hut and talk to the slaves. But those slaves who wished to go to the Protector to complain were required to have a pass from their owner or manager; and intimidation of slaves by their owners was deemed a misdemeanour. For the first time, provision was made for the investigation of the sudden and sometimes peculiar death of slaves. The Order provided that inquests were to be held ; and free persons were, on pain of a fine of £10, to report any sudden deaths of which they were aware to the Protector.

Sunday labour for profit was forbidden, except for domestic labour by regular domestics, or for necessity – a term which specifically excluded agricultural labour. The flogging of male slaves was limited to fifteen lashes, to be inflicted only after a minimum of six hours had elapsed. A new departure was made by the provision that such punishments could now be witnessed by one free person or three adult slaves. [36] Slave evidence was to be accepted as that of free persons, a provision which finally removed the necessity for certificates of competence, and did not make such evidence discretionary. False accusations by slaves were punishable only after conviction in a court of law, the penalties for all slaves being three months' imprisonment with hard labour or thirty-nine lashes for male slaves.

Slaves were also declared competent to marry, provided that they had a licence from the Protector of Slaves and the prior consent in writing from their owners. Marriage could be performed by any clergyman of the Church of England, minister of the Kirk of Scotland, any Roman Catholic priest, or any teacher of religion who functioned only as a schoolmaster. The marriage of slaves to free persons was permitted, except where consanguinity prevented it, and where such marriages did not rob the master of his rights to the services of the slave.[37]

Owners and managers were required to provide a specific quantity of food and clothing for their slaves. They were given the option of indicating, during the first week of January each year whether they intended to maintain the slaves by the provision of food or by cultivation of the land. As regards the former, slaves over ten years of age were to receive weekly twenty-one pints of either wheat flour, meal of Guinea corn or Indian corn; or fifty-six plantains; or fifty-six pounds of yams; as well as seven herrings or "shads". Those under ten years of age were to receive half that amount, which was to be given to their mothers. The food provided was to be "sound and fit for consumption," as well as of good commercial value; and slaves were to be provided with the means of preserving it.[38]

Those owners, who wished to maintain their slaves by allotting them provision grounds, were to give each slave over fifteen years of age half an acre of land, provided it was no more than two miles from the slave's residence. Each slave who was under fifteen years of age was allotted a quarter of an acre of land to be given to the slave's father or mother, or some other slave responsible for the child. The owners were to supply the tools and seeds; and they were not to dispossess the slaves until they had reaped their crops, while the crops were declared the absolute property of the slaves. These slaves were to have forty days per year in forty consecutive weeks to look after their grounds.

The clothing allowance recommended by the new Order was hardly different from that existing previously. The differences were as follows: whereas in the past adult slaves were allowed a hat and cap, they were now allowed a hat only. Blankets were to be provided annually instead of once in two years. Female slaves were to receive two gowns or wrappers instead of the one woollen wrapper previously allowed; and all adult slaves were given two pairs of shoes. This item was not mentioned in the Protector's report of 1830, but it does not necessarily mean that they received none. Male slaves also received a knife and a razor, while female slaves each received a pair of scissors.[39] The allowance for slaves under the age of fifteen was approximately half that of those over fifteen. In addition each family was allowed one saucepan, one kettle, or pot, or cauldron.[40]

There are two interesting points to be made regarding the foregoing provisions. In the first place, it is significant that it was actually stipulated that the food should be good and fit to eat; this seems to imply that less than an acceptable quality of food was given to the slaves by some persons. It is a well established fact that the salted cod usually imported from New Foundland was considered unfit for consumption by anyone else.[41] And this was probably the first serious attempt to regulate the diet of the slaves in Trinidad. In the second place, the clause regarding slave grounds declared the produce to be the "absolute property" of the slave. No restriction was placed on the slaves' growing the staple crop, sugar.[42] The possibility, therefore, that the slaves might not have been allowed the enjoyment of their labour was precluded – at least on paper.

Daily labour was fixed at twelve hours' duration, and this included the obligatory period of three hours for rest and meals. Females under fourteen years of age, or over sixty, were not to work in the fields; labour at night was permitted for manufacturing, provided that the slaves worked for no more than nine hours altogether.[43] By this Order slaves were entitled to free time to allow them to attend religious services within a radius of six miles from the estates on which they lived, provided that they were not absent for more than six hours. In a specifically liberal provision, they were to be allowed to attend divine worship on Sundays, Christmas day and Good Friday in any place belonging to the Church of England, Church of Scotland, or that of any other minister licensed by the governor. No slaves were to be allowed in any place of worship between the hours of 7.00 in the evening and 5.00 in the morning.[44] Every owner or manager who had forty or more slaves was required to engage the services of a medical practitioner. If he had less than forty, he was at liberty to share with another proprietor the services of the physician. The latter was to keep a detailed, fortnightly journal of his visits to the estates. Finally slaves were declared competent to purchase and dispose of property, provided that such property did not include slaves, boats, arms, and ammunition.

In transmitting the Order to Trinidad, Goderich explained painstakingly that the draft had been discussed with representatives of the West Indies in London. The final draft, therefore, had taken note of their comments and suggested corrections. In a detailed review of ameliorative efforts to date, he expressed the government's determination that the law must at last be vigorously carried into effect. Frustrated that no jurisdiction in the West Indies had adopted all the portions of the law or indicated an intention of doing so, he also criticised Trinidad in which he alleged that ill considered Proclamations and continual referrals to the Colonial Secretary had defeated the former law. As a result, some things had been determined in order to remove from Governors the discretion formerly given to them. In further explaining his position, he asserted: "This law ... proceeds throughout on the assumption that unlimited power will be abused, and ... supposes the necessity of subjecting the authority of an owner over his slaves to a constant and vigilant controul." A new philosophy began to emerge in the following statements: "Whatever property exists, or has ever existed in the Colonies, is the direct fruit of the labour of the Slaves." And later: "Property in inanimate matter and property in a rational being, cannot stand precisely on the same basis." A few days later, he added the observation that slave owners demanded a measure of respect which no man should give to another.[45] It was the most significant assessment of slavery to date, and was as clear a threat of emancipation as anyone made at that time.

REACTIONS TO THE ORDER

The Order was greeted with loud protests - initially from the Cabildo, which at that time was composed entirely of British personnel, none of whom could be identified as a capitulant. Their protest, which did not differ in substance from that of 1824, showed the common tendency to appeal to laws and precedents which did not apply to those who made use of them.

Thus they petitioned the Governor for some consideration for the pledge given to the capitulants that their rights, properties and religion would remain inviolate. They further claimed that the new Order had limited labour to an unprecedented extent, and in a manner that was not necessary for protecting the health and comfort of the slave. Appealing in vain to the Laws of the *Partidas* and of the Indies, they asked that the Order in Council be suspended until the King's pleasure be known.[46]

Protest meetings were the order of the day, as various groups of inhabitants sought to make their views known on this annoying subject.[47] They accused the British Government of violating the terms of the treaty of Capitulation and, in addition, of interfering with the master's rights of private property. A conciliatory chord was struck in Port of Spain, when a meeting of inhabitants proposed that there should be ten hours of agricultural labour and twelve of manufacturing labour during crop time; and that thirty free days per year, "including the four great festivals," be granted to the slaves.[48] Governor Grant declined to entertain the proposals, sent to him from this meeting, on the ground that he had no discretion in the matter;[49] but offered to represent the case of the delegation to the Colonial Secretary. Not satisfied with what they considered his refusal, the inhabitants of Port of Spain re-assembled in anything but a peaceful manner; one member was so rash as to propose that no further taxes be paid. After some time, this meeting approved a petition to the King seeking to have the right of the Protector or his assistant to enter slave houses limited to cases where complaints had been made. They pressed for acceptance of the proposals that the times of labour be fixed at ten hours' agricultural or twelve manufacturing labour daily; that the slaves be given a maximum of thirty days free in return for an allowance of three and a half pounds of salt fish; that "domestic" punishment be increased to twenty-five lashes; that the regulation of food and clothing be left to the Council; and finally that the clause refusing appeals for fines over £100 be rescinded.[50]

In the meetings which took place intermittently throughout 1832, various efforts were made to counteract this last ameliorative experiment. At one of these meetings, the slave proprietors accepted a motion by Edward Jackson, a lawyer, calling for someone to be appointed their representative to England. This person was to have "such full powers and authorities as might be necessary for the purpose of enabling him to protect and forward their interests, on all occasions, in the manner most useful and beneficial to the community".[51] The meeting then chose as their representative William Burnley, a leading planter and merchant, one of the most outspoken members of the Council, and a vociferous opponent of abolition.[52] A subsequent meeting, called to discuss an alleged act of misconduct by the island's agent,

Joseph Marryat, jr.,[53] adopted three resolutions as follows: the first stated, *inter alia*, that the Order in Council could not be enforced in Trinidad without ruining both master and slave. The second declared that Marryat could no longer remain the colony's agent. The third refused the boon offered by the British Government for assurance that the Order was in force in the island, the acceptance of which might imply submission to, or acquiescence in, the Order in Council, until their proposed modifications had been accepted.[54] This boon was the offer of a reduction of sugar duties for any colony in which the Order in Council had been implemented. However, the resort to venality failed of its intended effect in Trinidad and elsewhere.

At one of the first meetings of the inhabitants held in 1832, a small number of free coloured persons had been named to a newly formed Standing Committee of the slave proprietors.[55] The persons so selected had at first declined on the ground that such action as was contemplated would have been inconsistent with their own chosen course of action.[56] At the last meeting of that year, however, no fewer than fifteen of them were present, including a Dr. Philip. Up to a point, therefore, whites and the wealthier free coloured proprietors had become united in a common cause – opposition to the Order in Council of November 1831. On this occasion also, Henry Fuller – the former Attorney General - championed a tough line of action, suggesting that the Order be rejected or, alternatively, that slaves be compelled to work for twelve hours daily during the approaching crop.[57] The position taken by Fuller in this discussion cannot simply be put down to his recent loss of the office of Attorney General. Fuller seemed all along to have been an opponent of abolition; and, as will appear shortly, one of the improper cases before the courts involved the ill treatment of slaves on his own estate.

The meeting at which Fuller expressed his hostility to the new Order was steered back to a moderate course by Edward Jackson, whose four resolutions were unanimously adopted. These expressed the hope that the Government would give more sympathetic consideration to the evil circumstances which were sure to accompany the enforcement of the Order. They declared the firm commitment of those present to be guided by the Order in Council of February 2, 1830, until the Order of November 1831 had been modified. The free coloured spokesman, Dr. Phillip, pledged the willingness of his group to join their fellow-colonists in every measure aimed at the colony's prosperity. Their previous hesitation, he explained, was due to their unwillingness to oppose the wishes of Government on frivolous grounds, and to their belief that the Order would have operated without material injury to the community. But the experience of months had convinced them that it was their duty to oppose it by every means in

Noel Titus

their power.[58]

The entire proprietorial community, by their representatives, having now declared their opposition to the Order, the future of the programme under this new Order looked bleak. The opposition of the slave owners was aggravated in part by the agitation caused by another matter which was engaging public attention at the same time. In February 1832, a proclamation had been issued by Governor Grant aiming at the manumission of all slaves who had been illegally imported from Barbados and other islands.[59] Slave trials and planter protests occupied a considerable part of this year. In the midst of this protest, there were complaints about slaves leaving the estates on which they worked without the necessary passes; and that they refused to work on one occasion because they believed themselves to have been overworked.[60]   There were reports that some managers had been giving up in disgust because of the breakdown of discipline on the estates.[61] A writer, calling himself a "Perplexed Manager", complained of such trouble in the gang he supervised that he pleaded for the Order in Council to be explained to all slaves by a sworn interpreter sent by the Protector of Slaves for that purpose. According to him, inordinate demands for increased allowances of fish, rum, and time off eventually led to the neglect of the animals.[62] The "perplexed manager" suggests an important issue, which is, that there might have been a real language problem for some proprietors as well as for slaves.

The unrest in the slave population was reflected in a series of incidents which the press highlighted. Fire had broken out on the Concord estate in south Trinidad, destroying thirty-five acres of corn. There were also outbreaks of fire in Petit Bourg in north Trinidad, and on the Retrench estate.[63] All these fires were blamed on the slaves and reprisals were demanded. In the St. Joseph district over a period of one week, there was great loss of property on the estate of Noly Beaubrun, a free coloured proprietor. The gate of his estate was removed and placed in the road; five of his mules and nine of his cattle had been poisoned. The *Port of Spain Gazette* accused the slaves of thus avenging themselves because they had been unsuccessful in their demand for three free days per week.[64] This was a purely contrived explanation. Beaubrun was the planter against whom two of his slaves had complained of cruelty in 1823.[65] At that time the slaves had been punished for giving false information, although it is more likely that the Governor and his investigators were concerned only with defending someone whom they regarded under the circumstances as a fellow planter. His lack of cruelty was never established, and the action attributed to his slaves on this occasion was probably their retaliation against cruel treatment. Trinidad slave society was like a volcano on the verge of eruption.

OFFICIALS PROTEST

A serious obstacle to the operation of this Order was the interruption of a slave trial by one of the Alcaldes, in whose view the matters brought before the court were frivolous. An attempt to get the other Alcalde to sit in the trials was also unsuccessful, and the court was forced to adjourn, to the delight of the reporter.[66] This situation resulted from the change in judicial proceedings under the new Order in Council. Under that of March 1824, offences against slaves were to be tried in the Court for the Trial of Criminal Prosecutions. This clause had to be amended in order to conform to the Order of September 1822, where the Court of Criminal Inquiry was required to examine the evidence and determined whether it was strong enough to send the case to trial. But serious offences going before the Court of Criminal Inquiry seldom got any further. The newly constituted Supreme Court, before which cases were to be tried under the Order of November 1831, was bound to be rendered useless by the absence of the Alcaldes who had equal votes with the professional judges. The Alcaldes were not precluded from being slave owners, and some of the judges could not properly be excluded from that class.

It is now necessary to ask whether the cases were really as frivolous as the alcaldes claimed they were. In the first case under the new court – Rex v. Marie Catherine Vesprey – Browne, the second Alcalde, walked out of court and refused to be a party to what he termed the "persecution" of the defendant. In his prepared address to the court,[67] he objected to the criminality of "frittering away" the court's time to the detriment of the owner whose authority the slave was encouraged to defy. In addition, he considered that such trials only incurred great expense; and so he refused to let himself be used to injure the inhabitants of the colony.[68] Browne was saying, in effect, that he could not serve two masters; and it can reasonably be concluded that the welfare of the slaves weighed less heavily in his balances than the interests of the planters.

Why was this trial considered a persecution? According to Browne the accused, charged with striking a female slave with a "switch," had been the victim of gross provocation. Not only was the slave disobedient, but she was also obscene. She had thrown a vessel with urine into her mistress' face, and "exposed her person" in the face of her mistress and of the latter's husband. In all of this the Alcalde implied that both victims of the outrage had done nothing – a remarkable display of patience, if it were true. The complaint of the slaves under the existing circumstances could not be discharged by either the Protector of Slaves, the Judge of the Court of Criminal Inquiry, or any persons holding office under the Crown, he reasoned. Therefore he determined that those who were not dependent on the Government had the responsibility of discouraging any prosecutions which might appear both "impolitic" and "unjust."[69] What the alcalde did not explain was why a pro-slavery judge should send the case for trial after taking the evidence in the Court of Criminal Inquiry.

The first Alcalde declined to sit when called upon by the Chief Justice to do so. He was of the view that the 115th clause, which named the Supreme Court as the place for such trials was "ruinous". Since more serious offences were tried in the courts of the Alcaldes, he deemed it necessary to put an end to the system.[70] The Chief Justice, who was a recent arrival in the colony[71] and did not enjoy much popularity, believed that the case against three of the accused – Dessources, McChesney, and Robbins – was far from slight. But the indictment against McChesney had been so framed "as to afford the defendant a very reasonable prospect of acquittal".[72] This report was a sad reflection on Henry Fuller, then Attorney General, who was at once the framer of the complaint and the owner of the estate of which McChesney was manager.[73] Robbins, who was indicted on another charge, was Commandant of the Quarter of Chaguanas and a former Assistant Protector. He it was who dismissed the complaint against McChesney.[74]

In spite of their claim always to contribute to the administration of justice in the colony, and of their claim to neutrality with respect to the action of the two Alcaldes,[75] the Cabildo as a body must have supported the action of the two officers. There was not a word of censure from that body, nor any representation of regret at their disruption of the court. The Governor, however, disapproved of the course taken by the Alcaldes, preferring that their judgement should have been given on the cases in the normal way.[76] The Chief Justice had argued that the case had been unfairly prejudged since, prior to the trial, the officers in question could not have been acquainted with the facts. Such action, he thought, implied a distrust of the senior members of the court and assumed that they "were instruments to carry forward any ill-judged prosecution, which mistaken or crafty zeal might bring before them".[77] It would not be easy to reach a conclusion different from his – that there was collusion on the part of the Alcaldes; and members of the Cabildo as a whole were probably aware of what was afoot. The fact that neither the Chief Justice nor the Governor took any action against the offending alcaldes would seem to suggest that the law provided no sanction for the failure of any officer to perform his duties. If that were the case, the omission was a critical oversight.

INCENTIVE FOR COMPLIANCE

In the middle of 1832, while the opposition of the slave owners was building up, the British Ministers announced the offer of a boon to those Crown colonies in which it was apparent that the Order in Council had been in full operation. This boon was to take the form of remission of some taxes, as suggested by the Governor and Council and/or Court of Policy of the colony.[78] Governor Grant applied for Trinidad's share of it, claiming that the Order had been in force, and requesting that the action of the two Alcaldes should not be held against the colony.[79] Grant's anxiety to receive the boon might well have been due to a desire on his part to appease the irate slave owners; for he could not honestly assert that the Order in Council was the acknowledged law following the disruption of the court. Before the boon could be granted, however, the Secretary of State asked for a statement from the public officers – the Judges, the Public Prosecutor, and the Protector of Slaves – as to whether the Order in Council was being generally observed, or whether on the other hand, it was disobeyed and resulted in the failure of prosecutions.[80]

The public officers were divided in their testimony which, cumulatively, belied the assurances given by the Governor. The Chief Justice, who qualified his statement by saying that he had only been in the colony for ten months, denied that the Order had been substantially in force. No prosecution, he reported, had been allowed to succeed, a circumstance he attributed to the disposition of persons to evade it, and not to the lack of offences against it. He recommended an inquiry to ascertain whether the non-enforcement might not have been "in some degree the consequence of defects in some of the local institutions of the colony". Among the points needing study were that the office of the Protector of Slaves was expensive and inadequate for the visits, which in any case were not attempted; and further that the Principal officer should hold no other office, not even that of Registrar of Slaves, since the triennial returns were sufficiently taxing to distract his attention during the period of registration. He should not have a seat on the Council either, the Chief Justice asserted, since that was likely to impair his impartiality, and might also prevent the easy access of the slaves to him. In addition, it would have been better if the officers had not been resident in the colony for any long period, and had not been in financial difficulties there. The Chief Justice identified a further difficulty in the operation of the Order, which related to Grant's proclamation defining offences of slaves. He considered them harsh and vague, depriving the slaves of the "mitigated scale of discipline granted them by the Order of 1831".[81] The combination of offices and their consequences, the plurality of offices, the need for aloofness from the planter class – all of these were points noted by critics of the system. The fact that the Colonial Office went ahead with the appointment to a joint office of Registrar/Protector in 1833 bears eloquent testimony either to the slight regard which that office had for these arguments, or to pressure from the abolitionists.

Of the other officers, Judge Bent, one of the Puisne Judges, declined any opinion as he had not been in the colony very long and because his duties had been confined to Port of Spain.[82] Judge Hanley, the other Puisne Judge, considered the Order to be in force as a law; but he observed that, since he assumed office, no criminal prosecutions were instituted for any offence.[83] However, Hanley failed to comment satisfactorily on the reason for this – that is, whether there were no offences at all, or whether prosecutions had been obstructed. Finally Hanley believed that the law could easily have been enforced and that no prosecutions would have been defeated by improper means. The learned Judge arrived at this opinion from the ease with which prosecutions had been conducted under the previous Order; but Hanley had not been in the colony long enough to make such a comparison. The acting Attorney General, Wylly, arrived at a similar opinion – that the Order was substantially in force because of the paucity and nature of the cases being dealt with.[84] But not only was Wylly confined by his duties to Port of Spain, as was Judge Bent; he must certainly have been aware of the opinions published in the newspapers, the opposition in the case of the illegally imported slaves, and the opposition to Grant who tried to enforce this Order. The atmosphere was clearly not an encouraging one.

Perhaps the most significant statement was that of the Protector of Slaves, who reported that the Order had been carried into execution – by which he probably meant that it had been duly proclaimed. His claim that it had met with no obstruction on the part of the proprietors or managers is anything but correct, given his involvement in the failed slave trials. His mis-statement is apparent in his next comment – that the 88th clause, which concerned food, was universally rejected by the slave proprietors; and that labour was sometimes carried on beyond the hours required by the law, on promise of compensation. Add to the foregoing his complaint that many planters did not allow the free days granted by the Order; or that the quota of shoes had not been delivered to the slaves;[85] and the conclusion to which one is inevitably led is that the planters and managers obstructed the operation of the Order. Gloster's testimony, therefore, is not reliable.

The slave owners themselves contributed their own testimony to the debate; but it did nothing to justify their getting the boon, which even the editor of the *Port of Spain Gazette* was anxious that the colony should receive.[86] A heated discussion over the alleged misconduct of Joseph Marryat, jr., concerned his assurance to the British Parliament that the Order in Council was in force in Trinidad. The unfortunate Agent was branded a traitor, since the Order had allegedly not been given a trial on his own estates – Union and Marabella - or that of any owner.[87] The meeting at which all of this was discussed passed two resolutions moved by Henry Murray, erstwhile Registrar of Slaves. The first of them declared that Marryat's statement was wholly unfounded, and that the Order could not have been enforced in Trinidad without ruin to both planters and slaves. The second asserted that Marryat could no longer continue as the colony's Agent. In his place, therefore, W.H. Burnley was elected. At the same time a resolution was passed refusing the boon until the modifications, previously suggested, had been made.[88] Sir George Hill, who had replaced Sir Lewis Grant as Governor, pleaded for favourable consideration for the colony on the ground that there had been marked improvement in the general attitude toward the slave law. [89] This in itself was due partly to modifications to the Order, and partly to the establishment of inferior courts for certain offences against the Order.[90]

It must not be thought that the only response to the Order was one of protest. The Assistant Protector of Naparima[91] reported that several proprietors were paying well for his attendance on their estates once per month, but that financial embarrassment prevented a general adoption of the system. During his tenure of office, there had not been any reports of severe cruelty. The slaves, he indicated, were "rapidly advancing in the scale of civilization – their moral character is improving fast – their knowledge of the essential principles of religion very considerable…" But even he echoed a usual argument of the slave owners that the "slaves were better off than the peasants in Ireland."[92]

By this time a slave school was in operation in the colony. According to Grant, this school was re-established in 1832;[93] but there is no indication as to when it was first established. This school had a roll of some forty-three pupils, of whom one was white, and twenty-one each belonged to the free coloured and slave groups. That there should have been a white child in the school is very surprising, since racial distinction and segregation in the society were very carefully observed, even while limited privileges were being extended to the free coloured by law. The school was divided into three classes, their syllabus consisting almost exclusively of the alphabet, spelling, and instruction from special reading books as well as the Catechism of the Church of England. This school was under the supervision of the rector of Port of Spain.[94]

In the midst of all the confusion of protests, the Council undertook consideration of the substitution of provisions of food and clothing required by the Order. But getting members to apply themselves to the task was by no means easy for the Governor. As early as June 1832, Grant complained of the unsatisfactory behaviour of the unofficial members of the Council, Dr. Francisco Llanos being the sole exception. And it is important to note his complaint that official members, who had resided in the colony for some time, were not supporting the improvements but joining the unofficial members in proposing amendments.[95] Yet it is from this quarter that the improvements, recommended by the Order, needed support if amelioration was not to go the way it did in the older colonies. This would suggest that those who had been in judicial or related functions, like Fuller and Henry Murray, had not been doing much to promote the policy.

With respect to the provision of food, the Council allowed for maintenance in three categories: for slaves who were to be maintained by grounds alone, or by provisions only, or partly by provisions and partly by grounds. In the first category, that regarding slaves to be maintained by grounds alone, slaves over ten years of age were to receive half an acre of land within two miles of their home, and forty days per year to cultivate it. In the second category, that regarding provisions only, those over ten years of age were to receive weekly a fixed amount of flour and root vegetables, along with 3½ pounds of good salted cod. In the third category, that regarding part provisions and part grounds, they were to receive 3½ pounds of salt fish weekly, and twenty-six days in twenty-six consecutive weeks to look after their grounds. Slaves under ten years of age, in any of the three categories were given half of the allowances of food, or of land and time for cultivation.[96]

With respect to clothing, the annual allowance was set out as follows:[97]

Males over 5 years of age	Females over 5 years of age
1 felt hat	1 felt hat
1 Scotch bonnet	1 wrapper
1 cloth wrapper or jacket	2 neck kerchiefs
2 red flannel Oznaburgh or check shirts	2 linen or cloth shifts
2 cloth trousers	2 doulas or Oznaburgh petticoats
1 knife	1 pair scissors

All slaves under five years of age were given a Scotch cap and 2 shirts or shifts. Every slave was given one tin pan or "pannekin" annually, one blanket every two years, or more often if necessary. It will be seen, by comparison, that the new arrangement was a little more generous than that put in place in 1830; but it was less so than that required by the Order. In addition, these substitutions made no provisions for shoes, or razor.

Under the Order of 1831, the Governor had the authority to define the offences for which slaves were to be punished. An Ordinance, based on one from Demerara, and prepared by Fuller and Gloster,[98] was published by Grant in May 1832. This list of offences was so exhaustive that it prompted from the Chief Judge the remark that, with little ingenuity, any act could be construed into an offence.[99] There were thirty-six offences in the proclamation; the first eighteen of these were punishable by twenty-five lashes for male slaves, or one month in jail, or ten days' solitary confinement. The others were punishable by thirty-nine lashes for male slaves, or two months in jail, or twenty-six days' solitary confinement. For the purpose of this ordinance, all judges and members of the Cabildo and Council were declared magistrates, with the exception of the Chief Judge, the Attorney General, and the Protector of Slaves. The magistrates were given jurisdiction over all offences, and the power of the Protector or his assistants.[100] Notwithstanding the possibility that some of the provisions might have been abused, the Governor recommended that the law be given a trial for a period of one year.[101] The Proclamation had actually exceeded the limit of fifteen lashes stipulated by the Order in Council.

In the years covered by this new policy, there were thirty marriages, twenty-two of which took place between January and June 1834, by which time emancipation was imminent. This was a marked improvement on the period between 1824 and 1827.[102] In this period there were 425 manumissions, of which 325 were gratuitous and 100 by purchase. The majority of these took place in 1832, in which there were 189 altogether.[103] The average price of manumissions varied between £51.4. 0 and £79. 11. 0. But the high price fixed by appraisers was still a serious cause of concern, especially where one figure of £120 was double the amount eventually paid;[104] and where the sum of £173. 6. 8 sterling could not be paid.[105] In the last case, the Colonial Office again objected to the use of the same two appraisers in two out of three valuations.

There were numerous complaints against, and prosecutions of, free persons. In the majority of cases the offence was the usual one of beating or ill-treating slaves. The majority of these cases were dismissed, some in questionable circumstances, leading the Colonial Office to criticise the performance of the Protector of Slaves. For example, the Protector's performance was questioned when he dismissed, with a warning, an owner who had overworked two women with young children.[106] On another occasion a sick slave was forced to cut grass; but when the complaint was brought before the Protector, he did not ask for a medical certificate. Again, a slave was beaten and tied and, in the words of a Colonial Office commentator, "the investigation was clearly insufficient". In one other instance, a slave lost an eye as a result of ill-treatment; the accused was acquitted, even though the evidence was not contradicted. The observation on this case was: "It is unnecessary to make any comment upon the uselessness of such an administration of the Slave Law."[107]

After the publication of the 1831 Order, there were 61 prosecutions of free people. In the first half of 1832 there were fifteen, of which no fewer than nine were affected by the refusal of the alcaldes to sit in the trials. Only two cases were completed.[108] In the second half of that year there were eleven prosecutions, all before the courts of the alcaldes; but no explanation was given for this, having regard to their protest against the use of the Supreme court for the trial of minor cases.[109] In the first half of 1833 there were six prosecutions, of which three were dismissed. While one merited dismissal, and another needed further investigation, the dismissal of the third could not be justified. One of these dismissals involved a man called Besson who, being a foreigner, "pleaded ignorance of the Order in Council." [110] Twenty-eight cases were tried in the second half 1833, fourteen before the judges and fourteen before the lower courts. Of these no fewer than twenty-two were for beating or ill-treating slaves. In one case, where a gang had not been given clothes for two successive years, the offender was punished for the current year, while the charge for the previous year was dismissed.[111] It was an erratic administration of the law. Of the six cases for the last six months on which the Protector reported, January to June 1834, four cases of assault and one of beating a female slave were dismissed by the alcaldes but no explanation was given by the Protector of Slaves. The other two were inconclusive, the Protector only noting that there was no appearance of the persons charged.[112]

The Savings Bank reflected a similar pattern of performance as it did between 1824 and 1829. The following table illustrates this, the amounts being quoted in pounds sterling:

Table XIII:
Activities of the Savings Bank, 1832 - 34

Period	Deposits	Withdrawals	Balance
At December 1832			£261.5.4
Jan. to June 1833	£109.4.0	182.5.2½	210.12.8
July to Dec. 1833	12.2.8	4.18.9	217.16.7
Jan. to June 1834	77.0.11	10.6.8	251.5.11

Source: Report of the Protector of Slaves for the period ending: December 1832 (C.O. 300/30); June 1833 (C.O. 300/31); December 1833 (C.O. 300/32); June 1834 (C.O.) 300/33)

Another attempt at amelioration had proven to be a failure, even though stronger measures had been adopted to ensure its successful operation. The downfall, in this case, was due to the consistent attack on the Order by the slave owners of the colony, and their determination to have their own way. The exercise revealed that the slave owners were not prepared to let themselves be coerced, though they grudgingly agreed to some of the proposed improvements. The disruption of the court for the trial of misdemeanours against the slave laws showed that the slave owners had on their side the alcaldes – members of the influential Cabildo – who were also members of the judiciary. With the failure of this measure, and with the change of economic attitudes discussed by Eric Williams in his *Capitalism and Slavery*, emancipation was clearly indicated.

8. The Final Experiment

Over twenty years of amelioration ended in 1834 with the formal abolition of the state of slavery in the West Indies. It was less a victory than an admission of failure. The process of amelioration, beginning with the registration of slaves in 1812, was neither welcome in Trinidad nor was it well administered. A Registrar of Slaves with interests in slaves, multiple offices, little zeal, and faced with uncooperative planters, produced information that was no useful guide to those who developed the scheme, based on the notion that there was widespread smuggling. The adoption of registration was forced on the old West India colonies when, by virtue of an Act of July 1819, unregistered slaves became liabilities.[1] Except for the Order in Council of February 1830, the ameliorative Orders, especially that of 1831, met with stiff opposition from slave owners in Trinidad. The first was rejected by those colonies which had independent legislatures under the old West India system, while it ran into difficulties in Trinidad. The last was forcefully opposed by planters in Trinidad, officers of the Courts, and free coloureds who had previously held aloof from the opposition spearheaded by the whites. In the case of this last Order, there was forceful reaction elsewhere – in Jamaica and St. Lucia. In the latter island, business was brought to a virtual standstill.[2]

Protest was also strong in the United Kingdom itself, where growing disaffection with the process of amelioration was evident in the division within the abolitionist movement, which resulted in the formation of the Agency Committee in 1831. By that time, James Stephen had concluded that there was no hope for amelioration. The lecture programme instituted by this Committee whipped up enthusiasm in a public already tired of the West India question as it was called. In May 1832, a Parliamentary Committee was set up to investigate the state of slavery in the West Indies, and to recommend such steps as might be taken for implementing the abolition of the system.[3] The new Parliament of that same year was actively concerned with reform; and the presence in it of Irish members lent considerable support to the abolitionist cause.

In such an atmosphere, and with a history of recalcitrance on the part of the slave owners in the West Indies, it was not long before Parliament passed resolutions in 1833 calling for the abolition of slavery. The resolutions proposed that a loan of fifteen million pounds be given to the West Indian proprietors by way of compensation for the loss of their slaves; that stipendiary magistrates be appointed at the expense of the Crown to administer justice in the islands; and that assistance be given to the colonial legislatures to enable them to provide for the moral and religious education of the soon to be ex-slaves.[4] These resolutions reflected a number of plans from various sources, all of which incorporated a period of apprenticeship varying between two and twelve years, and a proposal by the Secretary of State – Sir George Stanley – that the slaves make half yearly contributions to their own freedom.[5] The basic argument for these proposals was that the owners stood to lose their property by the emancipation of the slaves and had to be compensated as a result. Where slave owners and Government officials differed was whether the compensation should have been a gift or a loan. Neither side took note of the basic premise of the amelioration programme, which was, that the slaves were persons. And no one seemed inclined to consider any compensation to the slaves, who had been exploited and deprived of their freedom all their lives.

The resolutions of Parliament reached the Lt. Governor of Trinidad, Sir George Hill, towards the end of June 1833. No sooner had they become known in the island than the slave proprietors became apprehensive of unrest; but the Governor, apart from promising vigilance, did not appear to share their fears.[6] The slave owners rejected Stanley's proposals, which they regarded as the "production of a few hours' speculation substituted in a moment of hurried confusion." Somewhat hysterically they appealed to positive legislation – the laws of the *Partidas* and of the Indies, as well as the *Cedula* of 1783 – as protecting their property in slaves.[7] They challenged the right of the state to appropriate such property; demanded compensation from Britain for having drained from the colony all the material benefits of the system; and charged the ministers of the crown with acting under the pressure of public feeling.[8]

In a last ditch effort at opposition, they pointed to what they considered two major obstacles in the establishment of an "artificial society". The first was that the slaves themselves were not likely to submit to it; the second was that, if they did, capital for their profitable employment would not have been forthcoming. Concerned with their own profit, the proprietors observed that the cost of Police to coerce the apprentices to regular work would have exceeded the value of the crop raised. It was their claim that the only distinction which the slave recognised between himself and a free man was that one had to work, while the other might do as he pleased. True to their tendency always to see the worst in any plan for the improvement of the condition of the slaves, and ironically true, they saw Stanley's proposed loan rapidly disappearing into the pockets of creditors. So they concluded that although they lacked the power to resist the "unjust" measure, the people of Trinidad would acquiesce only as men unable to oppose or avoid violence.[9] The protest was an exercise in futility, rendered all the more pathetic by the appeal to laws which were no longer applicable.

By this time the West Indians in England had taken up the cudgels in one last desperate stand. Their protest revealed two concerns only – continued trade, from which they were the beneficiaries and, equally selfishly, the impending ruin of their dependents.[10] They were willing to support emancipation if it conformed to the gradualism implicit in the resolutions of May 15, 1823; but they urged the Government to give careful thought to the future state of the ex-slaves, the continued cultivation of the West Indies, and the preservation of the inhabitants' lives.[11] The reference to the future state of the ex-slaves, to which they appealed, usually veiled the belief that degradation would follow the grant of freedom. It was more than just an appeal to let things remain as they were; it was a reflection of their fundamentally negative view of the African.

The Act which formally abolished the state of slavery[12] provided for the emancipation of all slaves over six years of age on August 1, 1834. However, following the discussions between the interests concerned, it provided for a period of between four and six years' apprenticeship for domestic and plantation slaves respectively. The slaves were still required to work on their former owners' estates under conditions stated in the Act. After the process of the preceding twenty years, the Act surprisingly excluded them from "the performance of certain civil and military offices, and from the enjoyment of certain political franchises". Thus their freedom, when judged by the other restrictions in the Act, was merely a limited personal freedom.

Following the arrival of this Act in Trinidad, Lt. Governor Sir George Hill reported to the Secretary of State that the public was "prepared to receive the Measure of abolition with serenity and to give it fair play".[13] This was not strictly true although, by that time, the slave owners had lost a great deal of their fire. Several matters had to be disposed of, the first of them being the final registration of the slaves. With emancipation only a few months away, some members of the Council raised the question as to whether the inhabitants might have been spared the trouble and expense attendant on that exercise.[14] But the Governor, considering that the registration was as important for the apprentices as it was for the slaves, determined that it should be completed for the safety of the owners.[15] Compensation for the "loss" of their slaves was a matter of far greater importance to the slave owners, so the numbers were crucial.

To carry into effect the provisions of the Act relative to this matter, a body of local Commissioners was set up. This body comprised the Governor, the Attorney General – Stephen Rothery, Henry Murray – a former Registrar of Slaves, J.W. Hobson and Thornton Warner, presumably a local planter. The main task of this Commission was twofold: to determine the number of slaves who actually were in the colony, and to calculate the average value of each slave in the colony for the eight years ending December 1830.[16] The first of these tasks proved to be an embarrassment in that the last triennial registration had taken place in 1831, but that the registers had not yet been completed; and, in any case, the date of completion still seemed to be somewhat distant. The fault, however, was not attributed to the Registrar. The Commissioners explained that there were 2,500 proprietors in the colony, each having to submit a separate return. These had to be collected and compared first with the previous returns of each proprietor, and secondly, with the returns of the former owner of any slave recently acquired. In addition, they explained with great justice, that the annexation of the offices of Protector and Registrar of Slaves had left the Protector with little time for dealing with the registration process.[17] The Governor asked the Protector to expedite matters, so that he might be able to send to London the appraised value of slaves for 1823 – 1830. Unfortunately up to one year later, the registers had not been completed, and the claims of many slave owners could not be settled.[18]

For the sake of convenience the colony was divided into eight districts, each with two valuers. These valuers were instructed to visit their districts on August 1, 1834, divide the ex-slaves into their proper classes and appraise them. The classification was to correspond with the Registry, and was to include runaways whose existence after 1832 had been proved.[19] It was also to include any slaves who were freed by virtue of the third clause of the Act of 1833, which stated that any slave carried to the United Kingdom before the passage of the Act was automatically free. Considering that the registers for 1831 were not complete, it is difficult to understand how they were to make the comparisons required of them.

Such valuations as they made ranged from £25 sterling for the aged or incapacitated to £170 sterling for "head people", a term embracing overseers or heads of gangs. The following table provides the various classifications and valuations arrived at:

Table XIV:
Classification and Valuation of Slaves, 1834

Praedial attached and unattached   Non-praedial

Classification	£ Sterling	Classifciation	£ Sterling
Head People	170	Head Tradesmen	150
Tradesmen	150	Inferior Tradesmen	130
Inferior Tradesmen	130	Field Labourers	110
		Inferior People	110
		Head Domestics	130
Inferior field labourers	90	Inferior domestics	90

Source: Port of Spain Gazette, July 15, 1834.

From the foregoing it should be observed that, on the whole, the labourer engaged in agriculture or manufacturing work brought a higher price than his counterpart in domestic work.

COMMUNICATING THE CHANGE

One of the important tasks to be performed before emancipation day was that of explaining to all concerned the changed relationship of masters and ex-slaves. For this purpose, letters were specially prepared and circulated throughout the colony so as to dispel the doubts of both classes.[20] Subsequently, the Governor issued a proclamation advising the slaves that they were still expected to work for their former owners, who were thereafter to be designated their employers. They were not to leave the estates of their employers or managers without the permission of the latter, except to go to church or market. In their turn, employers were instructed that they could no longer punish the apprentices; that could only be done by the magistrates appointed.[21] While the latter were to secure to the apprentices their due, they were also to punish the negligent, the insolent, the insubordinate, and those who absconded. Each Commandant was required to have the Proclamation explained to every slave in his Quarter; and each owner or manager was to be provided with a copy of it for the same purpose. Great care was enjoined on them so as to ensure that the apprentices got no "erroneous impression or misapprehension of the operation of the Abolition of Slavery Act."[22]

The editor of the *Port of Spain Gazette* tendentiously explained the Act to the future apprentices in these terms:

> As from August 1ˢᵗ you will no longer be slaves but free men. You will be punishable only by the Magistrates after a trial. You only have to work six more crops for your master, after which you may leave the estate or even the island. But when your masters are unable to make you work for them, you cannot compel them to give you your allowance of clothing; to care for you when you are sick or aged; or to provide you with your house or garden. These things you must do for yourselves.

Then after a few lines he concluded: "It is therefore better for you as it is."[23] At the same time he contrasted Hill's proclamation with that of Governor Smyth in British Guiana on the same subject, which latter he considered better.[24] But there was more shadow than substance in his distinction.

Governor Hill actively participated in the instruction of the slaves, doing a tour of that area in which unrest was anticipated. The task seemed to him a difficult one since the great discontent shown by the slaves was a hindrance to his making them understand the distinction between slavery and apprenticeship. "The King having told them," he wrote with great irony, "that slavery was to be abolished on the 1ˢᵗ of August, they are too much disposed to discredit that His Majesty requires them to work for six years more."[25] While he took precautions to forestall any possibility of a disturbance, he completely lost sight of the slaves' perception of the injustice of a freedom that was so severely circumscribed.

The attitude of the slave owners, as far as this was represented by correspondence in the press, indicated that even at that time they continued to be ill-disposed towards the emancipation of the slaves. A variety of opposition was expressed in the local press. What marked these views was the tendency to emphasise control of the apprentices or to restrict their activities wherever possible. Because of the number of emancipated ex-slaves in the colony, one writer claimed that it was impossible to hire labourers without running the risk of harbouring runaways; and also that the ex-slaves were being encouraged to hire themselves out to the loss of their "owners". He therefore suggested the adoption of a system, which originated with the French, to the effect that the apprentice be given a small book in which would be inserted his name, profession, description, and age. The employer would retain the book during the time that the labourer was employed by him. When his term of service was completed, the book would be returned to him with entries as to his length of service and the satisfactory performance of his duties. There was also to be an entry as to whether he was indebted to his last employer. No apprentice was to be employed without his book. This, the writer explained, would have afforded a means of keeping a check on the labourers, detecting fraud practised on the employers, and reducing the loss attendant on absconding.[26] But the very nature of the proposals suggests how easy it would have been for an employer to prevent the labourers moving to more lucrative jobs simply by holding onto the book. In other words, the proposals could have resulted in an even more severe restriction of the freedom of the labouring population than the apprenticeship entailed.

Another writer styling himself "Tobin Bashe, jr.," recommended that every free person seeking labour should get a ticket and pass book from either the Chief of Police or the Commandant of Quarter. This pass book was to state the name, country, colour, occupation, and residence of the labourer. Entries similar to those proposed by the last writer, were to be made with respect to labour and also about the labourer's indebtedness. Anyone hiring an indebted labourer was to be responsible for the debt; and any labourer working without the pass book was to be fined and deprived of his wages. The whole process, he asserted, was to be supported by good vagrancy laws. "The two grand points are to secure ample encouragement and protection to free labourers and apprentices, while at the same time the community is well guarded against all the evils and vices of idleness, vagrancy, and marronage." [27] With respect to the last evil his remedy was the enforcement of General Picton's regulations and the requirement that the Commandants furnish monthly lists of runaways for publication. He also suggested that there should be a corps of Colonial Rangers, to be raised by re-enlisting or re-employing members of the disbanded West India Regiments, with officers who knew the woods thoroughly. These actions were intended to deter the erection of maroon villages, and to open interior communications.[28]

Yet another writer, who thought that the Government was showing signs of inactivity, recommended conditionally the reduction of the period of apprenticeship. According to his reckoning, if the slaves were manumitted at the end of four years, there would remain a total of 2,256 hours for the balance of two years. He has not indicated how he arrived at this computation. The slave could be asked to pay the value of that period; but he did not indicate a price or the method of valuation to be used in his calculation. The employers could support the children, the old, and the infirm for six years without apprenticing them; and they could employ the apprentices at rates fixed by the Government rather than by competition. This he thought would have satisfied the ex-slaves and would have launched them into their new state with greater habits of industry. To his two questions – as to whether it was illegal to ask the apprentices to pay the value of the two years, and whether his proposal would have entailed the risk of compensation – no answer seems to have been given.[29]

These views are not to be ignored for two simple reasons. In the first place, they represent the general climate of opinion among the whites in the colony. In the second place, those who penned these views were of the class who were either to make or administer the ordinances which governed the lives of the apprentices. As will be shown later, except for a few officials sent out from England for emancipation, the majority of the officials either had slave interests or had been living in the colony for several years. These were the ones, therefore, whose influence would eventually be important.

SUBORDINATE REGULATIONS

The next aspect of the changed status to be dealt with concerned the framing of ordinances to give effect to the Act for the Abolition of Slavery. As a result of a discussion between the Governor and his friend Edward Jackson,[30] the latter submitted a form of apprentice laws for consideration by the Colonial Office. The Council, Jackson alleged, was unwilling to adopt any measures which had not been suggested by the British Government. He therefore produced a system of apprentice laws which, by his own admission, was not dissimilar to that of Tudor England.[31] The similarity of situations, in that there was a high demand for agricultural labour, was his sole justification for proposing that system.

Jackson's major concern seems to have been to extend the apprenticeship so as to include "other classes of society who in point of circumstance and civilization will be little if at all above the manumitted Apprentices."[32] And this meant not only the emancipated slaves, who were considered indolent, but other persons who were not of the propertied class – free coloureds and blacks. While admitting the possibility of opposition to such extension, he argued that force was necessary to ensure steady labour in a situation where labourers could acquire land cheaply. He doubted the likelihood of any investment without such safeguards; while with them European capital and skill would produce such wealth as would serve as an attraction to greater population. The provision of the necessary force was to have as its corollary some restriction in the occupancy of waste land. And he assured the Colonial Office that the Legislative Council would "anxiously" adopt the said laws, unless they failed to gain the approval of the Ministers.[33]

Behind these proposals lay the common belief that persons of African origin had to be forced to work, and the equally erroneous belief that the welfare of the colonies depended on European "skill". So that more time was spent in erecting systems to restrict the ex-slaves than in trying to develop a framework for a free peasantry. Moreover, the fact that these proposals were voiced by a member of the Council indicates that, at that level, the habit of controlling the slaves was not likely to be easily relinquished. Slavery, therefore, might legally come to an end, but apprenticeship – another system of forced labour – was to be its successor; the difference hardly went beyond terminology.

The Legislative Council adopted most of the proposed law sent out from Britain. Their report enunciated the principle, which presumably they believed, that slavery not only degraded those subjected to it, but unduly elevated other classes not so subjected. Hence the Council expressed the intention to correct both anomalies: to amalgamate "the present Slave population with the other classes of Society and to form from the whole a free and if possible a moral, religious and industrious population." Significantly the report adopted the argument advanced by Edward Jackson, stating:

> While therefore we are attempting to convert the coerced
> labour of the Slave into the voluntary exertions of a hired
> labourer we should also endeavour to reduce other classes
> of society not possessing property or other means of support
> to the same habits of regular industry. An *extension of the*
> *system of apprenticeship* at least to such persons as would
> come within the operation of the vagrant Laws as established
> in most countries in Europe and also to those who may choose
> to enter into voluntary contracts for the purpose appears to be
> a step and a material one towards carrying the above principles
> into operation. [34]

This report then listed various persons who were distinguished by lack of property, and who should be included in this extended apprenticeship.[35] If the principle had been accepted, it would have meant forced labour far more extensive in range than slavery had been; that is, the virtual enslavement of those who had been manumitted or many of those who had been settled as free persons. The prospects for the introduction of emancipation looked ominous.

In December 1833, an ordinance was published for the classification of apprentices. This required a procedure similar to that for the registration of slaves, the purpose being to verify the classification.[36] By another ordinance – the Order in Council of June 1834 – the colony was divided into five districts, each with a Special Justice and a Police settlement. The Special Justices were to reside in their respective districts, preside at hearings, visit the plantations fortnightly, keep details of all causes, the evidence presented, and the decisions given, and to make a quarterly return to the Lt. Governor.[37]

In the Order in Council of June 1834, apart from specifying the duties of the apprentices, provision was also made for additional labour up to a maximum of fifteen hours per week, to be imposed on the apprentices for their absence from work without reasonable cause. Absence for more than 7½ hours per week constituted desertion; for being absent two days in one week the labourer was considered a vagabond; while for being absent six days in the week he was considered a runaway. Penalties for these various degrees of absence were one, two, and four weeks' hard labour respectively; in the last case it was to be accompanied by flogging up to a maximum of thirty lashes.[38] Indolent, careless, or negligent work was punishable by extra work up to a maximum of fifteen hours;[39] but for non-praedial labourers the punishment was fifteen lashes. Wilful disobedience on the part of the ex-slave was to be punished by confinement or corporal punishment. Drunken or disorderly behaviour towards the employer or manager was punishable by one week's confinement or fifteen lashes. By comparison, the duties of the employers were extremely light. They were to indicate the beginning and end of the legal hours of work, and to pay one shilling per hour for overtime. They were to record all contracts for task work in a book which was to be open for inspection by the Special Magistrates. The contracts were limited to fourteen days' duration; and Special Magistrates were authorised to seize produce for the non-payment of the apprentices. Consent of the Special Magistrates was necessary for the removal of the labourers from one estate to another.

As a safeguard against the likelihood of crimes by the apprentices, the Order provided that three or more persons assembling in a riot might be dispersed by any Justice on his displaying some recognisable symbol. The Order also provided that no praedial labourer could be more than five miles from his estate without a pass; there should not be any unlawful settlement of labourers; squatting was made an offence punishable by three months' imprisonment; and the same punishment awaited those who fished without previously registering as fishermen. At the same time boats were only to be kept by those who had a licence from the Governor.

The conclusion to which all these regulations points is that the apprenticeship was a system not only of social control but of social strangulation. The additional restrictions put on fishing and owning a boat could have had the effect of preventing the apprentices from leaving the island or of pursuing an occupation they might previously have been engaged in. For it would have been no easy matter in those days to obtain the Governor's licence for a boat, as the fear of much needed labour absconding would have acted as a deterrent to the grant of a licence. This does not necessarily mean that the ex-slaves might not, through their masters, have been able to get the necessary permission at a consideration favourable to the master. But the restrictions would effectively have denied some apprentices the opportunity of setting themselves up as independent fishermen, and would have increased their dependence on the masters from whom they had recently been freed.

The administration of justice, as regards the apprentices, was placed under the direction of two Special Justices sent out from England. The Colonial Office provided rules of Procedure for their guidance, making a report of their performance necessary for the payment of their salary.[40] Up to a few days before emancipation day, none of the two Special Justices had arrived in the colony. The Governor, after consultation with the Council, pressed into service certain unpaid persons - Commandants, Adjunct Commandants, and the most "respectable" persons of each Quarter – to serve as Special Justices.[41] In so doing, he declared that he was acting under great embarrassment, because of his inability to explain to the slaves the absence of the Special Justices they had been expecting. The colony, in his opinion, needed ninety-two such Justices in order to prevent the overtaxing of officers, and also because of the area to be covered. These Justices were distributed among the following nine districts: Port of Spain, Western, St. Joseph, Tacarigua, Eastern, Carapichaima, North Naparima, South Naparima, and Southern.[42] The trouble is that he selected persons who had long been opposed to the amelioration programme, probably unaware of the role some of them had played in the past.

One Superintendent Special Justice was assigned to Port of Spain, together with a number of other Justices; in the other districts the "most respectable" person, provided he was living near the centre of the district, was appointed to act as Superintendent Special Justice. These latter were authorised to swear in as constables as many persons as would enable them to carry out their duties.[43] To preserve order, Hill fully equipped the militia in the rural areas; where there was no militia, he distributed arms to the "respectable and well disposed inhabitants". Like so many white persons in the island, he thought of the slaves as incorrigible insurgents, and so was preparing for the worst. The first Special Justice – McKenzie – arrived in the island by July 30; but he was so sick that the Governor assumed that he would not be able to function for some time.[44] The other, Capt. Hay, arrived a few days later.

In light of the fears and the preparations made in anticipation of violent disturbances, the events of emancipation day and after were distinctly anti-climactic. Such demonstration of disappointment as there was constituted only a minor incident in the activities which took place at that time. There assembled in Port of Spain and its environs a crowd of agitated ex-slaves, who were understandably unhappy with what they perceived to be their new state. The Special Justices[45] tried to explain to these people the new status of apprenticeship, emphasising that obedience was still due to their former owners. The restless, perhaps incredulous, crowd did not disperse even after a warning from the Governor, apparently labouring under the impression that they had been granted absolute freedom which was being denied them by the Governor and their masters.[46] This was the very point which Hill so sarcastically dismissed without addressing properly, and it is not surprising that they were incredulous. The explanatory proclamation, previously mentioned, had to be explained to them by their masters and commandants, since many of them would have been unable to read and probably knew little English in any case. Their reaction, therefore, was understandable. As their numbers increased during the day,[47] the Governor took the precaution of strengthening the guard, even though he seemed not to share the fears of the slave owners. There is nothing, however, to indicate any extensive mobilisation of troops, as was claimed by the *Port of Spain Gazette*.[48] Until dusk of that day there were no untoward events, nor did the former slaves exhibit any signs of belligerence.

The re-appearance of a group of the apprentices on the following day created great alarm among some of the former slave owners. The group did not show any tendency towards violence, nor did they carry any weapons with them. But Captain Hay read to them an Order declaring the assembly of three or more persons for over ten minutes a mob, then called on them to disperse. This was probably only a reflection of, and a response to, the fears of the class of former slave owners. His order failed of its intended effect, a fact which only tended to increase the apprehension of the already frightened ex-slave owners. Some of the apprentices were then arrested and hastily tried for breaches of the Order, perhaps in desperation; twenty-three of them received between fifteen and thirty-nine lashes, publicly administered, after which some of them dispersed.

In the meantime, petitions were presented to the Governor seeking the declaration of Martial Law.[49] A hastily convened meeting of the Council took place, with some members expressing their support for the petitions. The panic-stricken Council unanimously requested that the Governor seek two hundred soldiers from the Commander in Chief in Barbados, and a vessel of War from the Senior Naval Officer. The requests for Martial Law were unsuccessful, as the Governor did not consider the course justified. Although expressing the view that the apprentices would soon return to work and, incidentally, that the necessary reinforcements might not have been available,[50] Hill requested the reinforcements demanded by a unanimous vote of the Council. While it is true that Hill did not believe force was necessary, he was sufficiently influenced by the increasing panic about the security of the colony to make the request. And, in default of any other evidence, this seems to be the best explanation of his action both before and during the first days of emancipation.

At the height of all this agitation the senior military officer, Col. Hardy,[51] decided to withdraw the regular troops from the town. This naturally earned him the censure of an alarmed planter class and an anti-abolitionist newspaper, the *Port of Spain Gazette*. Hardy did not trouble himself to explain his action but was stoutly defended by one who styled himself "A Private of the 19th Regiment."[52] According to the latter, on the arrival of the troops in the town, they encountered only a "wretched assemblage of old black men, women and young children". These people had sat about smoking cigars and tobacco; and he questioned the need for military force or the proclamation of Martial Law.[53]

Whoever the writer was, his assessment of the situation does not conflict with what seems to have deterred Hill from using force. In addition to this, it is worth noting that Hill did not consider Hardy's conduct reprehensible, for there was no complaint against that officer. In contrast with Port of Spain, there was no report of any incidents in the south or any other part of the colony. The situation seems to have been expertly handled by the Special Justice for the district of Port of Spain, Capt. Burns, and all was quiet within a few days. By August 9 the Governor reported to the Secretary of

State that order had been restored on many estates;[54] and five days later, that only a few refractory apprentices had still to return to work. On this occasion he was quite optimistic about the compliance of the apprentices and, as events proved, was fully justified in not yielding to pressure and declaring Martial Law.[55] His conduct of the affair was warmly commended by the Secretary of State, in whose opinion the declaration of Martial Law was to be reserved for extreme cases of crime and violence.[56]

POSTSCRIPT

The principle on which the British Government proceeded from the beginning was that Trinidad was to serve as an island of experiment. For this reason, all ameliorative measures were to be given trial in the colony before being applied in other territories. But the history of the period shows that attempts were made to implement the various measures in the other islands even before they had proven to be successful in Trinidad. The programme of registration, begun in 1812, was actually instituted in Trinidad after the Government had failed to win Perceval's support for a Bill embracing the entire West Indies. However, its success in Trinidad had not been established when it was extended to the other British West Indian colonies. When the first annual returns from Trinidad were being prepared in 1815 the bill establishing the Colonial Registry in London was being debated in parliament. Subsequently, the old West Indian islands were asked to introduce aspects of the Orders in Council of 1824 and 1831 even though their effectiveness in Trinidad was still in doubt. Difficulties dogged the implementation of the first, at the same time that attempts were being made to secure its adoption in the other islands. While failure threatened the scheme of 1831, economic pressure was being used to impose the programme elsewhere. In the end neither experiment nor persuasion worked as they had been expected to do; and abolition became the only solution.

The structure of society within the colony militated against the successful implementation of the amelioration programme. In some respects it was a divided society: old colonists not united with new except in opposition to the British slave policy. And where constitutional changes were implemented in 1831, the religious affiliation of the old colonists was used as an objection to their membership of the Legislative Council. The white slave owners were concerned not only with keeping the slaves as they were, but with maintaining existing restrictions against the free coloureds – wealthy or otherwise - except where self interest demanded some measure of cooperation with them. The latter exhibited a rift within their own ranks whereby the richer and better educated ones looked towards the position of the whites as embodying the goal of their aspirations. This naturally meant that they were less inclined to identify themselves with the poorer free coloureds, and even less so with the slave class from which they had sprung. Their ambivalence eventually led them to support the white slave owners in their opposition to the Order in Council of November 1831.

This division within the society did not only influence negative attitudes during the process of amelioration, it set the stage for those developments which were to follow. Both the Act of 1833 and the attendant Ordinances indicated a desire to be restrictive; and this restrictive tendency was reflected in later legislation. These only served to keep old and new freemen apart. In addition, most slave owners were convinced of the inability of the African to provide for himself after emancipation or to commit himself to regular work – "habits of industry," as it was termed. Any vision slave owners may have had of an immediate return of their dependents to the plantations never materialised. Those who left the estates set themselves up as small proprietors and traders, and were apparently doing well.[1]

At no time, during the period 1812 -1834, were the West Indian slaves merely passive observers in the whole process. Their general restlessness could be seen in Barbados in 1816 when the Registration Bill was being debated; in Demerara in the slave uprising of 1823; and in Jamaica towards the end of 1831 and early 1832. The burning of canes and the withdrawal of labour in Trinidad in 1832 demonstrated the same restiveness. It may well be that the small size of the slave population and the novelty of the slave system in this island did not allow sufficient time for a strong tradition of combating the system to evolve. In every case of rebellion during this period, the unrest was based on the belief that the King had granted freedom and that their masters had withheld it.[2] The agitation demonstrated in Port of Spain during the first days of abolition was an indication of the disappointment of the slave population with the introduction of apprenticeship. They were no longer slaves; but to be compelled to work 45 hours weekly for people they were now to consider their "employers" rather than their owners, did not appear to present much of a difference. Such was the tension in the island that members of the Legislative Council were even prepared to consider expanding the apprenticeship so as to increase their labour catchment. The Committee of Inhabitants in 1833 had pointed out that being free meant, to the slaves, the ability to do as they wished. It is a paradox of the very scheme, which made Wilberforce rejoice, that those who were freed could not do as they wished. In fact, the members of the Council were inclined to limit even the freedom of those who were impoverished but had long ceased to be slaves. One thing should have been clear from the ameliorative exercise: slavery was of such a nature that it could not be ameliorated; it had to end.

So abolition came into force with the ruling classes anxious to retain the control they had always had over the labouring population. As was the case in the rest of the West Indies, the stage was set for the enaction of a very interesting drama. The whites, as their conduct on the first few days of emancipation showed, were apprehensive of the ex-slaves. Dissatisfied with the loss of their "property", the paying of regular wages did not appeal to them. The law, which was intended to effect the freedom of the slaves, was itself sufficiently limiting not to cause them undue concern; it allowed no more than personal freedom, and held out no real encouragement to the new class of freemen. As one writer aptly summed it up:

> The execution of this law demonstrated a basic economic,
> social, and political fact: the completely free colored man
> without land to work as an independent farmer would
> continue to be as oppressed and exploited as before.[3]

It is a tragic fact that the slaves, far from becoming free in 1834, were kept in virtually the same state of subservience as before – a state made even less tolerable because it was disguised as freedom.

NOTES

Introduction

1.   This assessment was made by Williams, Eric, in *History of the People of Trinidad and Tobago,* Trinidad: PNM Publishing Co., 1962, p. 10.

2.   Borde, P.G.L. *The History of the Island of Trinidad under the Spanish Government*, 1876 and 1883); English Translation, Paria Publishing Co., 1982, Vol. II, 176 – 184. On the involvement of St. Laurent, see Lavaysse, J.F.D. *A Statistical, Commercial, and Political Description of Venezuela, Trinidad, Margarita and Tobago*, (1820), Westport, Conn: Negro Universities Press, 1969, pp. 325, 326. Lavaysse suggests that the Spanish court feared that other colonies would follow the example of America, but he gives no source for his information. According to Jesse Noel, Roume has been excessively glorified by Borde. See his *TRINIDAD, Provincia de Venezuela*, Caracas: Fuentes para la Historia Colonial de Venezuela, 1972, pp. 46f.

3.   The *Cedula* of Population is to be found in Fraser, L.M. *History of Trinidad*, 2 Vols., (1891, 1896), London: Frank Cass & Co., 1971, Appendix, pp. i – v. See also Carmichael, Gertrude, *History of the West Indian Islands of Trinidad and Tobago*, London: Alvin Redman, 1961, App. pp. 363 – 9.   Borde, Vol. II, pp. 426 – 432 in Spanish. Campbell, Carl, *Cedulants and Capitulants*, Port of Spain, Paria Publishing Co., 1992, pp. 323 – 333.

4.   The statement was made by Eric Williams as a chapter heading in his *History*. See Chap. 5.

5.   The distribution of the population is discussed in some detail by Newson, Linda A., *Aboriginal and Spanish Colonial Trinidad*, London: Academic Press, 1976, pp. 184 – 194.

6. The population figures are cited in various texts: Fraser, L.M. *History of Trinidad*, I. 149, states that some people voluntarily left the colony, thus reducing the total to 17,643. Lavaysse's work creates a discrepancy, which it does not explain: that there was a high population of 18,627 as early as 1789. The evidence does not support him. Cf.. John, A. Meredith, *The Plantation Slaves of Trinidad, 1783 – 1816*, Cambridge: Cambridge University Press, 1988, p. 40, which gives the figures for 1789 as 13,053.

7. See the Report of Capt. Mallett, reproduced in Newson, Linda, *Aboriginal and Spanish Colonial Trinidad*, p. 210.

8. This calculation is based on the table of cultivable land prepared by Capt. Mallett.

9. C.O. 296/1: Picton to Dundas, December 17, 1797. Picton was left in command at Trinidad by the commander of the English expedition, General Sir Ralph Abercromby.

10. See for example, C.O. 296/1: Picton to Dundas, March 6, 1798; May 14 and July 30, 1800; June 26, 1801; and February 8, 1802. There was some concern in Parliament concerning the revival of the trade in the new colony. Manning, H.T., *British Colonial Government after the American Revolution, 1782 – 1820,* New York: Archon Books, 1966, p. 350.

11. C.O. 296/1: Picton to Dundas, April 18, 1800.

12. C.O.296/1: Picton to Dundas, May 14, 1799.

13. DeVerteuil, Anthony, *Begorrat ** Brunton .A History of Diego Martin, 1784 – 1884*, Trinidad: Paria Publishing Co., 1987, p. 43.

14. Parry, J.H.& P.M.Sherlock, *A Short History of the West Indies*, London: Macmillan, 1965, p. 15, stress the inextricable connection between sugar and labour.

15. This opinion was held by the white population generally; it was simply an excuse for the refusal to hire free blacks or free coloured persons.

16.   C.O. 296/1: Picton to Hobart, April 12, 1802.

17.   This observation is made by Goveia, E.V. in *Slave Society in the British Leeward Islands at the end of the Eighteenth Century*, New Haven: Yale University Press, 1965, pp. 5 and 6.

18.   Klingberg, F.J. *The Anti-Slavery Movement in England*, New Haven: Yale University Press, 1926, p. 120. Cf. Wilberforce, R.I. & S., *Life of Wilberforce*, 4 vols, London, 1838, II, pp. 369 – 70, and III. 37 for the change in attitude to the slave question by the leadership of government.

19.   C.O. 296/1: Dundas to Picton, May 5, 1799. Balcarres was also a planter. Dundas explained that the planters had identified themselves with British interests. See Millette, J.C.V. *The Genesis of Crown Colony Government*, Trinidad: Moko Enterprises, 1970, p. 100.

20.   C.O. 296/1: Picton to Dundas, May 1, 1800.

21.   C.O. 296/4: Hobart to Picton, February 4, 1802.

22.   C.O. 296/4: Hobart to Picton. July 22, 1802.

23.   Figures for 1798 to 1800 are from T.T.H.S. 876, an extract from C.O. 295/6: Population of the colony for the three years. Fraser, *History*, I. 288, cites figures which vary greatly from those of this document.

24.   The figures for 1801 – 1802 are quoted from T.T.H.S. 875, an extract of population figures for those two years, C.O. 295/6.

25.   See Capt. Mallett's Report; also Census of Agriculture, 1801 – 1802. For production figures, see Lavaysse, *op. cit.*, pp. 150, 151.

26.   Cf. also Hart, D. *Historical and Statistical View of the Island of Trinidad*, Trinidad: Chronicle Publishing Office, 1866, p. 148, for the statistics of the period after 1799.

27.   T.T.H.S. 7: Commission issued by Sir Ralph Abercromby to John Nihell as Chief Judge, March 1, 1797. Cf. T.T.H.S. 4: Oath of Allegiance required of all Inhabitants by Order of Sir Ralph

Abercromby.

28.   For a discussion of the corruption of the Trinidad officials in 1797, see Millette, *op. cit.*, ch. 2, *passim*.

29.   T.T.H.S. 844: Abercromby to Nihell, March 1, 1797.

30.   Abercromby to Nihell and Joseph Mayan, Commandants of Port of Spain, February 22, 1797. For the text, see Hollis, C. *A Brief History of Trinidad under the Spanish Crown*, Trinidad: Government Printer, 1941, pp. 97, 98.

31.   For a statement of the practice, see "Report of tHis Majesty's Commissioners of Legal Inquiry on the Colony of Trinidad," British Parliamentary Papers, *Colonies: West Indies* 3, Shannon: Irish University Press, 1971, pp. 51, 52. Hereafter *Legal Report*.

32.   C.O. 295/8: Gloster to Hislop, July 4, 1804, enclosed with Hislop to Camden, July 9, 1804.

33.   Prof. E. Goveia notes that slaves in the British Islands were considered property – a special kind of property. As chattels, the slaves could be sold for debts; otherwise, they were disposed of as real estate. See her *West Indian Slave Laws of the Eighteenth Century*, Barbados: Caribbean Universities Press, 1970, p. 21, and also note 47. By Orders in Council dated March 7, 1815, June 8, 1816, and August 5, 1822, the laws were changed to make them more conformable to the British system.

34.   Murray, D.J., The *West Indies and the Development of Colonial Government, 1801 – 1834*, Oxford: Clarendon Press, 1965, p. 69.

35.   C.O. 295/27: Liverpool to Munro, November 27, 1810 in Williams, Eric, *Documents on British West Indian History, 1807 – 1833*, Port of Spain: Trinidad Publishing Co., 1952, p. 6. For almost the full text, see Harlow, Vincent &   Frederick Madden, *British Colonial Developments, 1774 – 1834*, Oxford: Clarendon Press, 1953, pp. 93 – 96. The Royal *Cedula* on Population, Clause 25, allowed the settlers to recommend such regulations as they thought fit for the governing of the slaves.

36.   C .O. 296/4: Hobart to Picton, February 18, 1802. In suggesting European settlement, Hobart referred to the growing antipathy towards slave importation.

37.   M'Callum, P., *Travels in Trinidad,* Liverpool, 1805, p. 113. The deficiency laws of Jamaica, for example, required each plantation to maintain a specific proportion of whites to blacks. This policy enabled effective control over the slave majority on the estates. On the settlement of whites, see C.O. 296/1: Commissioners to Hobart, March 3, 1803, mentions 190; C.O. 296/4: Hobart to Commissioners, April 23, 1803 mentions 195. For their settlement, see C.O. 296/1: Commissioners to Hobart, March 3, 1803; and Picton to Hobart, March 28, 1803. C. O. 296/4: Hobart to Commissioners, October 18, 1802 – enclosure 20, and an unsigned modification of the plan in enclosure 22: "Hints for Cultivating Trinidad," by W.Layman; C.O. 295/17: "Secret Memorandum from Mr. Sullivan to the Chairs," February 18, 1803.

37.   Stephen, *Crisis of the Sugar Colonies*, (1802), New York: Negro Universities Press, 1969 p. 193.

38.   Stephen, *Crisis of the Sugar Colonies,* p. 164.

40.   Murray, D.J., *op. cit.*, pp. 70 - 72. Joseph, E.L. *History of Trinidad*, (1838), London: Frank Cass & Co., 1970, p. 242. Joseph notes that the West India body in England regarded the new colony with jealousy. This would also be true of the preceding period before that being referred to by him. Stephen believed that Trinidad could provide a means of demonstrating that sugar could be cultivated by free labour. See *Crisis of the sugar Colonies*, pp. 186 – 89.

41.   *The Crisis of the Sugar Colonies*, pp. 162 - 164. Stephen was responding to a report concerning the sale of crown lands in the colony, which he interpreted as a pledge to continue the slave trade, pp. 132, 149. He was anxious to restrict the "cart-whip empire", p. 161. Cf. Murray, D.J. *op. cit.*, pp. 13 – 24 for a discussion on the assemblies; and Manning, H.T. *British Colonial Government*, pp. 346 – 363.

42.   For discussions on European settlement, see M'Callum, *Travels in Trinidad*, pp. 113 – 117. C.O.296/4: Hobart to Picton, February 18,

1802; Hobart to Commissioners, October 18, 1802; C.O. 296/1: Picton to Hobart, April 12, 1802.

43.	The secrecy of the operation is well represented in C.O. 295/17: Hobart to MacQueen, April 1803; Draft Letter of the Secret Committee to the Governor General of Bengal (undated). For the manner in which they were settled, see T.T.H.S. 901: Proclamation dated October 18, 1806; also C.O.296/2: Hislop to Windham, October 28, 1806. The reasons for the failure of the project are represented in C.O. 296/2: Hislop to Windham, March 8, 1807; C.O. 295/17 Hislop to the Governor General of Bengal, March 14, 1807; Arch. Gloster to Joseph Marryat, April 3, 1807.; C.O. 295/20: Hislop to the Commissioners of the Treasury, December 4, 1807; cf. C.O. 296/4: Windham to Hislop, January 24, 1807, for the financial problem.

44.	Section VI was invoked by Henry Fuller, the Attorney General, in 1814 to support the introduction of slaves by fugitives from Venezuela. See T.D.D. 1: Fuller to Woodford, July 1, 1814; Fuller to A. Thompson & H. Outlaw, Searchers and Waiters of H.M. Customs, August 12, 1813. For the text of the Act, 47 Geo. III, c. 36, see Donnan, E. *Documents Illustrative of the History of the Slave Trade to America*, New York: Octagon Books, 1965, II. 659 – 669. Clause VI of the Act is the relevant one.

45.	Quoted from Medd, P. *Romilly*, London: Collins, 1968, p. 161.

46.	Williams, E. (Ed.,) *The British West Indies at Westminster, 1783 – 1823*, (hereafter *B. W.I.*) Trinidad: Government Printing Office, 1954, pp. 17ff.

47.	*B. W.I.*, p. 24.

48.	*B. W.I.*, p. 78. Cf. Williams, E. *Capitalism and Slavery*, London: Andre Deutsch, 1967, p. 182; Bandinel, J. *Some Account of the Trade in Slaves to Africa*, London: Frank Cass & Co., 1968, p. 109; Clarkson, T. *History of the Abolition of the Slave Trade*, London: Frank Cass & Co., 1968, II. 398.

49.	Fraser, *op. cit.*, I. 279f. This petition was presented to the House of Lords in February 1807.

50.	On this see Fraser, *op. cit.*, I. 278. The agent for the colony was Joseph Marryat, senior.

51.	Marryat to Council, February 19, 1807; cited in Fraser, *op. cit.*, I. 281.

52.	*B.W.I.*, p. 23.

53.	Joseph, E.L., *History of Trinidad*, (1838) London: Frank Cass & Co., 1970, p. 234, asserts that the imminence of the abolition of the slave trade led to slaves being imported and sold on long term credit.

54.	For 1807 figures see Lavaysse, p. 335 – approximate only. For 1808 see C.O. 295/21: Hislop to Castlereagh, July 1, 1809.

55.	Curtin, P.D. *The Atlantic Slave Trade*, Madison: University of Wisconsin Press, 1969, p. 71, states that the population of Trinidad "spurted very rapidly" after 1797.

56.	T.D.D. 2, 214: Woodford to Bathurst, November 23, 1816.

57.	For example, they were granted exemption from tithes and other duties on produce. See Articles 11, 12, 17, 18, and 27.

58.	Royal *Cedula* of Population, Article 25.

Chapter 1

1.	For a discussion of the full power of the master over the slave, see *Legal Report*, p.29. Cf. Stephen, *The Crisis of the Sugar Colonies,* p. 126.

2.	Goveia, Elsa, *West Indian Slave Laws in the Eighteenth century,* Kingston: Caribbean Universities Press, 1970, pp. 24, 25; cf. p. 22, where the owner was compensated for the judicial killing of the slave. Slave owners were seldom punished for offences against slaves. Cf. Dunn, Richard, S., *Sugar and Slaves,* Williamsburg, Virginia: University of North Carolina Press, 1972, pp. 238 -40.

3.   Manning, Helen, *British Colonial Government,* discusses the issue of judges on pp. 157, 158.

4.   Goveia, *West Indian Slave Laws*, pp. 44 – 48. Dubois, Laurent, *A Colony of Citizens*, Kingston: Ian Randle Publishers, 2004, p. 68, observes that the *Code Noir* had been consistently ignored by planters.

5.   Watson, Karl, *The Civilised Isle: Barbados, A Social History,* Bridgetown: Caribbean Graphics, 1979, p. 42; cf. pp. 118, 120.

6.   Davis, David Brion, *The Problem of Slavery in Western Culture*, Harmondsworth: Pelican, 1970, p. 122.

7.   The separation of families and the sexual exploitation of women were prominent among abuses practised in the West Indies. See Davis, *op. cit.*, pp. 75, 76. Cf. Patterson, Orlando, *The Sociology of Slavery*, London: MacGibbon & Kee, 1967, pp. 4, 159, 160.

8.   The expression was used by David Brion Davis, *The Problem of Slavery,* p. 288. For similar sentiments, see pp. 274 and 299. Davis states on p. 297, that statutes often contradicted judicial decisions.

9.   See C.O. 295/8: Report of Hislop to Camden, July 9, 1804. Cf. the *Legal Report*, pp. 20 -21.

10.   For the *Audiencia*, see the *Legal Report*, pp. 18, 19; for the other minor officials, pp. 21 – 28.

11.   See C.O. 295/8: Hislop to Camden, July 9, 1804. The freedom to choose magistrates posed the danger of causes being decided on the basis of personal acquaintance.

12.   For the Code of 1789, see Borde, *The History of the Island of Trinidad,* II, pp. 433 – 441.

13.   The instructions to Nihell were set out in T.T.H.S. 7, Abercromby to Nihell, March 1, 1797. see also Fraser, *History of Trinidad*, I. Appendix pp. xvii, xviii.

14.   Millette, James, *The Genesis of Crown Colony Government*, Curepe: Moko Enterprises, 1970, p. 37.

15.   Millette, *op. cit.*, p. 49. An Order in Council of June 19, 1813 reinforced the administration of justice in accordance with Spanish law "as nearly as circumstances will permit". See the *Legal Report*, p. 33.

16.   The work of this Commission is given extensive examination by Millette in "The Civil Commission of 1802," in *Jamaican Historical Review*, Vol. VI, 1966, pp. 29 - 111.

17.   Murray, D.J., *The West Indies and the Development of colonial Government, 1801 – 1834*, p. 82. Cf. Fraser, I. 352. Smith was suspended by Hislop and the latter was recalled. By the time news of his reinstatement had reached Trinidad in 1811, Smith had already left.

18.   Goveia, Elsa, *West Indian Slave Laws*, p. 19.

19.   *Legal Report*, p. 19.

20.   See chapter 4.

21.   *Legal Report*, p. 95: Answer of the Chief Judge to Question 200.

22.   C.O. 295/50: Woodford to Bathurst, July 29, 1820, No. 369. Woodford reported that the Attorney General of Barbados was not only against any prosecution, but that he was also uninterested because he was not apparently to receive fees. There is no record of his having solicited the assistance of his counterpart, the Governor of Barbados.

23.   T.D.D. 8, 19: Grant to Murray, July 29, 1829.

24.   For details see Grant to Law Officers, July 27, 1829. Gomez to Grant, July 29, 1829; Johnston to Grant, of the same date; Fuller to Grant, July 28, 1829; Llanos to Grant, and Gloster to Grant, both July 29, 1829. These are all enclosed with T.D.D. 8, 19, Grant to Murray, July 29, 1829.

25.   Gloster to Grant, July 29, 1829.

26.   This Order is dated September 16, 1822. See Legal Report, Appendix B, pp. 209 – 214. See also *Trinidad Gazette*, January 25, 1823.

27.   Order in Council, September 1822, clause 2.

28.   *Ibid.*, clauses 3 and 4.

29.   *Ibid.*, clauses 7, 8, and 10.

30.   *Ibid.*, clause 20.

31.   *Ibid.*, clause 18.

32.   For a discussion of this, see Millette, *op. cit.*, chapter 8.

33.   Legal Report, p. 28.

34.   *Ibid.*, for negative views, see p. 9.

35.   *Ibid.*, p. 28.

36.   C.O. 296/6: Bathurst to Woodford, March 25, 1824, No. 1.

37.   Order in Council, 1824, clause 41.

38.   See Warner to Woodford, September 14, 1824, enclosed with T.D.D. 4. 576: Woodford to Bathurst, September 15, 1824. Warner's opinion was upheld by Stephen. C.O. 295/76: James Stephen, jr. to R. Wilmot Horton, Whitehall, September 6, 1827.

39.   Protector of Slaves to Woodford, May 17, 1827; Johnston to Woodford, May   21 1827.

40.   T.D.D.   7: Johnston to Woodford, May 26, 1827.

41.   C.O. 295/76: James Stephen, jr. to R. Wilmot Horton, September 6, 1827.

42.   *Port of Spain Gazette*, July 21, 1830. The Proclamation was dated July 20.

43.   See below, chapter 6.

44.   T.D.D. 4. 550: Woodford to Bathurst, May 26, 1824. The enclosed

correspondence is as follows: Woodford to Fuller, *Procurador Syndic*; *Procurador Syndic* to Woodford; Certificate of Dr. Keith; all dated March 20, 1823. The sentence was signed by Woodford, A. Gomez, and J. Carter, escribano de Camara, March 21, 1823.

45.   T.D.D. 4. 570: Woodford to Bathurst, August 16, 1824. Woodford, in reply to Bathurst's request, stated that there was no record of their trial; the offence of which they were guilty was such, he said, as to allow no doubt.

46.   The excerpts cited were: 7th Partida, 1st Title, 28th Law; 3rd Law; and 3rd Partida, 2nd Title, 6th Law, enclosed as for note 35.

47.   See chapter 6, where the names of public officers and the extent of their ownership of slaves is discussed.

48.   The Alcaldes chosen by the Cabildo were usually planters, and would naturally have been slave owners.

49.   The Order of June 20, 1831, is enclosed with C.O. 295/92: Grant to Goderich, June 15, 1832. The Order is also to be found in the *Port of Spain Gazette*, June 9, 1832. The title Chief Justice, rather than Chief Judge, bcame current about this time.

50.   T.D.D. 9. 2: Grant to Goderich, December 10, 1831.

51.   T.D.D. 10: Grant to Fuller, June 11, 1832. Cf. T.D.D. 11: Fuller to Goderich, February 1, 1833, in which Fuller protested his loss of office, while Johnston and Gomez retained theirs.

52.   T.D.D. 11: Fuller to Goderich, February 1, 1833. Fuller protested the loss of his office, while Johnston and Gomez retained theirs.

53.   C.O. 295/93: Grant to Goderich (Separate and Confidential), July 10, 1832. Cf. Deeds of Antonio Gomez, date June 26 and 27, 1832.

54.   T.D.D. 11: Gomez to Goderich, January 30, 1833. The appointment of Gomez was not without its own difficulties. His suitability as a foreigner was questioned. But Chief Justice Scotland argued that he had, by long residence, become naturalized and therefore qualified for the office. Scotland to Grant, October 31, 1832.

55.   This irregularity is noted in chapter 2.

56.   *Port of Spain Gazette*, May 2, 1832, Article entitled "A Noble Act".

57.   T.D.D. 10. 54, Pt. 1: Grant to Goderich, July 3, 1832. By this time the alcaldes had absented themselves from a number of cases.

58.   T.D.D. 10. 54, Pt. 2: Grant to Goderich, July 3, 1832.

59.   See C.O. 295/93: Scotland to Grant, June 24, 1832, enclosed with the above. Grant gave his support to this change.

60.   T.D.D. 10. 54, Pt. 2 as above.

61.   *Ibid*. By an Order in Council of August 25, 1832, the Order in Council of June 20, 1831 on the appointment of Assessors was amended. See T.D.D. 10. 92: Grant to Goderich, November 3, 1832.

62.   This is the burden of the Address to the Cabildo by the First Alcalde. See Minutes of the Cabildo, May 22, 1832.

63.   Measures which may be adopted in the present state of affairs in Trinidad, British Guiana and St. Lucia, signed H.T.A note appended to C.O. 295/93: Grant to Goderich, July 3, 1832, Pt. 1. (The writer, Henry Taylor, is identified by Stephen. See below.)

64.   See comments by Stephen on the same despatch.

65.   Goderich to Grant, August 25, 1832, printed in *Port of Spain Gazette*, December 14, 1832.

66.   The Order is to be found in C.O. 295/97: Grant to Goderich, February 24, 1833.

67.   See C.O. 295/97: Grant to Goderich, February 25, 1833.

Chapter 2

1. Edwards, Bryan, *The History, Civil and Commercial, of the British West Indies*, London, 1819, IV. 445. Cf. Medd, P., *Romilly*, p. 167.

2. Wilberforce, R.I. & S. *Life of Wilberforce*, III. 482. Wilberforce's allegation must be treated with caution. Curtin, *op. cit.*, p. 233, has shown that the figures were often exaggerated in order to make the trade appear evil. That the figures were unreliable is a main thesis of his work.

3. Bandinel, *op. cit.*, p. 143.

4. The Act is 51 Geo. III, c. 23. Ragatz, *The Fall of the Planter Class in the British Caribbean*, (1928) New York: Octagon Press, 1971, p. 386, Ragatz makes the African Institution responsible for the Bill.

5. Wilberforce, *op. cit.*, III 482.

6. Wilberforce, *ibid*.

7. Wilberforce, *op. cit.*, III., 513.

8. Wilberforce, *op. cit.*, IV, 3. Cf. D. J. Murray, *op. cit.*, pp. 78, 79, 94 – 96.

9. Wilberforce, *op. cit.*, IV. 19, 20. Wilberforce "thought it would be prudent to wait till another year to see how the engine should work in Trinidad, and rectify any errors, supply any defects, etc., which experience should suggest". Perceval was not enthusiastic, and only reluctantly agreed to establish a Registry in Trinidad. Joseph Marryat, the colony's agent, was also opposed.

10. For the text of the Order, see Privy Council Register – P.C. 2, 193. Cf. *Legal Report*, Appendix D, pp. 160 – 176. The reference used is from the original Report.

11. *Reasons for Establishing a Registry of Slaves in the British Colonies: Being a Report of a Committee of the African Institution*, British Museum – PP 6199R, p. 323. The authors wrote that "neither the existence nor the measure of the infringement, can be taken with safety from the

returns ..." According to Coupland, *Wilberforce(1923)*, New York: Negro Universities Press, 1968, p. 455, neither Liverpool, Bathurst, nor Vansittart was willing to support the registration for lack of proof of smuggling. Vansittart was Chancellor of the Exchequer around 1814. See Griggs, Earl Leslie, *Thomas Clarkson, The Friend of Slaves,* Westport, Conn: Ngero Universities Press, 1970, p. 117.

12.   See Clause 7 of the Order.

13.   The need for this has been emphasised in Stephen, *The Crisis of the Sugar Colonies*, p. 189, when dealing with the issue of free Negroes.

14.   Clause 47.

15.   Clauses 6 to 8. The schedule required the following information: name, surname, colour, employment, age, stature, marks, relations. These are examined in detail in John, A. Meredith, *The Plantation Slaves of Trinidad*, Chs. 4 − 8.

16.   Clauses 14, 15, 17.

17.   Clauses 19, 21, 25 − 27.

18.   Clause 27.

19.   Clause 26.

20.   Clause 29.

21.   Clause 32, 34 − 37, 39.

22.   Clause 36.

23.   Clause 38.

24.   See the Schedule to the Order.

25.   Reasons for Establishing a Registry of Slaves, pp. 335, 338.

26.   Clause 44.

27. C.O. 296/5: Bathurst to Munro, July 4, 1812. Bathurst was the third Secretary, responsible for the colonies. Murray, *op. cit.*, Ch. VII. The title Colonial Secretary is used throughout to avoid the risk of confusion.

28. C.O. 298/5: Minutes of the Council, Trinidad, August 25, 1812.

29. The proclamation is enclosed with C.O. 298/5: Minutes of the Council, August 31, 1812.

30. C.O. 296/5: Bathurst to Munro, July 28, 1812.

31. These certificates are enclosed with C.O. 298/5: Knox to Munro, August 31, 1812. The copies were signed by Henry Murray, Deputy Clerk of the Council.

32. The date of issue of the certificates is August 31. The emphases are my own.

33. The members of the Council were: the Governor, a former Chief Judge in the person of John Nihell, Andrew Clarke and Philip Langton. Even at this early stage, the Council excluded those who were of Spanish origin. The *Escribano* was the officer responsible for keeping the records. On the Cabildo, see Millette, *The Genesis of Crown Colony Government,* Chapter 2.

34. C.O. 296/5: Bathurst to Munro, November 27, 1812.

35. C.O. 296/5: Bathrust to Munro, July 28, 1812.

36. C.O. 298/5: Minutes of the Council, Trinidad, March 6, 1813.

37. Joseph, E.L., *op. cit.*, p. 243, gives February 27 as the date of the Proclamation. This is mistaken.

38. T.D.D. I.5: Woodford to Bathurst, January 4, 1814. Elsewhere Woodford listed the slave population for three years previous to the Order as follows: 1809 – 21,475; 1810 – 20,279; 1811 – 21,288. See T.D.D. I. 23: Woodford to Bathurst, March 18, 1814.

39.   C.O. 295/34: *Facts and Observations as to the execution of the Order in Council of March 26, 1812*, pp. 7, 13, 14.

40.   *Facts and Observations*, p. 24. The emphases are his.

41.   *Ibid.*, pp. 25, 26.

42.   C.O. 296/5: Bathurst to Woodford, February, 10, 1814.

43.   T.D.D. I. 64: Woodford to Bathurst, November 23, 1814, enclosure dated April 28, 1814.

44.   T.D.D. I. 26: Woodford to Bathurst, May 9, 1814.

45.   T.D.D. I. 64: Woodford to Bathurst, November 23, 1814, enclosure dated April 28, 1814. The Commissary of Population functioned as a modern Registrar of Births, Deaths, and Marriages. For his duties, see Fraser, *History of Trinidad*, II. p. 83.

46.   Bigge's Report on the investigation, enclosed with T.D.D. 1. 64.

47.   *Ibid.*

48.   Joseph, *History*, p. 243.

49.   C.O. 296/5: Bathurst to Munro, November 9, 1812.

50.   The function of this officer in Spanish law was to protect minors and infants, and to keep surveillance over their guardians. However, because he was to appear in every cause involving a minor, and his fees took precedence over other expenses in the minors' estates, he frequently enriched himself at their expense. See *Legal Report*, 21.

51.   C.O. 300/21: Protector of Slaves' Report for the period ending December 1826, Appendix C. For the outcome, see C.O. 300/22: Report for the period ending June 1827, Appendix E. There is no reference to the third.

52.   C.O. 300/22: Report of the Protector of Slaves to June 1827.

53. T.D.D. 8. 34: Grant to Murray, October 1, 1829. The matter was submitted to H. M. in Council for special consideration.

54. Minutes of the Cabildo, January 27, 1814. In 1821 the salary of the Deputy Secretary of the Cabildo was increased to £300 sterling. By this time Murray was no longer Registrar. See Schedule of the Establishment, 1821, enclosed with C.O. 295/53: Woodford to Bathurst, April 11, 1821, no. 407. The spelling is that of the Registrar.

55. C.O. 295/43: Woodford to Bathurst, April 2, 1817, Schedule of Public Officers of Trinidad.

56. For actual proposals on Murray's salary, see C.O. 295/31: Stephen to Bathurst, August 24, 1813.

57. T.D.D.2.88: Woodford to Bathurst, March 10, 1815.

58. C.O. 295/43: Woodford to Bathurst, April 2, 1817.

59. C.O. 295/48: Woodford to Bathurst, March 30, 1819, enclosure.

60. C.O. 295/46: Woodford to Bathurst, October 13, 1818.

61. Murray to Woodford, September 23, 1818, enclosed with C.O. 295/46: Woodford to Bathurst, October 13, 1818.

62. C.O. 295/53: Woodford to Bathurst, April 11, 1821. In 1821 Murray blamed the late returns for 1819 partly on his father's absence, and his own ill health. See Ed. Murray to Young, June 29, 1821, enclosed with C.O. 295/53: Young to Bathurst, June 30, 1821. The application of 1819 will be found in C.O. 295/49: Henry Murray to Goulburn, October 20, 1819.

63. C.O. 296/6: Bathurst to Woodford, December 20, 1821.

64. T.D.D. 8. 37: Grant to Murray, October 3, 1829. Albert Murray thus signed a return showing the slave population January 31 1825 to January 31 1829.

65.   T.D.D. 1. 13: Woodford to Bathurst, February 19, 1814. Cf. Murray to Woodford, February 28, 1814, enclosed with T.D.D. 1.26: Woodford to Bathurst, May 9, 1814.

66.   T.D.D. 2: Murray to Woodford, February 1, 1815.

67.   C.O. 296/5: Adam Gordon to Woodford, November 19, 1814.

68.   Murray to Woodford, February 28, 1814, enclosed with T.D.D. 1. 26: Woodford to Bathurst, May 9, 1814.

69.   T.D.D. 2. 88: Woodford to Bathurst, March 10, 1815.

70.   T.D.D. 2. 137: Woodford to Bathurst, December 13, 1815. Sir Charles Smith, a later Governor, blamed planter unwillingness on the fact that the crop time was also the time of registration. T.D.D. 9. 122: Smith to Goderich, October 8, 1831.

71.   Murray to Woodford, March 1, 1815, enclosed with T.D.D. 2. 88: Woodford to Bathurst, March 10, 1815.

72.   C.O.296/5: Bathurst to Woodford, August 23, 1815.

73.   C.O.296/5: Bathurst to Woodford, October 3, 1816.

74.   C.O. 295/43: Woodford to Bathurst, April 2, 1817.

75.   C.O 295/46: Woodford to Bathurst, October 14, 1818.

76.   Edward Murray to Young, June 29, 1821, enclosed with C.O. 295/53: Young to Bathurst, June 30, 1821. He explained that his father had mentioned seeing them in London.

77.   *Ibid.*

78.   C.O. 295/53: Young to Bathurst, October 8, 1821.

79.   C.O. 296/6: Bathurst to Woodford, November 16, 1822.

80.   C.O. 295/65: Woodford to Bathurst, January 5, 1825.

81.   Murray to Woodford, January 4, 1825, enclosed with C.O. 295/65: Woodford to Bathurst, January 5, 1825.

82.   C.O. 296/8: Howick to Grant, December 9, 1830. Howick was Under Secretary to Lord Goderich, who had succeeded Sir George Murray as Secretary of State.

83.   *Ibid*.

84.   Registrar of Slaves to the acting Governor, February 25, 1831, enclosed with T.D.D. 9, duplicate, unnumbered: Smith to Goderich, March 5, 1831.

85.   C.O. 296/6: Bathurst to Woodford, March 9, 1825.

86.   C.O. 295/101: Hill to Stanley, March 9, 1834.

87.   See Murray, D. J., *op. cit.*, pp. 148, 179, 180, 183.

88.   T.D.D. 9. 122: Smith to Goderich, October 8, 1831. Smith was then acting Governor during the absence of Sir Lewis Grant from the colony. Cf. British Parliamentary Papers, *Slave Trade*, Vol. 81, p. 1085: "Copies of all the Population returns received from the Slave Colonies since the last were printed, up to the present Time."

89.   T.D.D. 2: Murray to Woodford, February 1, 1815.

90.   Murray to Woodford, March 1, 1815, enclosed with T.D.D. 2. 88: Woodford to Bathurst, March 10, 1815.

91.   Murray to Woodford, February 1, 1815.

92.   This deficiency had been pointed out by Sir Ralph Woodford, giving general support to the Registrar. See T.D.D. 2. 88: Woodford to Bathurst, March 10, 1815.

93.   C.O. 295/55: Edward Murray to Woodford, July 6, 1822.

94.   Commissary of Population to Woodford, November 3, 1823, enclosed with T.D.D. 4. 520: Woodford to Bathurst, November 6, 1823.

95.   *Ibid*.

96.   T.D.D. 4. 520: Woodford to Bathurst, November 6, 1823.

97.   *Slaves imported between 1813 and 1822;* signed by Edward Murray. Enclosed with T.D.D. 4. 520. Cf. C.O. 295/55: *Return of slaves imported between 1813 and 1821*, Murray to Young, July 6, 1822.

98.   *Proclamation* dated December 20, 1813, enclosed with C.O. 295/32: Woodford to Bathurst, January 4, 1814.

99.   C.O. 295/32: Woodford to Bathurst, January 4, 1814.

100.   Gloster to Grant, April 15, 1833, enclosed with C.O. 295/98: Grant to Goderich, April 19, 1833. In 1824 he was appointed Protector of Slaves under the Order in Council of March that year. In uniting the offices Goderich forbade the incumbent of the joint post having any other public office, or private practice. C.O. 296/10: Goderich to Grant, January 13, 1832.

101.   C.O. 295/97: Gloster to Grant, March 9, 1833. In that letter, Gloster welcomed the combination of the offices.

102.   Brougham, *Reasons for Establishing a Registry*, p. 335.

103.   Brougham, *Reasons for Establishing a Registry*, p. 338.

104.   For a discussion on the opposition in the West Indies, see R.L. Schuyler, *Parliament and the British Empire,* pp. 125 – 133, 139 – 149.

105.   The Act is 59 Geo. III, c. 120: *An Act for establishing a Registry of Colonial Slaves in Great Britain, and for making further Provision with respect to the Removal of Slaves from British Colonies.*

Chapter 3

1.   See Introduction above.

2.   See clause 21.

3.   59 Geo. III, c. 120, passed on July 12, 1819. This is to be found in the *Legal Report*, Appendix D, pp. 220 - 221. The printed Report in the *British Parliamentary Papers* does not contain the Appendices.

4.   Williams, *Documents of British West Indian History*, No. 417: C.O. 295/ 30: Woodford to Bathurst, October 18, 1813.

5.   T.D.D. 2. 88: Woodford to Bathurst, March 10, 1815; cf. T.D.D. 1. 55: Woodford to Bathurst, October 3, 1814.

6.   Williams, *Documents*, No. 423, C.O 295/53: Young to Bathurst, June 26, 1821; No. 424, C.O 295/53: Young to Bathurst, December 13, 1821; No.426, C.O. 295/62: Woodford to Bathurst, February 7, 1824.

7.   C.O. 296/5: Bathurst to Woodford, February 10, 1814.

8.   *Ibid*.

9.   C.O. 296/5: Bathurst to Woodford, August 5, 1815.

10.   See above, Introduction.

11.   T.D.D. 1. 55: Woodford to Bathurst, October 3, 1814.

12.   Frank Cassell, "Slaves of the Chesapeake Bay Area and the War of 1812", *Journal of Negro History*, Vol. LVII, No. 2, 1972, p. 150. Cassell tells us that they acted as guides, spies, messengers and labourers.

13.   See Cassell, "Slaves of the Chesapeake Bay Area," p. 150 for Cochrane's Proclamation of April 2, 1814. Cf. Horsman, Reginald, *The War of 1812*, London: Eyre and Spottiswoode, 1969, pp. 153, 154.

14.   Cassell, "Slaves of the Chesapeake Bay Area," pp. 150, 151. These marines are to be classified as refugees.

15.   Cassell, "Slaves of the Chesapeake Bay Area," p. 153, asserts that there were over 2,000 in Halifax. According to Horsman, *The War of 1812*, p. 263, the British had accumulated over 6,000 prisoners, including 1,000 American Negroes.

16.   C.O. 296/5: Bathurst to Woodford, October 24, 1814.

17.   C.O. 296/5: Bathurst to Woodford, November 3, 1814.

18.   T.D.D. 2.103:Woodford to Bathurst, June 6, 1815. The arrangements for settling them were not completed when they arrived.

19.   T.D.D. 2. 113:Woodford to Bathurst, August 5, 1815. There were 15 men, 14 women, and 29 children.

20.   T.D.D. 2.134:Woodford to Bathurst, November 30, 1815.

21.   T.D.D. 2. 189: Woodford to Bathurst, August 28, 1816. The arithmetic is slightly inaccurate.

22.   See T.D.D. 2. 113, 134 and 189 Woodford to Bathurst, August 8, 1816, and T.D.D. 2. 103:Woodford to Bathurst, June 6, 1815. Cf. 2. 131:Woodford to Bathurst, November 8, 1815.

23.   T.D.D. 2. 103: Woodford to Bathurst, June 6, 1815; cf. 2. 131 as above.

24.   T.D.D. 2. 113:Woodford to Bathurst, August 5, 1815.

25.   T.D.D. 2. 189:Woodford to Bathurst, August 25, 1816.

26.   *Ibid*. Cf. 295/47:Woodford to Bathurst, May 5, 1818.

27.   C.O. 295/47: Woodford to George Harrison, Trinidad, May 5, 1818. See *Address to the Rt. Hon. Earl Bathurst*, London, 1824, pp. 120, 121.

28.   Free Mulatto, *Address to Earl Bathurst*, pp. 133 – 42. Carl Campbell, *Cedulants and Capitulants*, Trinidad: Paria Publishing Co., 1992, pp.205, 206, 233 – 37.

29.   T.D.D. 2. 189:Woodford to Bathurst, August 28, 1816.

30.   C.O. 296/5: Bathurst to Woodford, December 19, 1816.

31.   C.O. 296/4: Hobart to Picton, February 18, 1802.

32. T.D.D. 2. 205: Woodford to Bathurst, November 18, 1816. Bathurst approved the arrangement, indicating that there was no need to change unless the refugees' conduct warranted it. C.O. 296/5: Bathurst to Woodford, December 19, 1816.

33. See below chapter 5, *passim*.

34. C.O. 295/44: Woodford to Bathurst, July 31, 1817. Woodford estimated that 80 of the last 500 (the largest group he meant) were industrious. The others were intelligent, but lazy. For a study of these settlements, see K.O. Laurence, "The Settlement of Free Negroes in Trinidad before Emancipation", in *Caribbean Quarterly*, No. 9, 1962, pp. 26 – 51.

35. C.O. 295/44: Woodford to Bathurst, July 31, 1817. Cf. 295/47: R. Lushington to Goulburn, January 24, 1818, concerning rates and authorizing rewards.

36. C.O. 295/47: Woodford to George Harrison, Trinidad, May 5, 1818.

37. C.O. 295/47: Lushington to Goulburn, Treasury, January 24, 1818.

38. C.O. 295/47: Woodford to Harrison, May 5, 1818.

39. T.D.D. 4. 478: Woodford to Bathurst, April 30, 1823.

40. T.D.D. 2. 205: Woodford to Bathurst, November 10, 1816.

41. C.O. 296/5: Bathurst to Woodford, January 17, 1817.

42. C.O. 295/47: Woodford to George Harrison, May 5, 1818.

43. C.O. 295/48: Woodford to Bathurst, December 12, 1819, No. 351. Cf. T.D.D. 4. 391: Woodford to Bathurst, December 16, 1820, where a similar request was made. Also C.O. 296/5: Bathurst to Woodford, July 6, 1820.

44. C.O. 295/54: James Kempt to Harrison, Halifax, August 21, 1821.

45.	Letter of Richard Inglis, August 20, 1821; the name of the recipient is not clear from the microfilm.

46.	C.O. 296/6: Bathurst to Woodford, May 12, 1825.

47.	C.O. 295/53: Report by the Commandant on the American Refugees, April 15, 1823. Enclosed with Woodford to Bathurst, April 30, 1823, No. 381.

48.	Free Mulatto, *Address to Earl Bathurst,* pp. 160, 164. Also C.O. 318/76: Memorial of Jean Baptiste Philip, M.D. and John T. Congnet, p. 27, enclosed with a List of Papers relating to the Claims of the Coloured Inhabitants of the said Island.

49.	Free Mulatto, *Address to Earl Bathurst*, p. 159 - 164.

50.	C.O. 295/57: Arch. Watherston to Bathurst, February 1, 1821.

51.	*Port of Spain Gazette,* April 5, 1833: Letter of M'Queen to Grant, St. Vincent, March 1, 1833.

52.	C.O. 296/10: Howick to Grant, September 6, 1831.

53.	*Legal Report*, pp. 8, 12, 31, 32. Given the role he played in the Council, a serious question arises as to whether Burnley should have been the Chair of this Committee. The questions were frequently not open, and seemed to prompt specific answers.

54.	*Legal Report*, pp. 7, 25, 32, 33, 43. Comments on the licentious-ness of female slaves completely ignore the roles of slave managers and other white personnel in violating slave women.

55.	*Port of Spain Gazette*, May 2, 1834: Tobin Bash to the Editor. The author probably used a pseudonym.

56.	Robinson to Woodford, May 9, 1817, enclosed with T.D.D. 3. 234: Woodford to Bathurst, May 13, 1817. Robinson was governor of Tobago.

57.	T.D.D. 3. 234: Woodford to Bathurst, May 13, 1817.

58.   *Ibid.*

59.   C.O. 296/5: Bathurst to Woodford, August 11, 1817.

60.   C.O. 295/46: Woodford to Bathurst, January 29, 1818. There were eight bitts in one dollar, the latter being equivalent to five shillings. See *British Parliamentary Papers, Slave Trade 2, 1831 – 1832*, Shannon: Irish University Press, 1968, p. 458: evidence of H.T. Bowen. Woodford in reply to Bathurst's letter, professed that he was not unwilling to receive the soldiers

61.   C.O. 295/46: Woodford to Bathurst, January 29, 1818.

62.   C.O. 295/48: Woodford to Bathurst, April 8, 1819, No. 321.

63.   T.D.D. 4. 584: Woodford to Bathurst, December 6, 1824. Cf. Report of the Committee of Council, p. 66.

64.   *Ibid.*

65.   *Ibid.* De Verteuil, *Begorrat ★ Brunton,* p. 99, has suggested that the Americans had been used to clear land in the region of the Oropouche River in East Trinidad. St. Hiliaire Begorrat profitted from this since he had large tracts of land in the area. Report of the Committee of Council, p. 55. The report indicates that some also planted coffee.

66.   T.D.D. 4. 584: Woodford to Bathurst, December 6, 1824.

67.   *Ibid.*

68.   T.D.D. 6. 56: Woodford to Bathurst, August 8, 1826. The emphasis is my own.

69.   *Port of Spain Gazette*, September 16, 1829.

70.   T.D.D. 1. 55: Woodford to Bathurst, October 1814. Cf. 2.88: Woodford to Bathurst, March 10, 1815.

71.   See Thompson, Alvin O., "African 'Recaptives' under Apprentice-ship in the British West Indies, 1807 – 1828," Seminar Paper No. 1,

1988 – 1989, Department of History, University of the West Indies, Cave Hill. On p. 3, Thompson estimates that 121 settled in Trinidad between 1807 and 1846. His estimate for 1807 – 1819 is 17.

72. Chas. W. Maxwell to Maj. Gen. Grant or the Officer Administering the Government, St. Christopher, June 4, 1831, enclosed with T.D.D. 9. 90: Smith to Goderich, July 13, 1831.

73. Smith to Maxwell, July 13, 1831, enclosed with T.D.D. 9. 90.

74. *Port of Spain Gazette*, July 23, 1831.

75. T.D.D. 9. 90: Smith to Goderich, July 13, 1831.

76. When asked to issue a Proclamation in favour of illegally imported slaves, Smith refused to do so. See the following chapter.

77. C.O. 296/10: Goderich to Grant, October 1, 1831.

78. C.O. 296/10: Goderich to Grant, December 2, 1831. The Judge of the Court of Vice-Admiralty was the one competent to try offences in breach of the laws for the abolition of the Slave Trade. Henry Gloster was Protector of Slaves under the 1824 and subsequent ameliorative Orders; Gomez was the Governor's Assessor or legal adviser, and later a puisne judge.

79. The Collector at the time was Benjamin Parkhurst. His involvement with slaves illegally imported from Barbados will be discussed in the following chapter.

80. C.O. 296/10: Goderich to Grant, December 2, 1831.

81. The Treaty is part of a body of legislation appended to the Consolidated Slave Trade Act, 5 Geo. IV, cap. 113.

82. Article 7.

83. C.O. 295/98: "Summary of the Negrita case and of the preceding correspondence with reference to Captured Negroes," September 2, 1833. Stanley subsequently dispensed with the month's notice,

but required that the Negroes be retained on board ship until accommodation had been provided for them. C.O. 296/11: Stanley to Hill, December 18, 1833.

84.   Stanley also recommended an equal number of the sexes, any shortfall to be made up in the following shipment. In C.O. 296/11: Stanley to Hill, December 18, 1833.

85.   C.O. 295/98: Hill to Stanley, July 1, 1833. Hill also mentioned accepting an offer from Commodore Farquhar, commander of naval forces in the area, to land Negroes in Trinidad while awaiting adjudication at Havana. Stanley censured this line of action in a minute to the despatch.

86.   Robert Lovelace to Parkhurst, August 26, 1833, enclosed with C.O. 295/99: Hill to Stanley, September 2, 1833.

87.   C.O. 295/99: Hill to Stanley, August 1, 1833.
In this despatch, he gave a return of the applications as follows:
    53 applications for 450 Negroes for cocoa estates/plantations
    12 applications for 243 Negroes for sugar
    1 application for 4 Negroes for cotton/rice
    13 applications for 18 Negroes for artisans
    76 applications for 118 Negroes for domestics
    29 applications for 218 Negroes for purpose unspecified

88.   C.O. 296/11: Stanley to Hill, December 18, 1833.

89.   C.O. 295/102: Hill to Stanley, April 7, 1834.

90.   *Ibid.*, Hill to Ricafort, March 31, 1834.

91.   *Ibid.*, Hill to Stanley, June 27, 1834. Hill reported receiving 1502 applications for their service.

92.   This fact was not clear from Hill's dispatch of July 1, 1833. C.O. 295/98.

93.   C.O. 295/102: Hill to Stanley, June 27, 1834.
94.   *Ibid.*

95.   Hill to McKay & McKenzie, February 27, 1834. Cf. The dispatch with which it was enclosed - C. O. 295/101: Hill to Stanley, March 9, 1834.

96.   C.O. 295/101: Hill to Stanley, March 9, 1834.

97.   C.O. 296/11: Stanley to Hill, May 10, 1834.

98.   C.O. 295/102: Hill to Stanley, June 27, 1834.

99.   C. O. 295/101: Hill to Stanley, March 9, 1834.

100.   C. O. 296/11: Rice to Hill, November 2, 1834.

Chapter 4.

1.   For details on the opposition of the various West Indian Assemblies, see Schuyler, R.L. *Parliament and the British Empire*, chapter IV; Klingberg, *The Anti-Slavery Movement in England*, pp. 173 – 81.

2.   The Act is 59 Geo. III, cap. 23.

3.   T.D.D. 1: Fuller to A. Thompson and H. Outlaw, Searchers and Waiters of H. M. Customs, August 12, 1813.

4.   *Ibid.*, Fuller to Woodford, July 1, 1814. On the Court of Vice-Admiralty and and the Court of Admiralty, see chapter 1.

5.   Woodford lamented Bathurst's decision in T.D.D. 1. 64: Woodford to Bathurst, November 23, 1814.

6.   C.O. 295/47: R. Johnson, Acting Collector & John Hudson, Comptroller of Customs, to Bathurst, January 5, 1818.

7.   C.O. 295/48: Woodford to Bathurst, August 31, 1819, No. 338.

8.   *Ibid.*

9.   C.O. 295/50: Woodford to Bathurst, July 29, 1820.

10.   C.O. 295/53: G. Wilson, J. Williams, W. Boothby, and J. H. Richardson to the Collector and Comptroller of Trinidad, Customs House, London, September 8, 1821. The Vice-Admiralty Court usually took cognizance of imports, while the Admiralty Court took cognizance of exports.

11.   C.O. 295/55: Edward Murray to Young, July 6, 1822, shows that 3,815 slaves had been imported during the period 1813 – 1821 alone; for the period 1823 – 1824, Burton Williams alone imported 125. See Appendix A, No. 4.

12.   C.O. 296/5: Bathurst to Woodford, August 27, 1816.

13.   C.O. 296/5: Bathurst to Woodford. January 20, 1820.

14.   C.O. 295/53: Young to Bathurst, June 26, 1821. See Williams, *Documents*, No. 423.

15.   C.O. 296/6: Bathurst to Young, September 8, 1821.

16.   Williams, *Documents*, No. 424, C.O. 295/53: Young to Bathurst, December 13, 1821. A quarree was approximately three acres of land.

17.   *Ibid.*

18.   C.O. 296/6: Bathurst to the Officer Administering the Government, February 15, 1822.

19.   T.D.D. 4. 498: Woodford to Bathurst, August 6, 1823.

20.   T.D.D. 4. 520: Woodford to Bathurst, November 6, 1823. A later dispatch gives the total as 329. See T.D.D. 7. 9: Woodford to Huskisson, March 7, 1828.

21.   C.O. 296/6: Bathurst to Woodford, September 29, 1823.

22.   T.D.D. 4. 526: Woodford to Bathurst, December 15, 1823.

23.   C.O. 296/6: Bathurst to Woodford, February 12, 1824.

24.   This Act is 5 Geo. IV. Cap. 113.

25. Clause 14. This will be compared later with the reasons for the violations noticed some three or four years after the Act came into force.

26. See clause 15.

27. Clause 17. The problems of later years arose out of the omission of the occupations of the domestics. See below.

28. T.D.D. 5. 610: Woodford to Bathurst, April 22, 1825.

29. *Ibid.*

30. *Ibid.* This last point is reminiscent of the Jeronymite Commission of 1516 – 1518, which judged the indigenous population on its capacity to function *"politicamente"* as did the Spaniards. *See Hanke, Lewis, The First Social Experiments in America,* Gloucester, Mass: Peter Smith, 1964, p. 29.

31. C.O. 296/5: Bathurst to Woodford, August 5, 1815.

32. See, for example, T.D.D. 6. Unnumbered: Woodford to Bathurst, April 13, 1826; Francis LaBarrie to Woodford, December 18, 1826; Memorial of Louis de la Grenade to Woodford, undated; also C.O. 296/8; Murray to the Officer administering the Government re MacQueen & Co., Messrs Dennistoun & Co., Capt. John Vernon – all dated August 21, 1828; also re Elizabeth Brathwaithe Threlfall, December 4, 1828. See also Williams, *Documents*, Nos. 440, 441, 442.

33. The application was enclosed with T.D.D. 5. 630: Woodford to Bathurst, June 12, 1825.

34. C.O. 296/6: Bathurst to Woodford, October 20, 1825.

35. T.D.D. 5: 630, Woodford to Bathurst, June 12, 1825. The proprietors involved here were Burton Williams and Robert Mitchell.

36. C.O. 296/6: Bathurst to Woodford, August 25, 1825.

37. C.O. 296/6: Bathurst to Woodford, January 18, 1826.

38. *Ibid.*

39. C.O. 296/6: Bathurst to Woodford, July 17, 1826. Bathurst was replying to Woodford's letter concerning the application of Burton Williams and his brother to import slaves from the Bahamas. Woodford's despatch was T.D.D. 6. 24: Woodford to Bathurst, April 13, 1826. A later Governor showed that it was not very difficult to circumvent this provision, if children of imported slaves were freed, by the simple expedient of importing females who were past childbearing age. It was not foolproof. T.D.D. 8 unnumbered: Grant to Murray, July 1, 1829.

40. C.O. 296/8: Murray to the Officer administering the Government, August 20, and August 21 1828 (six letters bearing the same date); and August 30, 1828.

41. Williams, *Documents,* No. 432: C.O. 295/72: Woodford to Bathurst, December 22, 1826, enclosing applications from Francis La Barrie (December 19), and Louis de la Grenade (undated).

42. C.O. 295/97: Grant to Goderich, January 2, 1833, appended note. The author admitted that the evidence was not clear before 1829. Cf. C.O. 28/100: Collector of Customs to Skeete, December 6, 1827, where the trade was said to have been excessive for some time. See Williams, Documents, No. 459.

43. C.O. 28/97: "A Return of Slaves exported from the 1st January distinguishing the Year, the Sex of the Slaves, together with the Place to which exported, and by what Authority." This was signed by Thomas Spencer, Ag. Collector, and John Straker, Comptroller.

44. C.O. 28/100: Aberdeen to Skeete, December 6, 1827; December 9, 1827, in which Aberdeen alleged that persons boarded with the Governor's licence, even when the Customs withheld a certificate.

45. C.O. 28/100: Skeete to Huskisson, November 30, 1827, with the following enclosures: W.B. Gibbons to Attorney General, November 16, 1827; Sharpe to Gibbons, November 17, 1827 and Sharpe to Gibbons, August 3, 1827, in which the Attorney General stressed that the law did not extend to visitors from another colony. In his letter of November 17, Sharpe recommended that Skeete report his

suspicions to H.M. government.

46.   T.D.D. 7. 10: Skeete to Woodford, March 1, 1828; enclosed with Woodford to Huskisson, March 8, 1828.

47.   C.O. 296/8: Huskisson to Woodford, January 19, 1828. Huskisson was Secretary of State in Goderich's Government. See Murray, *op. cit.*, p. 146.

48.   T.D.D. 7. 10: Woodford to Huskisson, March 8, 1828.

49.   C.O. 28/101: The offenders were Mary Jeffrey and Dorothy Coxall. The statement of facts was signed by James Stephen Jones, January 3, 1827.

50.   Fraser, *op. cit.*, II. 305. Carmichael, *op. cit.*, p. 166.

51.   C.O. 28/102: Skeete to Huskisson, March 24, 1828. Williams, *Documents*, No. 462. Cf. C.O. 295/97: Note appended to Grant to Goderich, January 2, 1833; and C.O. 28/100: Sharpe to Skeete, August 3, and 21, 1827.

52.   C.O. 28/100: Collector of Customs (Aberdeen) to Gov. Skeete, December 7, 1827.

53.   T.D.D. 8.2: Grant to Murray, April 14, 1829.

54.   C.O. 111/43: Memorandum of James Stephen, March 1823. Williams, *Documents*, No. 157.

55.   T.D.D. 8: Grant to Clogstoun, June 10, 1829.

56.   T.D.D. 8: Grant to Fuller, June 14, 1829.

57.   T.D.D. unnumbered: Grant to Murray, June 1, 1829. This despatch was headed "Separate and perhaps of a nature that ought not to be made public". The report on Hobson's application was embodied in this despatch.

58.   T.D.D. 8.16: Grant to Murray, June 25, 1829. Grant was reporting a complaint made to him by the Collector of Customs.

59. T.D.D. 8: Grant to Clogstoun, June 9, 1829. A similar point was made by the Secretary of State in C.O. 296/8: Murray to the Officer Administering the Government, December 29, 1829.

60. T.D.D. 8: Hobson to Grant, June 16, 1829. Cf. Undated affidavit attached.

61. T.D.D. 8: Hobson to Grant, July 3, 1829.

62. T.D.D. 8: Fuller to Grant, August 3, 1829.

63. C.O. 296/8: Murray to Grant, September 1, 1829.

64. T.D.D. 9: Fuller to Acting Governor Smith, July 30, 1830.

65. The portion due to the Crown was half of the penalty.

66. C.O. 296/8: Goderich to Smith, December 3, 1830. Goderich observed that, though he was a Judge, Hobson was not exempt from punishment.

67. T.D.D. 8.29: Grant to Murray, August 28, 1829. Parkhurst could not have been in office in Barbados for any long period, since up to December 1827, his name does not appear in the correspondence. Parkhurst was sent to investigate illegal importations. See C.O. 296/9: Howick to the Hon. J. Stewart, March 31, 1831.

68. T.D.D. 8: Parkhurst to Grant, August 13, 1829. In this letter, Parkhurst identified himself as Comptroller in Barbados.

69. *Ibid.* That the Barbados Customs were at fault was readily pointed out by Fuller. See Fuller to Grant, August 13, 1829.

70. James Stephen, jr., had objected at the time to the employment of Parkhurst in this investigation. C.O. 295/97: Grant to Goderich, January 2, 1833, appended note. Cf. C.O. 296/9: Howick to the Hon. J. Stewart, March 31, 1831, where an impartial officer was recommended for any future investigations.

71. T.D.D. 8: Grant to Parkhurst, August 25, 1829.

72. C.O. 296/8: Goderich to Smith, December 2, 1830.

73. T.D.D. 9. 51: Smith to Goderich, February 12, 1831. The emphases are my own.

74. Of Smith he wrote: "Sir Charles Smith writes on the subject as though the slave precisely resembled an inanimate or mute subject of property, and as if the purchaser of a human being therefore stood exactly in the same predicament as the Buyer of any other smuggled Goods." C.O. 296/10: Goderich to Grant, August 22, 1831.

75. *Ibid.*

76. C.O. 296/8: Murray to the Officer administering the Government, December 19, 1829.

77. Carmichael's claim is, in my opinion, unjustifiable. The evidence is forcefully represented in the dispatches which she used as her sources. It is very unlikely that Fraser would have had access to those dispatches. See C.O. 295/97: Grant to Goderich, January 2, 1833, where the traffic was said to have started in 1825.

78. For the text of the Proclamation, see *Port of Spain Gazette*, February 8, 1832.

79. *Port of Spain Gazette*, February 8, 1832. He decried the rumour in such a way as to suggest it as the reason for the Proclamation.

80. The free coloureds were not invited to such meetings.

81. Memorial of the Slave owners to Grant, February 1832, enclosed with T.D.D. 10, unnumbered: Grant to Goderich, February 18, 1832.

82. Governor's reply, appended to the above Memorial. See also his reply of March 20, 1832 to their Memorial of March 15, 1832.

83. T.D.D. 10. 102: Grant to Goderich, November 10, 1832.

84. C.O. 296/11: Goderich to Grant, December 14, 1832.

85. T.D.D. 10: Memorialists to Grant, March 15, 1832.

86. T.D.D. 10: Reply of Grant to the Memorialists, March 20, 1832. Cf. the reply of the Attorney General of Barbados to Gibbons, August 3, 1827.

87. C.O. 295/92: Grant to Parkhurst, March 20 and 24, 1832.

88. C.O. 295/92: Parkhurst to Grant, March 20, 1832.

89. *Port of Spain Gazette*, August 8, 1832.

90. *Port of Spain Gazette*, August 11, 1832. The Editor reported having heard that Parkhurst became Collector only in 1829.

91. T.D.D. 11. 13: Grant to Goderich, February 3, 1833, enclosure 2. The clearance for the "Beautiful Maid" was signed by Robert Aberdeen, Collector; and Benjamin Parkhurst, Comptroller. The date of the Certificate was not given, but there were two sailings of the "Beautiful Maid", one in 1829 when Parkhurst would have been in Barbados.

92. C.O. 296/11: Goderich to Grant, December 14, 1832.

93. T.D.D. 10: Extract of the Minutes of the Cabildo, August 7, 1832.

94. *Ibid.*, Memorial of the Proprietors of the Imported Slaves, February 1832.

95. Wylly to Grant, November 4, 1832,

96. T.D.D. 10: Petition of the Committee to Goderich, November 3, 1832.

97. T.D.D. 10. 89: Grant to Goderich, November 2, 1832.

98. T.D.D. 10. 90: Grant to Goderich, November 2, 1832.

99. T.D.D. 10: Parkhurst to Grant, November 3, 1832.

100. Minutes of the Cabildo, August 7, 1832. The Governor was President

of the Cabildo. "Unanimously" here probably means no more than that everyone except the Governor was in favour of the motion.

101.   C.O. 296/11: Goderich to Grant, December 14, 1832.

102.   Minutes of the Cabildo, December 18, 1832. The maintenance of the jail was the responsibility of the Cabildo. The supervision of this was the duty of an officer called the Provost Marshall.

103.   T.D.D. 10. 115: Grant to Goderich, December 30, 1832. See also dispatches 114 and 116 of the same date. He had earlier warned the Secretary of State that merely ascertaining the facts was not the end of the matter. See T.D.D. 10:90.

104.   The papers were thrown into a privy and covered with several pounds of lime.

105.   *Port of Spain Gazette*, November 16, 1832. The statement was that of the Editor.

106.   C.O. 296/11: Goderich to the Officer administering the Government, March 2, 1833 (Confidential).

107.   C.O. 295/98: Rothery to Hill, August 1, 1833.

108.   C.O. 295/99: Rothery to Hill, October 31, 1833, mentions 186 for the period August 1 to October 21, 1833; C.O. 101: Rothery to Hill, January 7, 1834 mentions 74 for the period October 31, 1833 to January 1, 1834.

109.   C.O. 296/11: Stanley to Hill, January 12, 1834. Stanley was appointed Secretary of State for the Colonies in the middle of 1833.

110.   C.O. 296/11: Stanley to Hill, January 12, 1834.

Chapter 5

1.   Free Mulatto, *Address to Earl Bathurst*, p. 45.

2.   See, for example, Davis, *op.cit.*, pp. 302 – 316, and Dubois, Laurent,

A Colony of Citizens, p. 54. Free coloureds and blacks could neither vote, hold office, get good jobs, nor own much land; they were generally stigmatized in the English islands. See also Dunn, *Sugar and Slaves*, p. 256.

3.   See Elisabeth, Leo, "The French Antilles," in Cohen, David W. & Jack P.Greene, *Neither Slave nor Free*, Baltimore: Johns Hopkins University Press, 1972, p.140. Failure to prove their free status in France could have led to their deportation to their deportation to the colonies. Cf. Dubois, *A Colony of Citizens,* p. 54.

4.   Bowser, Frederick,"Colonial Spanish America,"in Cohen & Greene, *Neither Slave nor Free,* p. 22 and note 11. Cf. Davis, 102 – 6.

5.   *Ibid.*, Bowser,"Colonial Spanish America," p. 23. Reference is made to Chapter VI of that *Cedula.*

6.   *Ibid.*, Bowser, "Colonial Spanish America," p. 25. The system of *coartacion* originated in Cuba.

7.   *Ibid.*, p. 38.

8.   *Ibid.*, p. 40.

9.   *Ibid.*, p. 39. On the Church's attitude towards freemen, see Davis, *op. cit.,* p. 310.

10.   *Ibid.*

11.   Elisabeth, Leo, "The French Antilles," p. 142, notes 32 and 33.

12.   *Ibid.*, p. 155.

13.   *Ibid.*, 161. On pp. 159, 160 Elisabeth argues that the edict aimed at discouraging concubinage; the aim might just as easily have been to deter coloured prosperity.

14.   Gaspar, David Barry,"The emancipation of the Free Coloureds in St. Lucia, 1824 – 1831," in papers of the Eleventh Annual Conference of Caribbean Historians, 1970, pp. 11, 12.

15.   Elisabeth, "The French Antilles," p. 162. Cf. Garrigus, John D., "Colour, Class and Identity on the Eve of the Haitian Revolution: Saint-Domingue's Free Coloured Elite as *Colons Americains*," in *Slavery and Abolition*, Vol. 17, No. 1, April, 1996, pp. 29, 30. In St. Domingue such titles were considered illegal for free coloureds.

16.   Hall, G.M., "Saint Domingue," in Cohen and Greene, *Neither slave nor Free*, pp. 183, 184. White families were jealous of the growing prosperity of the free coloureds.

17.   Hall, G.M. "Saint Domingue," p. 189.

18.   Garrigus, John D., "Colour, Class, and Identity" p. 34. Also Garrigus, "Some background to Free Coloured activism: Julien Raimond in Saint Domingue, 1744 – 1784," papers presented at the Annual Conference of the Association of Caribbean Historians, 1987, pp. 4, 13, 23, for references to free coloured property in slaves. Cf. Elisabeth, "The French Antilles," pp. 165, 166.

19.   The expression was used by Julien Raimond, and cited by Garrigus in "Colour, Class, and Identity," p. 36. For the protests, see "Some background to Free Coloured Activism," p. 27. According to Aline Helg, phenotypic distinctions were used in the census of 1777 in Cartagena. See "The Limits of Equality: Free People of Colour and Slaves during the First Independence of Cartagena, Colombia, 1810 – 15," *Slavery and Abolition*, Vol. 20, No. 2, August 1999, pp. 13 – 15, 17.

20.   Elisabeth, "The French Antilles," p. 166. According to Garrrigus, they were more successful at this than other colonists. See his "Catalyst or Catastrophe? Saint-Domingue and the Battle of Savannah, 1779 – 1782" in Papers of the 24th Annual Conference of Caribbeans Historians, 1992, p. 4.

21.   Elisabeth, "The French Antilles", p. 159.

22.   Hall, D.G., "Jamaica," in Cohen and Greene, *Neither Slave nor Free*, p. 195.

23.   Handler, Jerome, *The Unappropriated People*, Baltimore: Johns Hopkins University Press, 1974, p. 68.

24. Handler, Jerome and Arnold Sio, "Barbados," in Cohen and Greene, *Neither Slave nor Free*, p. 230. Cf. Handler, *The Unappropriated People*, pp. 67, 72.

25. Hall, "Jamaica," pp. 197, note 9, on Deficiency Laws.

26. Campbell, *Cedulants and Capitulants*, p. 100, shows that some 3,325 carreaux were granted. At approximately 3.2 acres to a carreaux, this was 10,640 acres.

27. On their inferiority, see Handler & Sio, "Barbados," pp. 230 – 239, 247 – 250 and Hall, D., "Jamaica," pp. 195 – 197, both in Cohen & Greene, *Neither Slave nor Free*.

28. For an assessment of their status in the West Indies, see Goveia, E.V., *Slave Society in the British Leeward Islands,* pp. 204 – 207. Cf. Hall, D. G., "The Social and Economic background to Sugar in Slave days", *Caribbean Historical Review*, Nos. III & IV, pp. 156 – 159; Millette, *The Genesis of Crown Colony Government*, chapters 1, 2, and 5.

29. That the free coloureds were not all republicans is beyond dispute at present. Fraser, I. 315 cites a very disparaging assessment of the free coloureds by Joseph Marryat, the colony's agent in London, an assessment widely held in the island.

30. On the first occasion they were forfeited; on the second, the penalty was perpetual banishment. See *Legal Report*, p. 28. One hundred lashes and a nail through the hand the first time; loss of the hand the second time.

31. See the penultimate article of that *Cedula*.

32. The concessions are discussed in Williams, *History of the People of Trinidad and Tobago*, pp. 43ff.

33. *Address to Earl Bathurst*, pp. 7 - 9, 17.

34. *Address to Earl Bathurst*, pp. 199, 200. Appendix A, No. 1 mentions three commissioned officers in 1796: Bartholomew Letren, Captain; Philip Borelie, Lieutenant; and Placide Dardene, Ensign.

35.   Fraser, *History of Trinidad*, I. 11 –14. Fraser's prejudice was obviously in favour of the English, and his efforts to explain away the actions of some Governors shows this clearly.

36.   Borde, *History of the Island of Trinidad*, p. 241. Borde says that, except for a few Royalists, the whole French population was suspect: "the whites, because they did not object to the new principles; the slaves because these principles might encourage them to revolt, and the free blacks and people of colour, because they had adopted the new principles in order to try and press for the emancipation of their brothers who were slaves, and also because they wished to emerge from the state of inferiority in which they found themselves vis a vis the whites."

37.   Campbell, *Cedulants*, p. 119.

38.   C.O. 318/76: "Memorial of Jean Baptiste Philip and John Congnet, Trinidad, enclosed with the List of Papers relating to the Claims of the Coloured Inhabitants of the said Island".

39.   "Appeal to the Imperial Parliament". Philip does not name the author or give any relevant details. *Address to Earl Bathurst*, pp. 17 – 23.

40.   C.O. 296/1: Picton to the Secretary to the Secretary of State, October 16, 1797. The Governor reported that justice was speedily administered.

41.   See *Address to Earl Bathurst*, pp. 24. 25.

42.   C.O. 296/1: Picton to Dundas, January 1, 1799.

43.   C.O. 296/1: Picton to Hobart, February 18, 1802.

44.   *Address to Earl Bathurst*, p. 10. Twelve officers were said to have been deprived of their Commissions, but no mention is made of civil officers being similarly removed from office.

45.   Prof. Goveia shows that, in the Leeward Islands, towards the end of the eighteenth century, free coloureds were admitted to the militia but never commissioned. *Slave Society*, p. 219.

46.   See above, Introduction, p. 6.

47.   *Address to Earl Bathurst*, p. 29. The Free Mulatto stated that Picton made use of St. Hiliaire Begorrat to prepare the regulations which, he said, were based on the *Code Noir* of Martinique. Begorrat was an early French settler from Martinique; according to de Verteuil, he arrived in 1784. See *A History of Diego Martin,* p. 10.

48.   C.O. 295/63: Woodford to Bathurst, September 3, 1824.

49.   This is contained in the 3rd Article of Des Alguacils. See the Memorial of Philip and Congnet in C.O. 318/76.

50.   This assessment was given by Fraser, *History of Trinidad*, I. 306. On the extension to the planter class, see Millette, J. "The Civil Commission of 1802," *Jamaican Historical Review*, Vol. VI, 1966, p. 40, n. 42.

51.   C.O. 295/63: Woodford to Bathurst, September 3, 1824. Picton did not have everything his way. Fullarton was no supporter of his with respect to free coloureds and slaves. See Millette, "Civil Commission," pp. 62f.

52.   Cited in C.O. 318/76: "Memorial of Philip and Congnet", p. 7. A similar demand was made of free coloureds in Guadeloupe during the regime of Daniel Lescallier. Lescallier's policy must be seen in the light of Napoleon's determination to re-establish slavery in that colony. See Dubois, *A colony of Citizens*, pp. 411 – 422.

53.   See T.T.H.S. 605: "A Law of Grenada directed at Persons from Trinidad who are suspected of stealing slaves." The date of this Act was 1784.

54.   C.O. 318/76: "Memorial of Philip and Congnet." The free coloured representatives claimed that some members of their class had been put up for sale in Trinidad and the other West Indian Islands.

55.   Prof. Goveia writes: "The social and political inferiority of free persons of colour was considered to be a necessary bulwark of the slave system." *Slave Society*, p. 222.

56.   J. Millette, *The Genesis of Crown Colony Government*, chapter 8. Fraser, *History of Trinidad*, I. pp. 307 - 309, is detailed but biased.

57.   For their response to Hislop's request that they specify what they wished, see Fraser, *History of Trinidad*, I. 309.

58.   The Governor asked the senior members of the Council for a comprehensive report on all coloured persons. A similar request was made to the Commandants. See Fraser, *History Of Trinidad*, I. 311.

59.   C.O. 296/4: Liverpool to Hislop, November 27, 1810.

60.   T.D.D. 2. 205: Woodford to Bathurst, November 18, 1816.

61.   *Address to Earl Bathurst*, Appendix F.

62.   For this, see L. M. Fraser, *History of Trinidad*, II. 139.

63.   T.D.D.4. 367: Woodford to Bathurst, July 29, 1820.
64.   E. Williams *Documents*, No. 319: C.O. 295/50: Woodford to Goulburn, July 30, 1820.

65.   *Ibid.*

66.   *Legal Report*, p. 66.

67.   *Ibid.*

68.   *Ibid.* p. 44.

69.   See chapter 1 above.

70.   The new body was set up by a Proclamation dated January 5, 1832. See *Port of Spain Gazette*, January 7, 1832.

71.   See T.D.D. 10. 47: Grant to Goderich, July 2, 1832, enclosing a Memorial of the "foreign" Inhabitants to Goderich.

72.   Abolition of Slavery Act, 1833, clause 22. The clause excluded them from civil and military office, and from the exercise of any franchise.

73. C.O. 318/76: Memorial of Philip and Congnet, pp. 15f. Cf. *Address to Earl Bathurst*, p. 124. The complaint comes from an interested party and might be exaggerated, but not necessarily false.

74. *Address to Earl Bathurst*, pp. 76, 77.

75. This is mentioned in the list of public measures later repealed, see *Port of Spain Gazette*, January 11, 1826.

76. This Order was published in the *Trinidad Gazette*, January 22, 1823.

77. These are clauses 18 and 19.

78. *Address to Earl Bathurst*, pp. 108 – 115.

79. J. Lewis, Advocate, to Woodford, March 1823, enclosed with T.D.D. 4. 469: Woodford to Bathurst, March 10, 1823. Their apprehension about alcaldes administering such justice was never answered by the Governor.

80. Circular to the Commandants of Quarters, March 3, 1823. Enclosed with T.D.D. 4. 469: Woodford to Bathurst, March 10, 1823.

81. T.D.D. 4. 469: Woodford to Bathurst, March 10, 1823.

82. *Legal Report*, p. 43.

83. Philippe tells of a court case in which a married woman was contemptuously questioned as to her right to use the title "Mme".

84. *Port of Spain Gazette*, April 2, 1833.

85. T.D.D. 3. 245: Woodford to Bathurst, July 12, 1817.

86. *Ibid*.

87. T.D.D. 3. 256: Woodford to Bathurst, August 3, 1817. The emphasis is my own.

88. The present writer has seen no trace of the Order referred to by Woodford.

89. T.D.D. 3. 256: Woodford to Bathurst, August 3, 1817.

90. The law in question is enclosed with the above despatch – in Spanish with an accompanying translation.

91. See T.D.D. 4. 585: Woodford to Bathurst, December 6, 1824, where Woodford speaks specifically of the devising of property by whites to their coloured children.

92. According to the Governor the coloured people believed that a married woman was not to work. A married white woman did not work, and that state was the attraction for some free coloureds as well as slaves.

93. M'Callum, *Travels in Trinidad*, Liverpool, 1805, pp. 72 – 75. Even a Governor, such as Governor Ricketts of Tobago and Barbados had his coloured mistress. See Hall, Neville, "Law and Society in Barbados at the turn of the 19th century," *Journal of Caribbean History*, Volume 5, November 1972, p.36.

94. M'Callum, *Travels in Trinidad*, p. 78.

95. Goveia, *Slave Society*, pp. 215, 216 has made reference to this feature in the Leeward Islands.

96. *Address to Earl Bathurst*, pp. 96 - 98.

97. C.O. 295/63: Woodford to Bathurst, September 3, 1824.

98. Williams, *Documents,* No. 316: C.O. 295/44: Woodford to Bathurst, August 13, 1817.

99. For the scale of the medical fees, see below, Appendix B, No. 3.

100. *Address to Earl Bathurst*, Appendix M, pp. 230 - 235.

101. C.O. 295/63: Woodford to Bathurst, September 3, 1824.

102. *Ibid.*

103. *Address to Earl Bathurst*, p. 100.

104.	In the Minutes of the Cabildo, entries of such licences are followed by the word *gratis* for whites, but not for coloureds. See Minutes for 1821 – 1824, *passim*.

105.	*Address to Earl Bathurst*, pp. 102 – 4. Cf. the enclosures to C.O. 295/56: Young to Bathurst, February 1822.

106.	C.O. 295/58: Dr. Williams' views are attached to Francis Williams' Memorial to the Royal College of Surgeons, February 26, 1822. Dr. Alexander Williams' interest was probably due to the fact that Francis was formerly his slave or might well have been his son.

107.	C.O. 295/58: Young to Alexander Williams, December 21, 1821. In so doing, Young appealed to the discretion allowed him by the Proclamation of December 20, 1814, which set up the Medical Board.

108.	T.T.H.S. 391: Young to Bathurst, February 27, 1822.

109.	C.O. 295/58: Garcia to Williams, February 26, 1822.

110.	Knox to Williams, February 26, 1822.

111.	C.O. 296/6: Bathurst to Young, May 4, 1822.

112.	*Address to Earl Bathurst*, Appendix BB, 283 – 88. An anonymous writer not only found their accommodation indistinguishable from that of the whites, but recommended its adoption in the other islands. *The West Indies in 1825*, London, 1825, p. 64.

113.	Clapham had certain reservations about consecrating the church, and was "roughly handled" by the Governor. Woodford virtually arranged Clapham's retirement. After an innocuous reference to the retirement in a sermon, Woodford demanded the extract and accused Clapham to Bathurst of prostituting the pulpit. C.O. 295/62: Woodford to Bathurst, February 8, 1824.

114.	C. O. 295/63: Woodford to Bathurst, September 3, 1824.

115.	The Commandant was Robert Mitchell, one whom Woodford held in esteem, and to whom he entrusted the superintendence of the American refugees. See *Address to Earl Bathurst*, Appendix AA, pp. 280 – 283 for the coloured point of view.

116.	T.D.D. 4. 469: Woodford to Bathurst, March 10, 1823.

117.	*Ibid.*

118.	*Ibid.*

119.	C.O. 295/63: Woodford to Bathurst, September 3, 1824.

120.	*Address to Earl Bathurst*, p. 183. It cannot be overemphasised that there was division among the coloured group.

121.	*Address to Earl Bathurst,* p. 168.

122.	T.D.D. 4. 550: Woodford to Bathurst, May 26, 1824. The two slaves were found guilty of falsehood and punished. See Chapter **2**.

123.	C.O. 318/76: Memorial of Philip and Congnet.

124.	*Ibid.*

125	For the details and the replies of the coloured nominees, see *Port of Spain Gazette*, January 18, 1832.

126.	*Port of Spain Gazette*, December 11, 1832.

127.	Williams, *Documents*, No. 334: Clunes to Goderich, January 1832.

128.	C. O. 296/6: Bathurst to Woodford, October 31, 1825.

129.	Published in *Port of Spain Gazette*, January 11, 1826, cf. Legal Report, Appendix D, pp. 240f. The following instruments were revoked:
	1.	Art. 1 of Des Alguacils, Picton to Commandants, August 20, 1800, making free coloureds exclusively alguacils.
	2.	Order of Government, August 15, 1807, imposing a tax of $16 on balls given by free coloured persons.
	3.	Order of Government, November 20, 1804, imposing a curfew of 9.30 p.m. on them.
	4.	Two Orders of September 1810 concerning the Police in Port of Spain.

5.   A regulation of June 30, 1813, regarding fees for passes in the Government Secretary's office, distinguishing fees for whites as against coloureds.

6.   Order of the Superior Court dated August 3, 1819, requiring persons to describe their conditions in presenting ptitions.

7.   Order of Government of April 11, 1821, on the fees for Medical practitioners.

130.   T.D.D. 6. 26: Woodford to Bathurst, April 26, 1826.

131.   Published in the *Port of Spain Gazette*, July 4, 1829.

132.   T.D.D. 9: Memorial to Sir Lewis Grant, July 29, 1829.

133.   *Ibid*. Grant to Horace Twiss, April 4, 1830.

134.   C.O. 296/8: Murray to Grant, March 18, 1830.

135.   *Ibid*.

136.   *Port of Spain Gazette*, August 15, 1834.

137.   C.O. 295/99: Hill to Stanley, November 25, 1833.

138.   *Port of Spain Gazette*, August 15, 1834.

139.   C.O. 296/8: Murray to Smith, November, 1830. I have not been able to find a list of those given commissions.

140.   C.O. 295/98: Hill to Stanley, August 1, 1833.

Chapter 6

1.   The extract is taken from Fraser, *History of Trinidad*, Vol. II, p. 174.

2.   *Legal Report*, p. 28. On the French Code Noir, see Davis, *The Problem of Slavery*, pp. 278 – 282

3.   Chapters II and III. For this code, which was published in 1789, see Borde, *Histoire*, II, Appendix, pp. 433 – 441. See n. 56. Joseph, *History*

of Trinidad, p. 238 refers to a trial in which it was successfully argued that the 1789 *Cedula* had not been approved by the Audiencia in Caracas, and hence was not in force; and also that Picton's Code of 1800 had not been approved in London and therefore was not in force. See Bryan Edwards, *History,* IV. 451, 452, where it is suggested that this code had fallen into disuse after the arrival of the British, but that it was reintroduced later. There is no corroboration of this in the literature.

4.   Chapters V to VII.

5.   For Picton's Code, see Carmichael, *History,* Appendix, pp. 379 - 83.

6.   The cases of Huggins and Hodge in the Leeward Islands are well known. See Murray, *The West Indies,* pp. 80f, 93f, 100 – 102. The details are given in British Parliamentary Papers, *Slave Trade,* Vol. 61, Shannon: Irish University Press, 1971., 471 – 51, and 515 – 530 respectively.

7.   See, for example, Mrs Carmichael, *Domestic Manners and Social Condition of the White, Coloured, and Negro Population of the West Indies,* (1833) New York: Negro Universities Press, 1969, II. 163.

8.   In 1823 Woodford submitted the testimony of three planters to this effect. T.D.D. 4. 518: Woodford to Bathurst, November 5, 1823, enclosures from Henry and Thomas St. Hill, and W. G. Pemberton.

9.   Minutes of the Cabildo, August 31, 1813.

10.   T.D.D. 2. 214: Woodford to Bathurst, November 23, 1816. This dispatch reported the opinion of the Commandants that the Abolition Act had been generally and faithfully observed – an opinion he actually contradicted.

11.   T.D.D. 3. 251: Woodford to Bathurst, July 31, 1817.

12.   See above pp. 197, 198. 200.

13.   C.O. 296/5: Goulburn to Woodford, May 22, 1817. Goulburn was Under Secretary   of the Colonial Office under Bathurst. See Murray, *The West Indies,* pp. 117f.

14.   C.O. 296/5: Goulburn to Woodford, December 1, 1817.

15.   Free Mulatto, *Address to Earl Bathurst*, p. 222. This statement was written in an atmosphere of controversy which should make us hesitate to attach too much weight to it.

16.   T.D.D. 3. 251: Woodford to Bathurst, July 31, 1817.

17.   *Appeal on behalf of the Negroes in the West Indies*, British Museum Papers, T 1137 (7), pp. 13f. This expression was a citation from Chief Justice Ottley of St. Vincent.

18.   *Ibid.* p. 15.

19.   *Ibid.*, pp. 17f. Wilberforce noted great licentiousness among other classes of the Society. He drew attention to the frequent employment of single men as   managers as a contributory factor.

20.   For the text of the motion, see R.L. Schuyler, *Parliament and the British Empire*, p. 151. See also *Substance of the Debate in the House of Commons, on the 15th May 1823*, New York: Negro Universities Press, 1969. p. xxvi, and for Canning's motion, p. xxviii.

21.   *Trinidad Gazette*, June 25, 1823. Cf. *Substance of the Debate*, pp. 18 – 20.

22.   *Trinidad Gazette,* June 25, 1823. Cf. Klingberg, *The Anti-Slavery Movement in England*, p. 196. Klingberg's estimate of Buxton and other abolitionists suggests that he might not have been entirely free of prejudice. On pp. 193f., he writes: "The difficulty with him and the other anti-slavery leaders was that they did not know negroes, and their policy was grounded on a too optimistic belief in the black man's capacity for rapid improvement. They believed that the negro was a white man enslaved, and based their crusade on this assumption."

23.   For the text of Canning's resolutions, see Newton, J.H., et al., *Cambridge History of the British Empire*, Cambridge: Cambridge University Press, 1940, Vol. II, 1783 – 1870, pp. 151f. Cf. *Substance of the Debate*, p. 34.

24.   Canning's resolutions were said by an anonymous writer to be intended to bind Parliament to a more practical course than Buxton's more enthusiastic resolution. See Anonymous, *The West India Question*, London, 1826, p. 7. The author of this document is believed to be R.J.W.Horton an Under-Secretary at the Colonial Office. Emancipation in his view was rashness.

25.   C.O. 122/5: Bathurst to Governor John Murray and Lt. Governor Beard, May 28, 1823. Taken from Harlow & Madden, *British Colonial Development*, p. 561.

26.   C.O. 296/6: Bathurst to Woodford, May 28, 1823.

27.   Williams, *Documents*, No. 186: Commandant at Chaguanas to Woodford, August 20, 1823.

28.   Williams, *Documents*, No. 190: Resolutions of the General Meeting, Arima, September 29, 1823.

29.   Williams, *Documents*, No. 191: Meeting of North Naparima, October 16, 1823.

30.   Williams, *Documents*, No, 192: Meeting of Pointe-a-Pierre, October 20, 1823.

31.   T.D.D. 4: 523: Woodford to Bathurst, December 5, 1823.

32.   *Ibid.*

33.   Proprietors of South Naparima to John Lamont, Commandant, October 9, 1823, enclosed with T.D.D. 4. 519: Woodford to Bathurst, November 6, 1823.

34.   T.D.D. 4. 523: Woodford to Bathurst, December 5, 1823. In an earlier despatch, Woodford chided the Commandants for indiscretion. See T.D.D. 4.518: Woodford to Bathurst, Nov. 5, 1823.

35.   C.O. 295/59: Extract of the Minutes of Council, July 9, 1823. Williams, Documents, No. 119.

36.   T.D.D. 6.7: Woodford to Bathurst, January 7, 1826, enclosure dated

September 4, 1823. Approval was given in C.O. 296/6: Bathurst to Woodford, April 12, 1826.

37.   T.D.D. 6.7: Extract of the Minutes of the Council, dated September, 1823.

38.   *Ibid*.

39.   C.O.296/6: Bathurst to Woodford, August 22, 1825 expressed reservations about approval. That approval was given in a dispatch dated April 12, 1826.

40.   *Ibid*., Bathurst to Woodford, October 4, 1823.

41.   *Ibid*., (Separate): Bathurst to Woodford, January 10, 1824.

42.   T.D.D. 4. 518: Woodford to Bathurst, November 5, 1823.

43.   Woodford to the Commandants, August 1823, enclosed with T.D.D. 4. 499: Woodford to Bathurst, August 6, 1823.

44.   T.D.D. 4. 499: Woodford to Bathurst, August 3, 1823.

45.   For the details of the discussions, see the Minutes of the Cabildo for September 29, October 13 and 20, and November 3, 1823.

46.   For the Proclamation embodying the new arrangement, see *Trinidad Gazette*, November 15, 1823.

47.   T.D.D. 4. 499: Woodford to Bathurst, August 6, 1823.

48.   Woodford to Howley, November 5, 1823. Fulham Papers, f. 868.

49.   C.O. 296/6: Horton to Woodford, July 9, 1823. The request was transmitted through the Under Secretary.

50.   He probably meant the Order based strictly on Bathurst's proposals.

51.   C.O. 295/59: Woodford to Bathurst, December 5, 1823. It is to this letter that Bathurst replied that he was not buying planter support for amelioration.

52.   C.O. 295/59: Woodford to Bathurst, December 5, 1823.

53.   The Order is enclosed with C.O. 296/6: Bathurst to Woodford, March 25, 1824, No. 1. An extensive portion is given in Harlow & Madden, *British Colonial Developments*, pp. 567 – 573. For a printed copy, see British Parliamentary Papers, Slave Trade, Vol. 68, 1969, pp. 166 – 80.

54.   The Protectorate is provided for in clauses 6, 7, and 8.

55.   See clause 12.

56.   Clause 24 was intended to confirm a Trinidad law permitting slaves to hold property. But the Chief Judge and the Judge of the Court of Criminal Inquiry were not agreed as to whether slaves were thus permitted under the existing laws. See *Legal Report*, p. 29

57.   It is difficult to say, from the available evidence, the extent to which slave families were separated. That there was a high proportion of judicial sales is evident from the following data: between 1808 and 1821, slaves sold for debt totalled 2,354, averaging 168 per year. Of that total, 2,112 were plantation slaves and 342 personal. See T.D.D. 4.526: Woodford to Bathurst, November 5, 1823, enclosure.

58.   C.O. 296/6: Bathurst to Woodford, March 25, 1824, No. 1.

59.   *Ibid*. The Order of November 1831 made these visits part of the Protector's duties. See chapter 7.

60.   C.O. 296/6: Bathurst to Woodford, March 25, 1824, No. 2. Woodford's reply to Bathurst indicated that it was impossible to reduce the Commandants to less than 20. T.D.D. 4.546: Woodford to Bathurst, May 7, 1824.

61.   C.O. 296/6: Bathurst to Woodford, March 25, 1824, No. 3.

62.   Vindex, *CONSIDERATIONS submitted in defence of the ORDERS IN COUNCIL for the MELIORATION OF SLAVERY IN TRINIDAD*, p. 154. The name Vindex was a pseudonym employed by a small group of abolitionists. See British Museum MSS, 522 f 31.

63.   Anonymous, *The West India Question Practically Considered*, London, 1826, p. 44.

64.   *Ibid.* Cf. Ragatz, L. J., *The Fall of the Planter Class,* p. 415, where the Spanish law in Trinidad was thought to have provided a more favourable atmosphere for the programme.

65.   Cabildo to Woodford, May 17, 1824. T.D.D. 4. 549: Woodford to Bathurst, May 26, 1824, enclosure 3. See also Minutes of the Cabildo, May 17, 1824. Woodford lost no time in pointing out that the laws quoted were irrelevant, though he found Spanish laws relevant for his punishment of Marquis and Regis.

66.   Remonstrance of the Council to Woodford, enclosed with T.D.D. 4. 549, as above.

67.   As a rule coloured persons were not included when the "inhabitants" held meetings. Surprisingly they used the description "free" which was usually confined to coloureds and blacks.

68.   Petition of the free Inhabitants to Woodford, enclosed with T.D.D. 4. 549.

69.   T.D.D. 4. 545: Woodford to Bathurst, May 7, 1824.

70.   Woodford to Howley, October 8, 1824, Fulham Papers, f. 870.

71.   Woodford to Howley, May 16, 1825, Fulham Papers, f. 881.

72.   Petition of Fuller to Woodford, May 18, 1824. Fuller, in August of the same year, claimed compensation for the post of *Syndic Procurador*, which he valued at $1,200 per year. Fuller's decision not to sell his estates is reported in T.D.D. 4. 546: Woodford to Bathurst, May 7, 1824.

73.   T.D.D. 4.546: Woodford to Bathurst, May 7, 1824. Woodford thought a lawyer was the best person for the job.

74.   For his election, see Minutes of the Cabildo, June 23, 1824. By -early 1825, he was referred to as one of the two Crown Officers. See *Trinidad Gazette*, April 9, 1825.

75. *Return of the Public Functionaries in the Island of Trinidad who are Proprietors of slaves, or of Plantations worked by slaves, or who are in the occupancy or concerned in the Management of slaves.* October 3, 1826. It is very likely that they possessed most of these slaves in 1824.

76. T.D.D. 4. 568: Woodford to Bathurst, August 16, 1824.

77. The Proclamation, dated March 6, was published in the *Port of Spain Gazette*, March 8, 1826.

78. T.D.D. 6. 23: Woodford to Bathurst, April 12, 1826.

79. For details on the discussion, see Legal Report, pp. 81, 111.

80. C.O. 296/6: Bathurst to Woodford, June 26, 1826. Bathurst considered the Proclamation to be at variance with the Order in Council, noting that there was no authority in Trinidad capable of altering an Order of the King.

81. See, for example, C.O. 295/48: Woodford to Bathurst, January 26, 1819; 295/50: Woodford to Bathurst, March 20, 1820. Also T.D.D. 4. 564: Woodford to Bathurst, August 4, 1824; 6. 23: Woodford to Bathurst, April 12, 1826. Cf. Legal Report, p. 29.

82. The estimates for 1828 provided for ten curates, and a Vicar Apostolic (Catholic); two clergy of the Protestant Church (Anglican), only one being in the colony at the time. See *Trinidad General Establishment, 1828. Ecclesiastical*, enclosed with T.D.D. 7: Woodford to Bathurst, (Private), August 31, 1827.

83. *Abstract of the Triennial Return of Baptism of Plantation Slaves, November 30, 1824,* enclosed with T.D.D. 4. 586: Woodford to Bathurst, December 6, 1824.

84. T.D.D. 6. 23: Woodford to Bathurst, April 12, 1826.

85. Clapham's retirement was largely arranged by Woodford. See chapter 5.

86. C.O. 300/19: Report of the Protector of Slaves for the period

ending December 1824; C.O. 300/20: Report of the Protector of Slaves for the period ending June 1826.

87.   This explanation was given by Carmichael, A. C., *Domestic Manners*, II. 177, 178; cf. pp. 214, 234, and 243.

88.   Carmichael, *op. cit.* pp. 177, 178.

89.   Orlando Patterson, *The Sociology of Slavery*, London: MacGibbon and Kee, 1967, p. 41, makes this point about Jamaica. It is no less true about Trinidad or anywhere else in the West Indies.

90.   A Letter Addressed to the Clergy ... 1829.

91.   Fuller to Woodford, December 1824.

92.   Fuller to Woodford, August 31, 1825, enclosed with T.D.D. 6. 17: Woodford to Bathurst, February 25, 1826.

93.   "A contract is the voluntary Agreement of two or more persons by which something is to be given or performed upon one part, for a valuable consideration either present or future, on the other part." The definition was given by Gloster himself; see Gloster to Woodford, February 3, 1825, enclosed with T.D.D. 6. 17 above.

94.   Gloster to Woodford, February 3, 1825 and April 3, 1826.

95.   C.O. 296/6: Bathurst to Woodford, August 15, 1826.

96.   The procedure to be followed was set out in a Circular to the Commandants. See the *Port of Spain Gazette*, November 29, 1826.

97.   The suggestions were enclosed in an appendix to T.D.D. 4. 580: Woodford to Bathurst, October 30, 1824.

98.   T.D.D. 6: Gloster to Woodford, August 4, 1826, enclosed with T.D.D. 6.57: Woodford to Bathurst, August 8, 1826. Gloster showed appraisals of £86.13.4, twice that amount by the second appraiser, and £150 by the umpire. Cf. C.O. 296/8: Murray to Grant, July 11, 1829. The rates were £173.6.8 for the appraiser and £250 by the umpire; and £130 by the appraisers and £260 by the umpire.

99.   T.D.D. 7. 9: Woodford to Huskisson, March 7, 1828. The figures cited here do not agree with those in the Protector's Reports. Cf. Protector of Slaves to Woodford, December 19, 1826, for the argument concerning the Consolidated Slave Trade Act, enclosed with T.D.D 6.82: Woodford to Bathurst, December 22, 1826.

100.   C.O. 296/6; Bathurst to Woodford, September 11, 1824.

101.   A Proclamation setting out guidelines appeared in the *Trinidad Gazette*, December 15, 1824.

102.   Statement of the number of Slaves manumitted in the Island of Trinidad from June 24 to December 24, 1827.

103.   "Appraisement of a Slave by Thomas Le Gendre and W. H. Burnley," enclosed with T.D.D. 6. 57: Woodford to Bathurst August 8, 1826. It never occurred to the appraisers that the slave had given her labour free to her owner, and that the appraisal was a gross injustice.

104.   Gloster to Woodford, August 4, 1826, enclosed with T.D.D. 6. 57: Woodford to Bathurst, August 8, 1826.

105.   Protector of Slaves to Woodford, December 19, 1826, enclosed with T.D.D. 6. 82: Woodford to Bathurst, December 22, 1826.

106.   Warner to Woodford, August 5, 1826.

107.   C.O. 296/8: Bathurst to Woodford, October 30, 1826.

108.   T.D.D. 7.8: Woodford to Huskisson, March 7, 1828.

109.   Protector of Slaves to Woodford, December 19, 1826, enclosed with T.D.D. 6. 82: Woodford to Bathurst, December 22, 1826.

110.   C.O. 296/8: Murray to Grant, July 11, 1829.

111.   T.D.D. 8. 38: Grant to Murray, October 1829.

112.   *Trinidad Gazette*, July 16, 1825. At the time of the application, the slave had run away. The Judge explained that the permission of the owner was not needed for marriage.

113.   C.O. 296/6: Bathurst to Woodford, September 11, 1824.

114.   For details, see his letter in the *Port of Spain Gazette*, October 12, 1825.

115.   T.D.D. 5. 600: Woodford to Bathurst, February 9, 1825, enclosure from the Protector of Slaves. On the Tread Wheel, see Minutes of the Cabildo, April to September 1823, passim; also C.O. 295/62: Report on the Tread Mill, February 6, 1824.

116.   Proclamation of June 23, 1824. Writing to Bishop Howley, October 8, 1824, Woodford said: "I certainly regret that the Order in Council was passed as it stands, but it has done no harm I hope & an order issued by me to show the ladies that they would be kept in order was considered of great service." Fulham Papers, f. 870. On November 27, 1826, Woodford confessed to Bishop Howley that the Order did not have the unfavourable results anticipated. Fulham Papers, f. 884b (i).

117.   The proclamation was published in the *Trinidad Gazette*, December 15, 1824.

118.   C.O. 300/20: Report of the Protector of Slaves for the period ending June 1826, Appendix B: Case of the King v. Regis Clark.

119.   *Trinidad Gazette*, December 8, 11, 1824. Cf. March 12, April 9, May 7, 1825, for the view that the proliferation of crimes was a direct result of the operation of the Order.

120.   *Trinidad Gazette*, March 30, 1825. In this issue, he announced his loss of office as Government Printer. Cf. Carmichael, *Domestic Manners*, pp. 129, 206.

121.   A Subsciber to the Editor, *Trinidad Gazette*, January 5, 1825. Cf. *Port of Spain Gazette*, June 14, 1826, where the new editor thought that the Order could be tried elsewhere, so beneficial had it been in Trinidad.

122.   *Port of Spain Gazette*, August 1, 1827. The writer did not indicate the source from which he drew his information; but no effort was made to contradict the facts given or his interpretation of them.

123.   These were assault and rape; assault and wounding; assault and sodomy.

124. C.O. 300/22: Report of the Protector of Slaves for the period ending June 1827, Appendix B, No. 2.

125. C.O. 300/23: Report of the Protector of Slaves for the period ending December 1827, Appendix B, No. 2.

126. *Ibid.*, Appendix B, No. 3.

127. T.D.D. 7: Protector of Slaves to Woodford, May 17, 1827. This case was not unlike that against Robert Gaston in 1824, in which the matter was heard in the same Court and passed on for prosecution. See C.O. 300/19: Report of the Protector of Slaves for the period ending December 1824, Appendix B.

128. Johnston to Woodford, May 21, 1827. In a subsequent letter, Johnston made reference to the trial of Marie Louise Dumaine in 1825, in which the following exceptions were successfully argued:
    1. Henry Gloster had no authority to make an accusation in the King's name;
    2. By the 6th clause of the 1824 Order, the Protector was a magistrate, and as such could not prosecute.
    3. By the 1822 Order, all criminal accusations were to be filed by the Attorney General or Law Officer of the Crown. Gloster held no such office, and was not competent o prosecute. For information on the office of Solicitor General, which he held, see note 69 above. T.D.D. 7: Johnston to Woodford, May 25, 1827.

129. The proclamation was issued on May 28. James Stephen recommended that the Proclamation be allowed as a matter of urgency, even though he did not see the need for it; see C.O. 295/76: Stephen to Horton, September 6, 1827.

130. Proclamation dated July 15, 1824, enclosed with T.D.D. 4. 567: Woodford to Bathurst, August 9, 1824.

131. A. Carmichael, *Domestic Manners*, p. 214. Carmichael had a very negative of slaves and was quite explicit about their inferiority.

132. T.D.D. 4. 545: Woodford to Bathurst, May 7, 1824. Cf. 5. 566: Woodford to Bathurst, August 6, 1824.

133.   C.O. 296/6: Bathurst to Woodford, June 24, 1824.

134.   T.D.D. 4: Woodford to the Commandants, August 21, 1824.

135.   C.O. 296/6: Bathurst to Woodford, September 11, 1824.

136.   The proclamation, dated October 29, 1824, is enclosed with T.D.D. 4. 580: Woodford to Bathurst, October 30, 1824.

137.   *Trinidad Gazette.* July 16, 1825. The minimum wages were:

Drivers, Boilers, and artificers of every description: per day	6s Cy.
For any time not exceeding 2 hrs	2s Cy.
For more than 2 hrs., but less than 4	3s Cy.
Field labourers, per day	4s Cy.
For any time, not exceeding 4 hrs.	2s Cy.

138.   T.D.D. 4. 549: Woodford to Bathurst, May 26, 1824.

139.   T.D.D. 4. 545: Woodford to Bathurst, May 7, 1824.

140.   C.O. 296/6: Bathurst to Woodford, June 25, 1824.

141.   T.D.D. 4: Warner to Woodford, September 14, 1824, enclosed with 4. 576: Woodford to Bathurst, September 15, 1824.

142.   Only one case can clearly be mentioned – that of John Fitzgerald in 1826. For the Governor's action, see *Port of Spain Gazette*, February 1, 1826. Cf. Williams, *Capitalism and Slavery*, London: Andre Deutsch, 1967, p. 259, note 15.

143.   See the *Trinidad Gazette*, September 14, 1825. On this day the name was changed to *Port of Spain Gazette*.

Chapter 7

1.   For details on the activities in these colonies, see Murray, *The West Indies*, pp. 146 – 165. G.R. Mellor, *British Imperial Trusteeship, 1783 – 1850*, London: Faber & Faber, 1951, pp. 98, 99; Schuyler, *Parliament and the British Empire*, pp. 156 – 170.

2. The Order in Council is printed in the *Port of Spain Gazette*, April 14, 1830, as well as in the British Parliamentary Papers, Slave Trade, Vol. 77, 1969, pp. 27 – 43. Attention is drawn only to departures from the 1824 Order in this and the later Order.

3. C.O. 296/6: Bathurst to Woodford, September 11, 1824. The clauses in question are 52 – 67 for manumissions generally.

4. Clause 21. The incidents involving the slaves Marquis and Regis, noticed in chapter 1, are sufficient justification of this.

5. C.O. 296/8: Murray to Grant, February 4, 1830. Murray also warned Grant to avoid vagueness in the proclamations he was framing.

6. For a discussion on the supervision of public officials, see Murray, *The West Indies*, pp. 151f.

7. C.O. 296/8: Murray to Grant, February 18, 1830.

8. Except here, there is no indication as to how many slaves did a task. This writer assumes, therefore, that only one person was intended.

9. The report appears in the *Port of Spain Gazette*, April 19, 1830. This issue also published a Report of the Protector of Slaves enclosed with a despatch: Smith to Goderich, October 9, 1830.

10. "Throwing grass" probably refers to the late evening task of bringing grass for the animals. See Picton's Code, Article 7.

11. The report mentions "head people", which probably means heads of groups, and therefore drivers of gangs.

12. A small amount, probably a half pint.

13. These provisions will later be compared with those demanded by the 1831 Order, as well as with the substitutions authorised subsequent to that Order.

14. C.O. 296/8: Murray to the Officer Administering the Government, November 18, 1830.

15.   *Port of Spain Gazette*, February 4, 1831. The Proclamation also indicated that Assistant Commandants were to become Assistant Protectors. One does not know Grant's authority for this.

16.   *Port of Spain Gazette*, July 31, 1830.

17.   T.D.D. 9. Unnumbered: Grant to Murray, April 21, 1830.

18.   T.D.D. 9: Gloster to Smith, August 27, 1830, enclosed with Smith to Murray, September 11, 1830. Smith was acting Governor in the absence, on leave, of Grant.

19.   C.O. 296/8: Murray to the Officer administering the Government, November 17, 1830. Murray noted with satisfaction the dissent of the professional judge. The latter case involved St. Hiliaire Surieux, the owner of the slave. He also found nothing in the Order in Council to support the distinction being drawn between domestics and other slaves.

20.   T.D.D. 9 unnumbered: Smith to Murray, July 20, 1830. The opinions are given in Smith's dispatch.

21.   C.O. 296/8: Goderich to Grant, May 10, 1831.

22.   The Order is enclosed with C.O. 295/92: Grant to Goderich, June 15, 1832. Cf. also the *Port of Spain Gazette*, May 30, 1832, and British Parliamentary Papers, *Slave Trade*, Vol. 79, Shannon: Irish University Press, 1969, pp. 93 – 138.

23.   For a fuller discussion of this, see chapter 1 above.

24.   See chapter 6.

25.   C.O. 295/87: A list of public officers owning slaves was made by the Registrar on March 7, 1831.

26.   C.O. 296/10: Goderich to the Officer administering the Government, August 18, 1831. The circuit system was omitted from Woodford's draft of the 1824 Order. C.O. 295/59: Woodofrd to Bathurst, December 5, 1823. Cf. C.O. 296/5: Bathurst to Woodford, March 25, 1824, No. 1.

27. T.D.D. 9: Extracts of the Minutes of the Council. October 1, 1831. The seven circuits were:
    1. Eastern – the 14 districts east of Port of Spain, Aricagua to Mayaro in a semi-circle
    2. Northwest – Maraval to Carenage
    3. South east – Chaguanas to Pointe-a-Pierre
    4. Naparima – San Fernando, North & South Napaima, Savana Grande
    5. South west – Oropouche to Erin
    6. Toco – including Cumana
    7. Moruga

28. *Ibid.*

29. *Ibid.*

30. T.D.D. 9. 122: Smith to Goderich, October 8, 1831. His tours were:
    1. Aricagua to Arouca and eastwards, also Maraval to Carenage
    2. The coastline from Chaguanas to Erin
    3. Toco and Mayaro.

31. C.O. 296/10: Goderich to Grant, January 13, 1832. Goderich stressed that the Protector was to hold no other office, and to have no private practice. In a memorandum to Grant, Chief Justice Scotland disapproved of the combination of such offices; the Protector should have not other office.

32. By the term "south" was meant the whole region from Chaguanas to Erin, and across to Mayaro.

33. C.O. 296/10: Goderich to Grant, January 13, 1832.

34. The Order was printed in the *Port of Spain Gazette*, January 4, and 7, 1832.

35. *Port of Spain Gazette*, March 25, 1832. The Order was so named because of its 121 clauses.

36. Section XXXVII. The previous Order required only one free person to be a witness.

37. The sections on Marriage are LIV to LVIII. On mixed marriages, see LVI, where it is stated that such marriages could only be declared invalid on grounds of consanguinity.

38. The food and clothing allowances are to be found in clauses LXXXVIII, LXXXIX, and XCVII respectively.

39. See Appendix C, Nos. 1 and 2 for a comparison of all allowances.

40. This was one of the clauses which gave great offence to slave owners,

41. On this point, see Williams, *Capitalism and Slavery*, p. 59.

42. In 1824, J. Cadett claimed that there was a law to this effect. See T.D.D. 4. 549: Woodford to Bathurst, May 17, 1824, enclosure.

43. These provisions were included in clauses XCII – XCVI.

44. The framers of the Order were reflecting the fears of the Trinidad and, indeed, West Indian slave society, where the presupposition was that the slaves would use the cover of darkness to plot the murder of the whites.

45. C.O. 296/10: Goderich to Grant, November 14, 1831. For the last point, see Goderich to Grant, November 17, 1831.

46. Minutes of the Cabildo, January 4, 1832. Cf. *Port of Spain Gazette*, January 18, 1832. The Address was unanimously adopted, Gloster being one of those present.

47. *Port of Spain Gazette*, January 11, 1832 reporting on North Naparima, Guapo, and Port of Spain; February 4, 1832, reporting on Savana Grande.

48. *Port of Spain Gazette*, January 14, 1832.

49. Goderich had relieved Grant of any discretion concerning this Order, on the ground that Grant could not then yield to solicitations. C.O. 296/10: Goderich to Grant, November 14, 1831.

50. *Port of Spain Gazette*, January 14, 1832. At this time similar action

was taken in St. Lucia where, eventually, sugar manufacture and mercantile operations were brought to a standstill. See, for example, *Port of Spain Gazette*, January 18 and April 11, 1832.

51.   *Port of Spain Gazette*, June 27, 1832.

52.   According to Sir Norman Lamont, Burnley had owned eight estates and had interests in several others. He also had interests in mercantile establishments. He also had interests in mercantile establishments. See his *Burnley of Orange Grove*, Port of Spain Gazette, 1947.

53.   For further details, see below.

54.   *Port of Spain Gazette*, October 12, 1832.

55.   *Ibid.*, January 18, 1832.

56.   Carmichael, G., *History*, p. 162, where the letter is cited in full.

57.   *Port of Spain Gazette*, December 11, 1832.

58.   For a brief mention of this issue, see chapter 5.

59.   *Port of Spain Gazette*, February 29 1832. On March 7, 1832 it reported the absenteeism on eight estates in the Carapichaima district. See also T.D.D. 10.72: Grant to Goderich, September 20, 1832. Grant also reported that the slaves saw no need for passes and that some were being prevented from visiting husband or wife if they belonged to different estates.

60.   *Port of Spain Gazette*, May 26 and June 6, 1832. The charge of overwork was made on the Plein Palais estate, Pointe-a-Pierre.

61.   *Ibid.*, February 29, 1832.

62.   *Ibid.*, March 17, 1832.

63.   C.O. 295/94: Colpoys to Elliott, Admiralty, Antigua, April 19, 1832. For charges of arson, see the *Port of Spain Gazette*, March 25, 1832. The estates involved were Concord (Naparima), St. Andre near Petit Bourg, and Retrench.

64. *Port of Spain Gazette*, July 11, 14, and 18, 1832. The Protector's report does not record any complaint against punishments as was also claimed by the paper.

65. See chapter 1.

66. *Port of Spain Gazette*, May 2, 1832.

67. Browne's address was delivered at the beginning of the session.

68. *Port of Spain Gazette*, May 2, 1832, under the caption "A Noble Act". We must also take note of the emphasis which Browne placed upon the authority of the owner, a subject on which was based much of the objection to amelioration on the whole.

69. Minutes of the Cabildo, May 22, 1832.

70. *Ibid.*, Letter of the First Alcalde to Chief Justice Scotland, May 5, 1832. Mellor in *British Imperial Trusteeship*, p. 102, has overlooked this point – that some of the cases could have been tried in minor courts. There was wanton opposition as well as good sense in the objections.

71. According to Joseph, *History of Trinidad*, p. 258, Scotland arrived on February 12, 1832.

72. C.O. 295/93: Scotland to Grant, June 24, 1832.

73. *Ibid.* By June, Fuller had lost his appointment as Attorney General. A Colonial Office note to Grant's despatch of July 3, 1832, noted that Gloster was legal adviser to the Cabildo, and recommended that he give up one of the offices.

74. C.O. 300/29: Protector's Report for the period ending June 24, 1832

75. Minutes of the Cabildo, July 3, 1832. The Minutes indicate that the Governor had got the wrong impression, for they neither approved nor disapproved of the actions of the alcaldes.

76. *Ibid.* May 15, 1832: Governor's address to the Cabildo.

77.   *Ibid.* May 22, 1832. Chief Justice to the First Alcalde, May 6, 1832.

78.   C.O. 295/93: Goderich to the Governors of Crown Colonies (Circular), May 13, 1832.

79.   T.D.D. 10. 61: Grant to Goderich, August 30, 1832.

80.   Goderich to the West India Governors, September 5, 1832, CIRCULAR. Published in the *Port of Spain Gazette*, January 4, 1833.

81.   T.D.D. 11: Scotland to Grant, December 31, 1832.

82.   *Ibid.* Bent to Grant, December 22, 1832.

83.   *Ibid.* Hanley to Grant, December 22, 1832.

84.   *Ibid.* Wylly to Grant, December 29, 1832.

85.   T.D.D. 11: Gloster to Grant, December 29, 1832. Barely two months later, Gloster referred to Grant the following protest by slave owners: "I make the following declaration under protest, and without in any manner admitting the legal validity of the Order of His majesty in Council dated 2nd Novr. 1831 or the Proclamation of His Excellency the Governor, dated the 25th January last, but adhering to and renewing the protest made by me against the Order in Council and registered in the Archives of the Illustrious Board of Cabildo – 22nd February 1833". T.D.D. 11. 29: Grant to Goderich, February 25, 1833.

86.   *Port of Spain Gazette*, January 4, 1833.

87.   *Ibid.* September 19, 1832. The editor threatened anyone following Marryat's example with appropriationof his crops by the planters, leaving the merchants to have estates if they so desired.

88.   *Ibid.* October 12, 1832. In the last resolution they denied submission to, or acquiescence in, the Order in Council. The meeting was chaired by Henry Fuller, former Attorney General; the mover of the resolutions was Henry Murray, former Registrar of Slaves. T.D.D. 10. 107: Grant to Goderich, December 30, 1832, acknowledged

receipt of the Order in Council of November 6, 1832, concerning alterations to that of November 2, 1831.

89. C.O. 295/99: Hill to Stanley, November 25, 1833. Compared with the reports at the end of 1832, those at the end of 1833 indicate greater co-operation on the part of the slave owners.

90. See Scotland to Hill, November 3, 1833; Gomez to Hill, November 24, 1833; Johnston to Hill, November 25, 1833 reported that the Order as amended was in force. Stephen Rothery to Hill, November 23, 1833, claimed that the Order was in force since his arrival in April, and that no case had been defeated by improper means. He also claimed to have had contact with owners and slaves from every estate. They were all enclosed with C.O. 295/99: Hill to Stanley, November 25, 1833. See also Gloster to Hill, December 2, 1833, enclosed with C.O. 295/101: Hill to Stanley, January 8, 1834.

91. This officer was a Roman Catholic parish priest named R.P. Smith.

92. *Port of Spain Gazette*, January 15, 1833.

93. C.O.295/97: Grant to Goderich, April 4, 1833, enclosure.

94. T.D.D. 11.6, enclosure: Report on the Slave School, by the Revd. Mr. Cummins, December 20, 1832.

95. T.D.D. 10, unnumbered: Grant to Goderich, June 10, 1832. The Council at this time consisted of six official members – senior public officers – and six unofficial members, who were prominent citizens.

96. The provisions for food and clothing were published in a proclamation dated January 25, 1833. See *Port of Spain Gazette*, February 1, 1833.

97. For a comparative table, see Appendix C, No. 2.

98. C.O. 295/93: Proclamation defining Slave Offences, May 12, 1832; enclosed with Grant to Goderich, July 3, 1832.

99. C.O. 295/93: Scotland to Grant, June 24, 1832, enclosed with Grant to Goderich, July 3, 1832.

100. These punishments, in some instances, exceed the punishments allowed by the Order. See Appendix D, for a list of the offences.

101. C.O. 295/93: Grant to Goderich, July 3, 1832.

102. There were two in 1830 – C.O. 300/25: Report of the Protector of Slaves for the period ending December 1830; one during the following year – C.O. 300/27: Report of the Protector of Slaves for the period ending December 1831; five in 1833 – C.O.300/31: Report of the Protector of Slaves for the period ending June 1833; and for the first half of 1834 – see C.O. 300/33: Report of the Protector Slaves for the period ending June 1834.

103. There were 78 in the first half of 1832 – C.O. 300/28: Report of the Protector of Slaves for the period ending June 1832; and 11 in the second half of the year – C.O. 300/30: Report of the Protector of Slaves for the period ending December 1832.

104. C.O. 300/30: Colonial Office comments on the Protector's Report for the period ending December 1832.

105. C.O. 300/26: Report of the Protector of Slaves for the period ending June 1831, with comments attached. Cf. C.O. 300/30: Report of the Protector of Slaves for the period ending December 1832, where the sum of £65 was paid while the valuation was £130. For similarly high figures, see C.O. 300/26: Report of the Protector of Slaves for the period ending June 1831. The figures are: £104, £119.13.4; and £173. 6. 8.

106. C.O. 300/25: Report of the Protector of Slaves for the period ending December 1830.

107. C.O. 300/27: Report of the Protector of Salves for the period ending December 1831.

108. C.O. 300/28: Report of the Protector of Slaves for the period ending June 1832.

109.   C.O. 300/30: Report of the Protector for the period ending December 1832. All except one were for assault. Five were dismissed, four fined £1 or $5. The defendants in the last two were imprisoned for 7 and 14 days respectively.

110.   C.O. 300/31: Report of the Protector of Slaves for the period ending June 1833. He was charged with inflicting twenty lashes on a slave.

111.   C.O. 300/32: Report of the Protector of Slaves for the period ending December 1833. Fines ranged from £1 in the lower courts to £11 before the Chief Judge.

112.   C.O. 300/33: Report of the Protector of Slaves for the period ending June 1834.

Chapter 8

1.   59 Geo. III, cap. 120: *An Act for establishing a Registry of Colonial Slaves in Great Britain, and for making provision with respect to the Removal of Slaves from British Colonies.* See *Legal Report,* Appendix D, pp. 200 and 201. Clauses 8 and 9 state that unregistered slaves could not be legally purchased, sold, mortgaged, or insured.

2.   Reports on this were carried in the *Port of Spain Gazette* of January 18 and May 12, 1832; and on May 19 about Dominica where the legislature expressed the view that the Order in Council should be rejected..

3.   For a discussion on this, see Ragatz, *The Fall of the Planter Class*, p. 453.

4.   The text of the resolutions may be found in Augier, F. R., and S. C. Gordon, *Sources of West Indian History,* London: Longmans, Green & Co., 1962, p. 191.

5.   Murray, *The West Indies*, pp. 198 – 202; *Port of Spain Gazette*, July 2, 5, and 16, 1833.

6.   C.O. 295/98: Hill to Stanley, July 2, 1833. Some proprietors had

asked for troops to be stationed in their Quarter, but Hill was unwilling to divide the troops. Hill was designated Lt. Governor in a short lived combination of the governments of Barbados and the Windward Islands. See Murray, *op. cit.,* p. 181.

7.   This same appeal was made when ameliorative Orders were issued in 1812, 1824, and 1831. See above.

8.   C.O. 295/98: Inhabitants to Grey and Stanley, 1833.

9.   *Ibid.*

10.   By this time Britain had also been under pressure because of protective duties on West Indian sugar. See Mellor, G.R., *British Imperial Trusteeship*, p. 100.

11.   *Port of Spain Gazette,* July 16, 1833.

12.   3 & 4 William IV, cap. 73. *An Act for the Abolition of Slavery throughout the British Colonies; for promoting the Industry of the manumitted Slaves; and for compensating the Persons hitherto entitled to the services of such slaves.*

13.   C.O. 295/99: Hill to Stanley, October 12, 1833. Hill expressed the view that slavery could only have been ended by imperial legislation, and complimented the Secretary of State on the success of the measure.

14.   C.O. 295/99: Hill to Stanley, November 25, 1833.

15.   The Colonial Office Memorandum to Hill's despatch in November referred to the Registrar's fees being paid into the Treasury, but not to Hill's query nor to his suggestion.

16.   C.O. 295/101: Hill *et al* to the Commissioners of the West India Compensation Fund, January 3, 1834, enclosed with Hill to Stanley, January 9, 1834. The other writers included John Welch Hobson, a free coloured man. See Fraser, *op. cit.,* I. 309 for the signatories of a petition of the free coloured community.

17.   The Protector himself had welcomed the combination in 1833.

18. The Secretary of Sstate asked Hill to investigate the delay. If it arose from neglect, he was to deduct the expense of additional staff from the salary of the Registrar. C.O. 296/11: Aberdeen to Hill, January 26, 1835

19. *Port of Spain Gazette*, July 15, 1834. How this was to be proved was not specified; but presumably some verbal testimony as to their having been seen would have been considered sufficient.

20. For a comprehensive table, see *Port of Spain Gazette*, July 15, 1834. It is not clear what the distinction between "head people" and "head tradesmen" was; the terms did not arise before this time.

21. C.O. 295/102: Proclamation dated July 11, 1834, enclosed with Hill to T. Spring Rice, July 20, 1834. Cf. *Port of Spain Gazette*, July 22, 1834.

22. C.O. 295/102: Hill to the Commandants, July 12, 1834.

23. *Port of Spain Gazette*, July 18, 1834. This is not a verbatim account, but a summary of his text. Cf. *Port of Spain Gazette*, August 2, 1833, Hill to Jackson, July 19, 1833. The latter had written to Hill asking for information as to how the resolutions would be carried into effect.

24. For this document, see the *Port of Spain Gazette*, October 25, 1833.

25. C.O. 295/102: Hill to T. Spring Rice, July 30, 1834.

26. *Port of Spain Gazette*, February 7, 1834.

27. *Ibid.*, April 29, 1834.

28. *Ibid.*, April 25, 1834.

29. *Ibid.*, May 30, 1834, letter of Gardez to the Editor, dated May 28, 1834.

30. C.O. 295/101: Hill to Lefevre, February 12, 1834.

31. C.O. 295/101: Jackson to Lefevre, April 8, 1834.

32.   C.O. 295/101: Jackson to Lefevre, February 12, 1834. Cf. See the classification approved by the Legislative Council below.

33.   C.O. 295/101: Jackson to Lefevre, April 8, 1834. In a minute to Hill's despatch of February 12, 1834, the proposals were set aside, but only because an Order in Council had been approved on the same matter. A Legislative Council had been set up towards the end of 1831.

34.   C.O. 295/101: Proposed Report on the System of Apprentices Laws. The emphasis is my own.

35.   The list is as follows:
1. Slaves manumitted by the 1833 Act
2. Children apprenticed under the Act
3. Persons entering into voluntary contracts to become apprentices
4. Free vagrants, without visible means of support
5. Free persons condemned to hard labour, employers entering security for their good behaviour
6. Slaves condemned to the Crown in the Vice Admiralty Court
7. Slaves (fugitives) from other colonies
8. Apprentices sent out from Europe

36.   *Port of Spain Gazette*, January 7, 1834; This Proclamation is dated December 24, 1833.

37.   By a Proclamation of July 22, 1834, Hill increased the number of districts to nine. C.O. 295/102: Hill to Lefevre, July 24, 1833.

38.   Order of June 1834, cap. 5, sections 4, 5, and 6. *Trinidad Almanac, 1832 – 1870*, pp. 84, 85.

39.   Presumably for one week as above.

40.   Procedure to be followed by Special Magistrates, Downing St., October19, 1833. Cf. *Port of Spain Gazette*, December 17, 1833.

41.   C.O. 295/102: Hill to Rice, July 20, 1834. For approval of these arrangements, see C.O. 296/11: Rice to Hill, September 5, 1834. A substantial list of the Special Justices is published in the Port of

Spain Gazette, August 12, 1834. Among them are R. Bushe and Frederick Browne, the alcaldes who frustrated the court system in 1832 as assessors. The list also included Henry Murray, the first Registrar.

42. Proclamation dated July 12, 1834 in the *Port of Spain Gazette*, July 22, 1834. See also *Trinidad Almanac, 1832 – 1870*, pp. 112, 113.

43. C.O. 295/102: Souper to Acting Superintendent Special Justices, July 1834, enclosed with Hill to Lefevre, July 24, 1834.

44. C.O. 295/102: Hill to Rice, July 30, 1834.

45. These Special Justices would have been those persons appointed earlier. Hill reported to the Colonial Secretary on August 7, 1834, that Capt. Hay had only then arrived.

46. C.O. 295/103: Hill to Rice, August 7, 1834.

47. The exact size of the crowd is not certain.
48. *Port of Spain Gazette*, August 5, 1834.

49. Three petitions were presented to the Governor. One was signed by 50 people; another by 78, including Special Justices and the Chief of Police; another by 69 persons. See C.O. 295/103: Hill to Rice, August 7, 1834, enclosures.

50. C.O. 295/103: Hill to Rice, August 7, 1834. Cf. C.O. 28/115: Hill to Smith, August 3, 1834, where he requested the assistance while indicating his own resistance to the demand for martial law. Smith expressed his inability to help. C.O. 28/115: Smith to Hill, August 13, 1834.

51. Col. Hardy was Commanding Officer of the regular troops in the colony at the time of emancipation.

52. See *Port of Spain Gazette*, August 15, 1834, for this letter.

53. *Ibid.* This assessment was supported by Lt. Col. Capadose, *Sixteen Years in the West Indies*, London, 1845, 156 – 164.

54. C.O. 295/103: Hill to Rice, August 9, 1834. In his dispatch of August 7, Hill expressed confidence that the apprentices would return to work.

55. C.O. 295/103: Hill to Rice, August 14, 1834. In C.O. 28/115: Hill to Smith, August 15, 1834, Hill reported that no troops were needed, and commended Cols. Hardy and Doherty.

56. C.O. 295/103: Hill to Rice, October 8, 1834. This dispatch follows that mentioned in the previous note.

Conclusion

1. W. G. Sewell shows that those who left the estates fared better than those who remained on them; and that, contrary to the general opinion, those who left the estates, were neither thriftless nor vagabond. See his *The Ordeal of Free Labour in the British West Indies*, London: Frank Cass, 1968, pp. 110 – 112.

2. See, for example, Williams, *Capitalism and Slavery*, p. 203, for a discussion on this point.

3. Guerra y Sanchez, R., *Sugar and Society*, New Haven: Yale University Press, 1964, p. 24.

APPENDIX A
REGISTRATION

No. 1

General State of the Whole Number of Slaves returned for Registration at each Period of Registry (enclosed with T.D.D. 4. 520: Woodford to Bathurst, November 6, 1823).

	Adults		**Children**		
Year	Males	Females	Males	Females	Total
1813	10,917	8,206	3,255	3,339	25,717
1815	10,018	7,944	3,161	3,206	24,329
1816	10,110	7,983	3,914	3,864	25,871
1819	9,419	7,868	3,329	3,165	23,691
1822	9,017	7,732	3,225	3,253	23,227

Sgd. Edward Murray
Registrar of Slaves

Figures of the Commissary of Population
(enclosed with the same dispatch as above)

Number of Slaves:

1813	none
1815	none
1816	24,846
1819	22,854
1822	22,328

No. 2

Births and Deaths of Slaves, 1813 – 1822

(Taken from Returns of the Registrar, enclosed with T.D.D. 4.520 above)

Period	Births		Deaths	
	Males	Females	Males	Females
1813 – 1815	599	599	876	618
1815 – 1816	350	341	509	365
1816 – 1819	753	700	1,727	1,126
1819 – 1822	767	727	1,425	986
	2,469	2,356	4,537	3,094

No. 3

Extract from the Return of Marriages, Births and Deaths

Class	Births		Deaths		Marriages
	Males	Females	Males	Females	
Free Coloureds	2,443	2,171	998	1,111	448
Slaves	2,506	2,474	240	215	3
Whites	808	700	949	508	–

Total Births and Deaths, based on the above:

Class	Births	Deaths
Free Coloureds	4,614	2,109
Slaves	4,980	455
Whites	1,508	1,457

No. 4

Return of Slaves imported, 1812 – 1821. Enclosed with C.O. 295/55: Edward Murray to Young, July 6, 1822.

Year	Amount of Slaves	Highest Numbers	Origin
1813	51	237	Barbados
1814	294	1,079	Dominica
1815	842	1,173	Guadeloupe
1816	813	296	New Providence
1817	327		
1818	438		
1819	338		
1820	368		
1821	344		
	3,815	TOTAL	

Return of Slaves imported 1813 – 1822
(as in T.D.D. 4. 520, enclosure):

Males	1,678	
Females	1,561	
	3,239	

No. 5.

Returns showing the Slave Population, January 31, 1825 – January 1829 (Enclosed with T.D.D. 8. 37: Grant to Murray, October 3, 1829).

	Males	Females	Total
Births	1,079	767	1,846
Deaths	710	759	1,469
Whole number registered	12,405	11,280	23,685

Sgd. Edward Murray

Dep. Registrar of Slaves.
    No. 6

Extract – Return of Population,
January 1825 – January 1829.

Dates	Males	Females	Total	Tax Roll	Births	Deaths
1825	11,908	11,209	23,117	24,402	431	622
1826	12,602	11,165	23,227	23,072	457	632
1827	12,008	11,115	23,123	23,661	415	682
1828	11,772	11,292	23,064	23,859	454	641
1829	11,528	10,908	22,436	23,002	342	589

These figures were submitted by Edmonstone Hodgkinson, Commissary of Population.

APPENDIX B
FREE COLOUREDS

No. 1

Docket of fees for the Governor and Secretary
(Extract from the Council Minutes, June 30, 1813)

| Departures from the Island | White passes | $2.00 | |
| | Coloured passes | $1.00 | C.O 295/42 |

No. 2

Enclosure to 295/53, No. 405:
Woodford to Bathurst, April 11, 1821.

Each pew holding six persons to let at £36 Cy.

Side " " " " "48 "

" " " " four

" " " eight " £8 ea. 64"

Free colored Population each seat 5"

For servants each seat 4"

White Population 356 pews

Free coloreds and slaves 312 pews, including 14 long open benches for 168, and other seats.

APPENDIX C

No. 1

COMPARATIVE TABLE OF FOOD ALLOWANCES –
by provisions only.

For Slaves over ten:

In 1830	By the 1831 Order	By Substitutions
4 – 6 qts. of meal	21 pts. Of Flour, Indian or Guinea corn,	6 pts. Of flour or rice (1) or 9 qts of corn meal.
	56 plantains or 56 lbs of yams.	7 lbs of biscuits, or 20 plantains (2) or 21 lbs of yams, sweet potatoes, eddoes, or tannias (3)
31/2 lbs of salt fish	7 herrings or shads	31/2 lbs of salt fish
1 glass of rum in crop time.		

Part provisions and part grounds:

By the substitutions of 1833

3½lbs of salt fish weekly
26 days in 26 consecutive weeks.

Support by grounds only:

By the 1831 Order	By Substitutions
½ acre land – 2 miles or less from home	½ acre land – 2 miles or less from home
40 days per year	40 full days per year

seeds and tools

Comparison with British Guiana: (1) 10 pts. (2) 2 bunches of 35 lbs each. (3) 25 lbs. (4) 1 day per week. See *Port of Spain Gazette*, February 1, 1833.

No. 2

COMPARISON OF CLOTHING ALLOWANCES
For male slaves over 15

In 1830	By the 1831 Order	By Substitutions
2 shirts	2 cotton shirts	2 shirts
2 trousers	2 trousers	2 trousers
1 cloth jacket or wrapper	1 jacket	1 jacket
1 hat	1 hat	1 hat
1 woollen bonnet or cap	1 cap	1 cap
1 blanket every 2 years	1 blanket	1 blanket every 2 years
	2 pairs shoes, 1 knife, 1 razor	

Female slaves over 15

2 petticoats	2 petticoats	2 petticoats
1 woollen wrapper	2 gowns, or wrappers	1 wrapper
2 shifts	2 shifts	2 shifts
1 hat	1 hat	1 hat
1 Kilmarnock cap		2 kneck kerchiefs
1 blanket every 2 years	1 blanket	
	1 pair scissors	1 pair scissors
	2 pairs shoes	

Except where otherwise stated, the provisions were for one year. The allowances for those under 15 were roughly half that of the others.

Appendix D

SLAVE OFFENCES AS DEFINED BY GRANT'S PROCLAMATION OF MAY 12, 1832.

1. Wilful self wounding, neglect of health.

2. Carelessness with clothes, provisions, or tools.

3. Gambling of any sort.

4. Meetings or dances without their owners' permission

5. Furious riding or driving on the public roads.

6. Crowding public places to the annoyance of passengers or others.

7. Burning grounds without their owners' or managers' consent.

8. Carrying weapons in the streets without their owners' or managers' consent.

9. Possessing weapons without their owners' or managers' consent.

10. Firing guns, ringing bells, blowing horns, making bonfires, or causing alarms

11. Having more than one pound of sugar, coffee, cocoa, or one imperial quart of molasses unknown to their owners.

12. Trading in canes, sugar, rum, molasses, coffee, etc.

13. Neglect of work.

14. Refusing or neglecting to serve on Sundays as domestics, watchmen,

cattlemen, *et al.*

15.   Violent language or gesture. Insolence to those in charge of them.

16.   Indecent or violent conduct.

17.   Intoxication.

18.   Trespassing.

19.   Absconding more than 48 hours, or 5 miles beyond their place of work without a pass.

20.   Refusing to prevent the damage of their owners' property.

21.   Resisting the infliction of punishment.

22.   Harbouring runaways.

23.   Gross insubordination.

24.   Refusing to work on their grounds.

25.   Wilfully damaging their own provision grounds.

26.   Wilfully damaging machinery, carts, bridges, boats.

27.   Wilfully damaging property in their care.

28.   Arson.

29.   Conspiracy not to work.

30.   Causing a riot.

31.   Obeah.

32. Being present at a meeting to administer unlawful oaths, etc.

33. Assaulting their owner, or the person in charge of them.

34. Running away and any other offence.

35. Attempting to leave the colony.

36. Neglecting or ill-treating their children.

BIBLIOGRAPHY

Government Papers in Trinidad

Minutes of the Cabildo, 1813 – 1834. These were not always in good condition, particularly those for the mid-1820's.

The Register of Ordinances and Orders of Government, 1813 –1835. This was very useful, but contained some gaps.

Duplicate Despatches from Trinidad Governors, 1813 – 1835. Very useful, but also containing some gaps.

Colonial Office Papers (Microfilms at UWI, St. Augustine)

Despatches incoming from the Secretary of State for the Colonies, C.O. 296/1 – 11: 1797 – 1834.

Despatches outgoing from Trinidad Governors, C.O. 295/1 – 103: 1797 – 1834. These were usued to supplement gaps from the Trinidad Duplicates.

Reports of the Protector of Slaves, C.O. 300/19 - 33: 1824 – 1834.

Minutes of the Council, C.O. 298/1 – 9: 1801 – 1834. Only some of these were available, the rest being taken from excerpts in the despatches.

Printed Collections of Documents

S.C.Gordon & F.R.Augier,   *Sources of West Indian History*
                           London: Longmans, 1967.

Donnan, Elizabeth   *Documents Illustrative of the History of*
                           the Slave Trade to America. Vol. II:
                           The Eighteenth Century.
                           ( ) Octagon Books, 1965.

Harlow, V. & F. Madden   *British Colonial Developments,*
                           1774 – 1834 London: 1953.

Williams, E.	*The British West Indies at Westminster, 1783 – 1823*
	Trinidad: Government Printing Office, 1954.
_____	*Documents on British West Indian History, 1807 – 1833.*
	Substance of the Debate in the House of Commons, on the 15th May 1823, on a Motion for the Mitigation and Gradual Abolition of Slavery Throughout the British Dominions. New York: Negro Universities Press, 1969.
	Trinidad Publishing Co., 1952.

British Parliamentary Papers

All publication information is the same, except the date. Shannon: Irish University Press.

Colonies, West Indies, Vol 3, (1971).
Reports from the Commissioners of Inquiry on the Administration of Justice in the West Indies and South American Colonies, 1825 – 1829.
- Report of His Majesty's Commissioners of Legal Inquiry on the Colony of Trinidad   pp. 285 – 341.

Slave Trade, Vol. 61, (1971).
Correspondence Returns and other Papers relating to the Slave Trade.
- Papers relating to the trials of Hodge and Huggins
- Adrican Slave Trade Accounts 1806 (265) Vol. XIII

Slave Trade, Vol. 62: (1971)
Returns and Papers Relating to the Slave Trade, 1816 – 18.

Slave Trade, Vol. 65 (1969)
Returns and Papers relating to the Slave Population of the West India Colonies and the Abolition of the Slave Trade 1821.
- Return of Slaves imported into Trinidad, 1813-1821.

Slave Trade, Vol. 66 (1969)
Correspondence and Papers relating to Slavery and the Abolition of the Slave Trade, 1823 – 24

- Return of the Slave Population in each of H.M. colonies in the West Indies as received in the Office of the Registry of colonial Slaves 1815 – 1822. (424) Vol. XXIV.

Slave Trade, Vol. 67 (1969)
Correspondence and Papers relating to Slavery in the West Indies and the Abolition of the Slave Trade, 1825.

- Copy of the Proceedings in the trial of Marquis and Regis pp. 11 – 16.
- Accounts and Papers relating to Slaves in the West Indies 1825 (66) Vol. XXV.

Slave Trade, Vol. 68 (1969)
Papers Relating to the Conditions of Slaves in British Possessions and Other Papers Relating to Slavery and the Slave Trade, 1825 – 26.

- The Order in Council of March 1824.   pp. 166 – 180.
- Spanish laws regarding the rights of owners.   pp. 190 – 92.

Slave Trade, Vol. 70 (1969)
Papers and returns Relating to the Slave Population of the West Indies, 1826.

- Return of Slaves imported into Trinidad in the last four Years 1822 – 25.
- pp. 706 – 712.
- Despatch of Sir Ralph Woodford to Earl Bathurst, February 28, 1826, with 18 enclosures, pp. 705 – 752.

Slave Trade, Vol. 72 (1969)
Report on Apprenticed Africans at Antigua and Other Papers Relating to Slavery and the Slave Trade, 1826 – 27.

- Return of Public Functionaries who are owners of Slaves, pp. 42 – 43.

Slave Trade, Vol. 73 (1969)
Papers relating to the Condition of Slaves in British Possessions and other Papers relating to Slavery and the Slave Trade, 1826 – 27.

- Extract from the Committee of Council, appointed on the

4th of November 1824,"for the purpose of obtaining a more correct knowledge of the Negro Character, as exhibited in this Colony, in the state of slavery and of freedom. 1826 – 27 (479) Vol. XXIII.

- Papers outlining the Measures adopted by Great Britain for improving the Condition of the Slave Population. 1826 – 1827 Vol. XXVI. pp. 611 – 47.

Slave Trade, Vol. 75 (1969)
Reports Correspondence and Papers Relating to Slavery in the Colonies and to the Slave Trade, 1828. Irish University Press

- Return of the amount of the Slave Population in each of His Majesty's Colonies as received in the Office of the Registrar of Colonial Slaves since May 9, 1826.

Slave Trade, Vol. 76 (1969)
Reports from Protectors of Slaves and from Commissioners of Inquiry and other Papers relating to the Condition of Slaves in British Possessions and to the Slave Trade, 1828 – 29.

- Return for 1824 of Free Labourers and Manumitted Slaves 1829 (336) Vol. XXV pp. 425 – 34.

Slave Trade, Vol. 77 (1969)
Papers relayting to the Condition of Slaves in British Possessions and other Papers relating to Slavery and the Slave Trade, 1830 – 31.

- Order of the King in Council for consolidating the laws pertaining to Slaves.   1830 (8) Vol. XXI. pp. 27 – 43.
- Report showing Slaves imported by Burton Williams since Jabuary 1822. pp. 62, 63.
- Return of the Slave Population in the Registry of Colonial Slaves since March 1830.   1830 – 31 (91) Vol. XVI. p. 469

Slave Trade, Vol. 79 (1969)
Papers relating to Measures adopted for the Melioration of the Conditions of Slaves in British Possessions, 1831 – 32.

- Proclamation for effecting the Order in Council of 1830
- Proclamation for effecting the Order in Council of November 1831. pp. 29 – 31.
- Despatch of Goderich to Grant concerning the Order in Council of 1831. pp. 59 – 88.

- Order in Council of November 2, 1831. pp. 93 – 138.

Slave Trade, Vol. 80 (1969)
Papers relating to the Abolition of Slavery, 1835.
- Return of Slaves imported into Trinidad, 1825 – 1830.
- Return of Slaves in the Office of the Registry of Colonial Slaves.

Secondary Material

Anonymous	*The West India Question Practically Considered* London, 1826.
Augier, F.R., et al	*The Making of the West Indies,* London: Longmans, 1964.
Bandinel, J.	*Some Account of the Trade in Slaves from Africa* London: Frank Cass & Co., 1968.
Borde, P.G.L.	*Histoire de l'Ile de la Trinidad sous le Gouvernement Espagnol,* Paris: Maissoneuve et Cie., 1876.
Bowser, Frederick P.	"Colonial Spanish America," Cohen, David and Jack Greene, *Neither Slave Nor Free*, Baltimore: Johns Hopkins University Press, 1972, 19 – 58.
Burn, W.L.	*The British West Indies* London: William Brendon & Son, 1961.
Burns, A.	*History of the British West Indies* New York: 1965.
Campbell, Carl	*Cedulants and Capitulants* Trinidad: Paria Publishing Co., 1992.
_____	"Ralph Woodford and the free coloureds: the transition from a conquest society of

settlement, Trinidad 1813 – 1828", *Journal of Caribbean Studies,* Vol. 2, Nos. 2 & 3, 1981, pp. 238 – 249.

_____ "The rise of a free coloured plantocracy in Trinidad, 1783 – 1813", Boletin de Estudios Latinoamericanos y del Caribe, No. 29, Dec. 1980, --. 33 -54.

Capadose, Lt. Col. (Henry) *Sixteen years in the West Indies*, 2 Vols. London, 1845.

Carmichael, A. *Domestic Manners and Social Condition of the White, Coloured, and Negro Population of the West Indies,* Vol. 2 London: Frank Cass & Co., 1969.

Carmichael, G. *History of the West Indian Islands of Trinidad and Tobago* London: Alvin Redman, 1961.

Clarkson, T. *History of the Rise, Progress & Accomplishment of the Abolition of the Slave Trade by the British Parliament,* 2 Vols. London: Frank Cass & Co., 1968.

Cohen, David W. & Jack P, Greene, ed. *Neither Slave nor Free* Baltimore: Johns Hopkins University Press, 1972.

Coupland, R. *The British Anti-Slavery Movement* Frank Cass & Co., 1964.

Corwin, A.F. *Spain and the Abolition of Slavery in Cuba* University of Texas Press, 1967.

Curtin, P.D. *The Atlantic Slave Trade* University of Wisconsin Press, 1969.

Day, C.W. *Five Years' Residence in the West Indies* London, 1852

Deerr, Noel	*The History of Sugar*, 2 Vols. London: Chapman & Hall Vol. 1, 1949; Vol. 2, 1950.
de Verteuil, Anthony, C.S.Sp.	*Begorrat* ** *Brunton A History of Diego Martin, 1784 – 1884.* Trinidad: Paria Publishing Co., 1987.
Dubois, Laurent	*A Colony of Citizens: Revolution and Slave Emancipation in the French Caribbean, 1787 – 1804,* Kingston, Jamaica: Ian Randle Publishers,, 2004.
Duncker, Sheila	*The Free Coloured and the Fight for Civil Rights in Jamaica,*
Dunn, Richard S.	*Sugar and Slaves* Chapel Hill: University of North Carolina Press, 1972.
Edwards, Bryan	*The History Civil and Commercial, of the British Colonies in the West Indies*, 5 Vols. London, 1819.
Elisabeth, Leo	"The French Antilles," Cohen & Greene, *Neither Slave Nor Free*, 134 – 171.
Fraser, L.M.	*History of Trinidad*, 2 Vols. (1891, 1896) London: Frank Cass & Co., 1971.
Free Mulatto	*Address to the Rt. Hon. Lord Bathurst,* (1823) Trinidad: Paria Publishing Co., 1987
Garrigus, John D.	"Colour, Class and Identity on the Eve of the Haitian Revolution: Saint Domingue's Free Coloured Elite as *Colons americains.*" Slavery and Abolition, Vol. 17, No. 1, April 1996, 20 – 43.

| | "Some Background to free coloured political activism:Julien Raimond in Saint Domingue, 1744 – 1784," paper presented at the 19th annual Conference of Caribbean historians, 1987. |

Gaspar, David Barry — "The emancipation of the free coloureds in St. Lucia, 1824 – 1831," paper presented at the 11th Annual Conference of Caribbean historians, Curacao, 1979.

Gaston-Martin — *Histoire de L'esclavage dans les Colonies Francaises*
Paris: Presses Universitaires de France, 1948.

Geggus, David — "Slave Society in the Sugar Platation Zones of Saint Domingue and the Revolution of 1791 – 1793." *Slavery and Abolition*, Vol. 20, No. 2, August 1999, 31 – 46.

Goveia, Elsa — *Slave Society in the British Leeward Islands at the end of the Eighteenth Century*
New Haven: Yale University Press, 1965.

_____ — *West Indian Slave Laws of the Eighteenth Century*
Caribbean Universities Press, 1970.

Griggs, Earl Leslie &
Clifford H. Prator — *HENRY CHRISTOPHE and THOMAS CLARKSON*
A Correspondence
New York: Greenwood Press, 1968.

Guerra y Sanchez, R. — *Sugar and Society in the Caribbean*
New Haven: Yale University Press, 1964.

Hall, D.G. — "The social and economic background to sugar in slave days," *Caribbean Historical Review*, Nos. III – IV, Dec. 1954, 20 – 45.

————————	"Jamaica," Cohen & Greene, *Neither Slave Nor Free*, 193 – 213.
Hall, Gwendolyn,	"Saint Domingue," Cohen, David and Jack Greene, *Neither Slave Nor Free,* 172 - 192.
————————	*Social Control in Slave Plantation Societies*
Hall, Neville	"Law and society in Barbados at the turn of the 19th Century," *Journal of Caribbean History,* Vol. 5, 1972, 20 – 45.
————————	"The Judicial System of a Slave Plantation Society – Barbados on the eve of emancipation," Colloque d'Histoire Antillaise, T 1
Handler, Jerome & Arnold A. Sio	"Barbados," Cohen & Greene, *Neither Slave Nor Free,* 214 – 257.
————————	*The Unappropriated People,* Baltimore: Johns Hopkins University Press, 1974.
Harlow, V. & F. Madden	*British Colonial Developments, 1774 – 1834* Oxford: Clarendon Press, 1953.
Hart, D.	*Trinidad and the Other West Indian Islands and Colonies.* Trinidad: Chronicle Publishing Office, 1866.
Helg, Aline	"The Limits of Equality: Free People of Colour and Slaves during the First Independence of Cartagena, Colombia, 1810 – 15." Slavery and Abolition, Vol. 20, No. 2, Aug. 1999, 1 – 30.
Higman, Barry	"Growth in Afro-Caribbean Slave Populations," *American Journal of Physical Anthropology* (1979) 50: pp. 373 – 386.

Hollis, C.   *A Brief History of Trinidad under the Spanish Crown*
                                  Trinidad & Tobago Government Printers, 1941.

Horsman, R.   *The War of 1812*
                                  Eyre and Spottiswoode, 1969.

James, C.L.R.   *Black Jacobins*
                                  New York: Vintage Books, 1963.

John, A. Meredith   *The Plantation Slaves of Trinidad, 1783 – 1816*
                                  Cambridge: Cambridge University Press, 1988.

Joseph, E.L.   *History of Trinidad, ( )*
                                  London: Frank Cass & Co., 1970.

_____   *Warner Arundell: The Adventures of a Creole*
                                  London, 1838.

Klingberg, J.L.   *The Anti-Slavery Movement in England*
                                  New Haven: Yale University Press, 1926.

Knaplund, Paul   *James Stephen and the British Colonial System, 1813 – 1847.*
                                  Madison: University of Wisconsin Press, 1953.

Lamont, N.   *Burnley of Orange Grove* (Lecture)
                                  Port of Spain Gazette, 1947.

Laurence, K.O.   "The settlement of free Negroes in Trinidad before Emancipation," *Caribbean Quarterly*, No. 9, 1962, 26 – 51.

Lavaysse, J.F.D.   *A Statistical, Commercial, and Political Description of Venezuela, Trinidad, Margarita and Tobago* (1820)
                                  Westpoint, Conn: Negro Universities Press, 1969.

Long, Edward — *History of Jamaica*, 3 Vols.
London: Frank Cass & Co., 1970.

M'Callum, P. — *Travels in Trinidad*
Liverpool, 1805.

MacKenzie-Grieve, A — *The Last Years of the English Slave Trade ( )*
London: Frank Cass & Co., 1968.

M'Queen, J. — *The West India Colonies*
London, 1825.

Manning, H.T. — *British Colonial Government after the American Revolution, 1782 – 1820*
Archon Books, 1966.

Mannix, D. & P. Cowley — *Black Cargoes*
London: Longmans, 1962.

Mathieson, W.L. — *British Slavery and Its Abolition, 1823 – 1838*
London: Longmans, Green & Co., 1926.

Medd, P. — *ROMILLY: A Life of Sir Samuel Romilly Lawyer and Reformer*
London: Collins, 1968.

Mellor, G. R. — *British Imperial Trusteeship, 1783 – 1850.*
London: Faber and Faber, 1951.

Millette, J.C.V. — *The Genesis of Crown Colony Government*
Trinidad: Moko Enterprises, 1970.

_____ — "The Civil Commission of 1802," *Jamaican Historical Review*, Vol. VI, 1966,

Murray, D.J. — *The West Indies and the Development of Colonial Government, 1801 – 1834*
Oxford: Clarendon Press, 1965.

Newson, Linda A — *Aboriginal and Spanish Colonial Trinidad*
London: Academic Press, 1976.

Newton, J.H., et al.

The Cambridge History of the British Empire
Vol. 2, The New Empire, 1783 – 1870
Cambridge: Cambridge University Press, 1940.

Noel, Jesse A.

Trinidad, Provincia de Venezuela
Caracas: Fuentes para la Historia Colonial de Venezuela, 1972.

Ottley, C. R.

Slavery Days in Trinidad.
Trinidad, 1974.

Parry, J.H. & P.M. Sherlock

A Short History of the West Indies
London: Macmillan, 1965.

Patterson, Orlando

The Sociology of Slavery
London: MacGibbon & Kee, 1967.

Ragatz, L.J.

The Fall of the Planter Class in the British Caribbean, 1763 – 1833
New York, 1928.

Roberts, G.W.

"Movements in Slave Population of the Caribbean During the Period of Slave Registration," in Rubin & Tudin, pp. 165 – 182.

Rubin, Vera & Arthur Tudin

Comparative Perspectives on Slavery in New World Plantation Societies
New York: New York Academy of Sciences, 1977.

Saunders, Gail

Slavery in the Bahamas, 1648 – 1838
Bahamas: Nassau Guardian, 1985.

Schuyler, R.R.L.

Parliament and the British Empire

Sewell, W.G.

The Ordeal of Free Labour in the British West Indies
Frank Cass & Co., 1968.

Southey, T.

Chronological History of the West Indies, 3 Vols.
London, 1827

Stephen, James

The Crisis of the Sugar Colonies (1802)
New York: Negro Universities Press, 1969.

───────────

The Slavery of the British West India Colonies Delineated (1824)
New Yrok: Kraus Reprint Co., 1969.

Turner, Mary

"The 11 O'Clock Flog: Women, Work and Labour Law in the British Caribbean," *Slavery and Abolition*, Vol. 20, No. 1 Apr. 1999, 38 – 58.

Vindex

Considerations submitted in Defence of the Orders in Council for the Melioration of Slavery in Trinidad, 1825.
British Museum, 522 f. 31.

Waddell, D.A.G.

The West Indies and the Guianas
New Jersey: Prentice-Hall, 1967.

Ward, W.E.F.

The Navy and the Slavers
London: Allen & Unwin, 1962.

Wilberforce, R.I. & S.

The Life of William Wilberforce, 4 Vols.
London, 1838.

Wilberforce, W.

Appeal on behalf of the Negroes in the West Indies
British Museum Papers, T 1137 (7)

Williams, E.

History of the People of Trinidad and Tobago
Trinidad: P.N.M. Publishing Co., 1962.

───────────

From Columbus to Castro
London: Andre Deutsch, 1970.

───────────

Capitalism and Slavery
London: Andre Deutsch, 1967.

INDEX

Printed in Great Britain
by Amazon